THE PRINCIPLES OF FAMILY BUSINESS LAW

The Principles of Family Business Law offers an accessible approach to legal issues that shape family businesses. Drawing on years of research, the book introduces three principles – intimacy, integration, and inheritance – that explain why family businesses are distinctive and how, with proper guidance, they can thrive. The book examines recurring problems such as role conflicts among family members, succession planning obstacles, and ownership disputes. Vivid case studies illustrate how legal rules interact with family dynamics in practice. Designed for scholars, students, lawyers, and business advisors, the book integrates insights from corporate law, family law, and estate planning, while remaining readable and grounded in real-world concerns. Whether used in the classroom or in practice, it provides essential tools for navigating the complex interplay of law and family business. By supporting the resilience of family businesses, the book affirms the family and community values they help to sustain.

Benjamin Means is John T. Campbell Chair in Business and Professional Ethics at the University of South Carolina Joseph F. Rice School of Law. He is the founding director of the United States' first law-school-based family business program, where he has developed an innovative curriculum to prepare law students to represent family business owners. His scholarly work, published in top journals, has established a new field of legal academic inquiry.

The Principles of Family Business Law

BENJAMIN MEANS
University of South Carolina Joseph F. Rice School of Law

CAMBRIDGE
UNIVERSITY PRESS

CAMBRIDGE
UNIVERSITY PRESS

Shaftesbury Road, Cambridge CB2 8EA, United Kingdom

One Liberty Plaza, 20th Floor, New York, NY 10006, USA

477 Williamstown Road, Port Melbourne, VIC 3207, Australia

314–321, 3rd Floor, Plot 3, Splendor Forum, Jasola District Centre, New Delhi – 110025, India

103 Penang Road, #05–06/07, Visioncrest Commercial, Singapore 238467

Cambridge University Press is part of Cambridge University Press & Assessment, a department of the University of Cambridge.

We share the University's mission to contribute to society through the pursuit of education, learning and research at the highest international levels of excellence.

www.cambridge.org
Information on this title: www.cambridge.org/9781009354530

DOI: 10.1017/9781009354547

When citing this work, please include a reference to the DOI 10.1017/9781009354547

First published 2026

Cover credit: Illustration by Norma Mazo © Benjamin Means

A catalogue record for this publication is available from the British Library

Library of Congress Cataloging-in-Publication Data
NAMES: Means, Benjamin, 1973– author
TITLE: The principles of family business law / Benjamin Means.
DESCRIPTION: Cambridge, United Kingdom ; New York, NY :
Cambridge University Press, 2026. | Includes bibliographical references and index.
IDENTIFIERS: LCCN 2025032575 (print) | LCCN 2025032576 (ebook) |
ISBN 9781009354530 hardback | ISBN 9781009354547 ebook
SUBJECTS: LCSH: Family-owned business enterprises – Law and legislation | Inheritance and succession | Corporate governance – Law and legislation | Dispute resolution (Law)
CLASSIFICATION: LCC K1348 .M43 2026 (print) | LCC K1348 (ebook) |
DDC 346/.0668–dc23/eng/20250721
LC record available at https://lccn.loc.gov/2025032575
LC ebook record available at https://lccn.loc.gov/2025032576

ISBN 978-1-009-35453-0 Hardback
ISBN 978-1-009-35456-1 Paperback

Contents

Preface

In 2014, at the invitation of Thomas Rutledge, a well-regarded business-law attorney, I convened a panel on family businesses for the American Bar Association's annual LLC Institute. The panelists included Professors Eric Chiappinelli and Robert Thompson, as well as Peter Mahler, the founder of the invaluable New York Business Divorce blog.

Toward the end of our conversation, I asked the panelists and the audience whether they thought a book on family business law would be a useful contribution, and, if so, what they thought the central message should be. The sentiment in the room was strongly in favor of such a book, and I still recall Professor Thompson's counsel that my task would be to explain how intimate relationships among participants can be reconciled with their business obligations.

Now, more years later than I had intended, I have written the book. Whether the organizing principles for family business law that I propose here – intimacy, integration, and inheritance – are sufficient to the task set by Professor Thompson, the reader can judge.

Please be aware that I submitted this book to Cambridge University Press in the Spring of 2025, and I have not attempted to update it subsequently to keep track of ongoing events. Perhaps most notably, the Market Basket case study in Chapter 8 needs a coda because the Demoulas family members have, once again, gone to war with each other. If history repeats itself first as tragedy and then as farce, the Demoulas family may be well positioned to show us whatever comes after that.

Acknowledgments

I am grateful to Inge Kutt Lewis for steadfast administrative and editorial support, including the occasional nudge to get to work, and Grace Phillips for top-notch research assistance. The many business owners who have spoken to me about their businesses over the years also deserve my thanks. This book benefits from their wise observations. I would also like to thank Josie Brown and Douglas Moll for reading and commenting on many of the articles that preceded this book. Their feedback helped me to see how the ideas contained in those articles could be combined and extended. I appreciate Matt Gallaway's encouragement (and patience) as my editor at Cambridge University Press. The words encouragement and patience are also apt, though they hardly do justice to my wife, Susan Kuo, who reads all my work and is my sharpest, most loving critic.

While this book presents new ideas, it is deeply rooted in my previous scholarship. Many of its insights build upon and repurpose portions of several law review articles, all reprinted with permission. Most notably, *Solving the "*King Lear *Problem,"* 12 U.C. IRVINE LAW REVIEW 1245 (2022); *The Value of Insider Control*, 60 WILLIAM & MARY LAW REVIEW 891 (2019); *Wealth Inequality and Family Businesses*, 65 EMORY LAW JOURNAL 937 (2016); *The Contractual Foundation of Family-Business Law*, 75 OHIO STATE LAW JOURNAL 675 (2014); and *Nonmarket Values in Family Businesses*, 54 WILLIAM & MARY LAW REVIEW 1185 (2013). The book also incorporates material from *A Contractual Approach to Shareholder Oppression Law*, 79 FORDHAM LAW REVIEW 1161 (2010); *A Voice-Based Framework for Evaluating Claims of Minority Shareholder Oppression in the Close Corporation*, 97 GEORGETOWN LAW JOURNAL 1207 (2009); *Logan Roy as Lear: How Not to Succeed*, 73 DEPAUL LAW REVIEW 921 (2024) (symposium); and *How Not to End Up like* King Lear*: A Family-Business Succession Case Study*, 24 TENNESSEE JOURNAL OF BUSINESS LAW 391 (2023).

Finally, I am deeply grateful to my great-grandfather George Mazo for giving up his academic ambitions so that I could one day pursue mine.

Introduction

I.1 "I'M A STREET FIGHTER"

Weighing in on legal strategy, a client once told me to kick his brother in the balls. "I'm a street fighter," he explained. The client was embroiled in a family business dispute concerning a real estate development company in New Rochelle, New York. The brothers – let's call them Saul and John – each owned half. Saul, my client, ran the business. John expected to share equally in the profits, but he did not work for the business, so he was not paid a salary. He was also reported to have an alcohol problem, which was part of the reason that he was not employed in the family business. John thought that Saul was taking too much salary, leaving little or nothing left to distribute as dividends – which are how profits get paid to owners. So, John did two things. First, he took steps to acquire the fractional share interest held by Saul's estranged daughter. That would allow John to claim a majority interest, fire his brother, and take control. Also, in case that stratagem failed, John filed a petition in court alleging that he was an oppressed shareholder and asking the judge to dissolve the business.

Under New York law, which governed the dispute, the rights of the minority and the majority were defined solely by their shareholder relationship. Yet, the lawsuit had everything to do with a sibling rivalry. Complicated family relationships can heighten the emotion in a business dispute, making it harder to resolve sensibly. The litigants know how to hurt each other, as when John solicited his niece's help against her father. Clients will tell their attorneys, "It's not just the money, it's the principle of the thing." Until the legal fees start to add up. Saul eventually tired of paying his lawyers by the hour and sent John a letter stating that they should dispense with the "bullshit and the bottom feeders" and work out their differences in person. I appreciated the poetic alliteration, even if, as an attorney, I was classified as a "bottom feeder." I didn't take it personally. After a lot of posturing on both sides, and at least two years of legal fees, Saul purchased John's half of the business. The price was about what it would have been if the brothers had gotten a neutral business valuation in the first place.

If you have ever been involved in a lawsuit, especially when family matters are at stake, you know that the courtroom should be the last resort. In a family business lawsuit, everyone can lose. Even victory in court means little if you have killed the golden goose along the way. And, instead of finding a sympathetic ear, litigants in a family business dispute must submit to harsh scrutiny during discovery and an impersonal legal system that treats much of what matters to them as irrelevant. More than once, I have heard a family member explain a lawsuit this way: "Mom loved you best." But litigators are not therapists. Nor are judges. Even so, lawyers should be sensitive to the family dynamic and try to curb their clients' less rational impulses. For example, when Saul insisted on hitting John below the belt, the partner in charge at my law firm told him that we could continue to spend his money but that gratuitously aggressive litigation would not help. Less scrupulous counsel might not have raised the objection.

I don't mean to suggest that family business ownership is a bad idea. That is not the book's message. Far from it. A family enterprise is often a source of pride and can strengthen familial relationships and support communities. During hard times, family ties make it easier to sustain a business. For example, a family restaurant has a built-in staffing advantage: The restaurant can ask family members to show up and help when needed. If there is a revenue shortfall, family employees may take pay cuts or forgo salary without complaint. Intrafamilial flexibility can also keep business debts to a minimum. I recently interviewed the mother and son co-owners of a dance studio that funded an expansion by mortgaging the mother's personal property rather than taking out a separate commercial loan. Studies suggest that family ownership is a competitive advantage in the marketplace, especially in the first generation – unconditional support helps when you are trying to launch a new product or service and need time to establish a market for it.

Yet, when there is significant conflict, whether it starts with a business disagreement or a personal issue, family relationships may get in the way of resolution. My background is as a litigator, and the dispute between the two brothers Saul and John was my introduction to family and small businesses. My first law review article on the subject sought to provide guidance for courts adjudicating similar disputes, and I have returned to the topic of shareholder conflict in various ways ever since. In this book, although I take a broader view of the societal value of family business, I retain the habits of a litigator and temper optimism with an appreciation for what can go wrong. The subject of dispute resolution is one area where legal academics have a comparative advantage and can contribute usefully to the wider family business literature. From a legal perspective, the question is how to maximize the benefits of family business ownership, for the family and for a wider set of stakeholders, while putting into place appropriate guidance to handle conflicts when they cannot be avoided.

I.2 FAMILY AND SMALL BUSINESS PROGRAM

These days, apart from occasionally serving as an expert consultant, I have left the realm of litigation behind. I teach law students at the University of South Carolina Joseph F. Rice School of Law, where I have created a family business curriculum that includes specialized coursework and externships. That curriculum dovetails with my research on the governance of closely held businesses, especially those in family hands. I meet people with ties to family businesses everywhere I go. Most are glad to talk about how their family started a business venture, how many generations of family members are involved, and what makes it all worthwhile. A common refrain: "I wouldn't do this if it were just about money." Business owners have been generous in sharing life and business lessons that might benefit others. I have interviewed the second- and third-generation owners of a funeral home in Wilson, North Carolina, to better understand how their business draws strength from the black community it supports. I have received a guided tour of a third-generation family farm in Allendale, South Carolina, where the owners trace their connection to the land to a plantation house built by slaves before the Civil War. And I have talked to the owner of a billion-dollar South Carolina-based trucking business whose father still goes to the office every day and consults on major decisions, even though he is ninety years old.

Before I became a law professor, one of my mentors at Michigan Law School, Carl Schneider, told me that a legal academic can go almost anywhere, get to know people, and ask them questions. Our curiosity is our passport. He wanted me to avoid the trap of pursuing theory for its own sake and emphasized the importance of learning how things really work. As the director of a Family and Small Business Program, I find myself in a terrific position to put Professor Schneider's advice into practice. I am in constant contact with family business owners and those who work with family businesses. I ask not only what it takes to build a business, but what it takes to sustain it. I ask business owners about their plans and what they worry about most. I ask about family conflicts that may have arisen in the past and how those conflicts were addressed.

This book benefits greatly from the wisdom of the business owners that I, my students, and other members of the Family and Small Business Program have interviewed and relies on original family business case studies throughout to illustrate key points. I have also included, often verbatim, theories and arguments first developed in law review articles that I have published since I became a law professor more than fifteen years ago. Although each of those articles was meant to stand alone, I can see now, with the benefit of hindsight, how they relate to one another. At a broad level of generality, my work to date supports one central claim: that family business law is a distinctive field of study, one that situates business law, theory, and practice within a family context.

I.3 MAZO'S DELICATESSEN

So far, I have touched on my background as a litigator in New York, and my more recent work as a law professor and director of the Family and Small Business Program at the University of South Carolina Joseph F. Rice School of Law. This book is not about me, but I wanted to say something, by way of introduction, about who I am, what qualifies me to write this book, and why I have chosen to do so. For that reason, I should also mention my family's delicatessen, which operated for decades in Charleston, South Carolina. The delicatessen closed before I was born but remains a source of family pride and explains how my grandmother's parents escaped religious persecution in Eastern Europe, and how, despite not speaking English, they made a new home for themselves and their children in the United States of America. As was the case for my family, the story of a family business is often also a story about immigration.

When she was five years old, my grandmother, Norma Mazo, crossed the Atlantic Ocean on a Cunard liner, the *Berengaria*, with her parents, an older sister, and a younger brother. The seas were rough, and it was not a pleasant crossing. The Mazos were quartered below deck. Norma's parents were Shmuel-Gershon Mazo and Sonia, née Portugal. The children in birth order were Frances, Norma, and Earl. They came from Warsaw, Poland. According to a December 10, 1922, *New York Times* article, the *Berengaria* had "512 third class passengers. Among the latter 110 Russian immigrants, 86 Hungarians and 56 Poles." Also 5,072 bags of mail.

The Mazo family's voyage was miraculous, even if they did not fully realize it at the time. In 2022, my cousin Joseph Butwin, Frances's son, sent an email to mark the 100th anniversary of the crossing. His brother David responded with details about how the trip was arranged, quoting a letter from Earl adding "a footnote to our family's emigration: Uncle Dave in Charleston had sent the money for the whole family, including Papa's old mother, to come over." Then, as David summarized, "the old woman got sick, Papa wanted to see her well, Sonia famously said 'No, we are going,' Papa meekly gave in, soon of course the immigration laws changed." In Earl's words, "There were no more arrivals of our sort from Poland." David completed the account with a grim coda: "The old woman was still alive when Hitler took Poland. You know the rest."

Shmuel-Gershon (known in America as George) had two older brothers, Dave and Eli, who immigrated around the turn of the century. By the 1920s, Dave and Eli had established a successful delicatessen business in Charleston with two storefronts. Soon after his arrival, George was established as the proprietor of Mazo's Delicatessen at 171 King Street, the smaller, downtown location. George and Sonia lived above the store with their children. Although George was a scholar by inclination, and had been employed in Poland as a scribe, he and Sonia sacrificed their personal ambitions to provide opportunities for their children. Frances, Norma, and Earl were not expected to take over the family business and instead went on to college and independent careers in literature, art, and journalism. Frances and her husband owned a bookstore in St. Paul, Minnesota, and she translated the work of Sholem Aleichem into English, including the stories that would inspire *Fiddler on the Roof*. Norma and her husband were artists in Washington, DC. Earl wrote for *Stars and Stripes* during World War II and was later a reporter for *The New York Times*.

George and Sonia closed Mazo's Delicatessen in the 1950s when their health declined. By then, the business had served its purpose. One of our family's treasures is a series of paintings Norma created as a wedding anniversary present for her parents, documenting their life together in ten-year increments: in Warsaw, newly married, and then with young children; in Charleston, fledgling delicatessen owners, then well established and relatively prosperous; and then, a last look, older, contented, with pictures of children and grandchildren adorning the walls. In Norma's paintings, as in reality, Mazo's Delicatessen was pivotal to the story of the Mazo family. It was George and Sonia's legacy, a foundation supporting the aspirations of future generations.

My faculty office in Columbia is only a two-hour drive from Charleston. On a recent visit I walked down King Street with my family to the old store, now Beau & Ro, a women's clothing brand. Across the street stands the Charleston Library Society, frequented by my grandmother. Inside the shop, I found that the delicatessen was now arranged as a showroom. As I wandered around the second floor, formerly the living quarters, my son settled in a corner with a book amid racks of overflow clothing. Perhaps it was the same corner my grandmother would have chosen with one of her library books or a sketchbook. It was possible for a moment to envision Norma there, in that place, and to feel the proximity connecting her life to mine.

Many Americans could tell a similar story about their family: immigration, business ownership, and a move upward in society. Sometimes, the story involves overcoming racial or religious prejudices. In Charleston and elsewhere, Jews were often unwelcome. They sometimes arrived as itinerant peddlers, selling their wares from a cart, and eventually building up enough capital to open a storefront. This was true, for example, of the Lehman brothers in Alabama, who eventually led a global financial institution. I do not know if the older Mazo brothers started with a cart, but they would have had few resources when they came to the United States at the turn of the twentieth century. Barriers of language, culture, and religion would have made it hard for them to obtain a college education and to gain access to professional status. All they had to sell was their labor. Rather than work for others, however, they were able to establish their own business venture and to accumulate the capital they needed to change the family's circumstances.

Today, small businesses serve the same function for many families and communities. The United States remains a nation of immigrants in many respects, and newcomers may still find their way much as the Mazos did a century ago. A recent article in the *New York Times* about Chinatown traced several business ventures across generations and described how more assimilated children and grandchildren found meaning in what the older generation had built, carrying on some of those traditions while also adapting and innovating.[1] In the South, black-owned businesses are a crucial mechanism for accumulating capital and building community. There are funeral homes like Leevy's and Carrons; grocery stores like Uncle Willy's, whose owner told me that she picked the name in homage to her uncle's roadside stand. For those who have been locked out of the opportunity structure, starting a new business venture can be a way in.

I.4 OVERVIEW

It is sometimes assumed that the family business is a phenomenon of the past and out of step with modern business practices. Yet, roughly one out of every

[1] *See* Ligaya Mishan, *Saving Chinatown, While Also Making It Their Own*, N.Y. Times Style Mag. (Sept. 19, 2023).

three businesses is family owned, including those listed in the Fortune 500.[2] That US business law scholars have paid little attention to family businesses is a major oversight.[3] In family businesses, family considerations influence governance, financing, succession planning, and strategy. Laws concerning marriage, divorce, and inheritance can sometimes dictate business outcomes. Conversely, corporate governance arrangements can upend family and estate law expectations, as when a testamentary bequest is void because it violates a shareholder transfer restriction.

In a family business, as I define it, effective control rests in the hands of a single family and at least two family members are active in the business. Family businesses range from small owner-operated establishments to publicly traded behemoths, but they all share the need to reconcile two systems – a family system and a business system. Consequently, apart from challenges that all businesses face, the success of a family business depends on whether its constituents can successfully navigate two sets of values, role expectations, and legal rules. In some cases, the two systems create an expanded set of resources for creative problem solving. In other cases, conflicts between the two systems *are* the problem. Either way, greater scrutiny of family businesses is long overdue.

This book argues that the field of family business law consists of three overarching principles: (1) intimacy; (2) integration; and (3) inheritance.

Intimacy: Family ties, personal history, and emotional connections shape decision-making in ways that standard corporate governance frameworks cannot fully explain. Rather than forcing family businesses into the traditional corporate arm's-length economic model, family business law

[2] Some commentators cite much higher figures. *See, e.g.*, Dwight Drake, Business Planning: Closely Held Enterprises 314 (5th ed. 2018) ("Family dominated businesses comprise more than 80 percent of U.S. enterprises, employ more than 50 percent of the nation's workforce, and account for the bulk … of America's gross domestic product."). Regardless of "what criteria are used, family businesses represent a substantial portion of the U.S. economy": Joseph A. Astrachan & Melissa Care Shanker, *Family Businesses' Contribution to the U.S. Economy: A Closer Look*, 16 Fam. Bus. Rev. 211, 217–18 (2003).

[3] Setting aside my own work on the subject, the legal academic literature on family businesses can be captured in a single footnote of only moderate length. *See* Carrie Stanton, *Scrutinizing Succession*, 2025 Wis. L. Rev. 741; Allison Tait, *Corporate Family Law*, 112 Nw. U. L. Rev. 1 (2017); Eli Bukspan & Eylon Yadin, *Marrying Corporate Law and Family Businesses*, 66 Drake L. Rev. 549 (2018); Karen E. Boxx, *Too Many Tiaras: Conflicting Fiduciary Duties in the Family-Owned Business Context*, 49 Hous. L. Rev. 233 (2012); Eric A. Chiappinelli, *Stories from Camp Automotive: Communicating the Importance of Family Dynamics to Corporate Law Students*, 34 Ga. L. Rev. 699 (2000); Steven H. Hobbs & Fay Wilson Hobbs, *Family Businesses and the Business of Families: A Consideration of the Role of the Lawyer*, 4 Tex. Wesleyan L. Rev. 153 (1998).

recognizes that participants in a family business are typically motivated by more than just the pursuit of mutual economic advantage. Intimacy is a defining and distinguishing characteristic.

Integration: Family business law integrates consideration of corporate law, trust and estate law, and family law, as all may apply simultaneously. To the extent possible, contractual bargains and fiduciary duties among the parties should be interpreted and applied in a consistent fashion across doctrinal categories and with an appreciation for the broader family and business relationships at stake.

Inheritance: Family business owners often see themselves as stewards and care deeply about the legacy they leave behind, whether that involves a transfer to the next generation of family owners or sale to a buyer who shares their values. By promoting sound corporate governance, with particular attention to the risks associated with inadequate succession planning, family business law seeks to enhance the resilience of family businesses and to support the creation of long-term value. At their best, family businesses thrive in a competitive marketplace while setting the foundation for a sustainable enterprise capable of contributing to society across generations.

The book proceeds as follows. Part I begins with theory, contrasting corporate law's economic framework, which assumes a narrow focus on profit maximization, with family business law's more capacious approach. Part II demonstrates the explanatory value of family business law in three common scenarios: (1) co-ownership of a business by a married couple; (2) the hiring and promotion of employees who are also family members; and (3) the transfer of ownership and control across generations. Part III focuses on dispute resolution, reviewing existing legal oversight mechanisms, considering the possibility of legislative reform, and describing the appropriate judicial role when lawsuits cannot be avoided. Part IV evaluates the role family businesses play in society. In particular, Part IV offers evidence of a stewardship perspective that focuses on long-term benefits over short-term profits, and asks whether, on balance, family businesses reduce wealth inequality in society or contribute to it. This inquiry is meant not only to describe the world as it now exists but to envision how the values of the marketplace can be better aligned with the needs of society at the level of the individual, the family, and the community.

PART I

THEORY

I am not the first legal scholar to recognize the importance of family businesses. When I was a visiting professor at the University of Alabama School of Law in the fall of 2011, the office next door was occupied by an emeritus member of the faculty, Steven Hobbs. He was a quiet person and mostly kept to himself, but, on one memorable occasion, invited me to walk over to Bryant-Denny Stadium to see a football game. Along the way, Professor Hobbs asked about my scholarship. At the time, I was working on my first article on family businesses and told him why, based on my practice experience and previous academic work on closely held businesses, I intended to argue that family ownership deserved greater attention. With a twinkle in his eye, Professor Hobbs mentioned that he had done some work previously that I might find of interest. As I soon discovered, his article, "Family Businesses and the Business of Families: A Consideration of the Role of the Lawyer," co-authored with his spouse, Fay Wilson Hobbs, was published in 1998, when I was still a law student. Their focus was different but anticipated my interest in the subject.

Nor was Professor Hobbs the only other legal scholar whose interest in family businesses preceded mine. Notably, Professor Eric Chiappinelli published an essay in the *Georgia Law Review* arguing that the standard business law curriculum should include coverage of crucial family business dynamics.[1]

[1] A quarter century later, at least one law school has taken heed of the admonition. At the University of South Carolina Joseph F. Rice School of Law, we have created a curriculum that

There are other scholars I might mention whose work on corporate governance sometimes touched on family business concerns, including Robert Thompson and the late F. Hodge O'Neal. Yet, for the most part, family businesses remained peripheral in legal academic scholarship. Given the economic importance of family businesses, the lack of scholarship on the subject surprised me. In a series of law review articles, starting with the nascent idea I discussed with Professor Hobbs in Tuscaloosa, Alabama, I have worked to develop the descriptive, methodological, and normative contours of family business law. This book weaves together more than a dozen years of my scholarship and articulates the principles – intimacy, integration, and inheritance – that define family business law as a field.

As I review the current status of the field, I'm heartened by the growing number of law professors who are engaging with my scholarship and taking up family business law questions in their own work. For example, in 2017, Professor Allison Tait published an article in the *Northwestern University Law Review* arguing that family law principles should inform corporate law because closely held businesses are often family owned.[2] Professor Tait was emphatic that "we can and should build" a body of what she termed corporate family law.[3] Professor Carrie Stanton's work on family business succession, published in the *Wisconsin Law Review*, marks the continued development of the field.[4] Professor Stanton contends that corporate law fiduciary duties, especially as they have been developed and refined in the context of mergers and acquisitions law, could be applied to require careful and timely succession planning so that family businesses would have a greater chance of managing the transition from generation to generation.

Before turning to specific arguments of the kind advanced by Professors Tait and Stanton, this section of the book makes a broader case for the study of family businesses in the legal academy. Chapter 1 addresses fundamental methodological limitations of corporate law scholarship that may explain why family businesses have been overlooked. If businesses are perceived as economic ventures defined by the statutory parameters of existing forms of business association, then family concerns will remain invisible. There is no form of business association designed for families. In the marketplace, the objective is earning profits, not preserving family relationships. Thus, by definition, family concerns may appear to fall outside the proper scope

includes family business law, advanced topics in family business law, and a family and small business externship.

2 Allison Tait, *Corporate Family Law*, 112 Nw. U. L. Rev. 1 (2017).

3 *Id.* at 8.

4 Carrie Stanton, *Scrutinizing Succession*, 2025 Wis. L. Rev. 741.

of inquiry for business law scholars. Within a law-and-economics framework, family connections matter only to the extent that they might facilitate greater profitability.

To rebut the mistaken impression that family relationships are extraneous in a business setting, Chapter 2 brings to bear decades of research in other academic disciplines to argue that family businesses have distinctive characteristics that are not captured by existing legal categories or the simplified assumptions of law and economics. This is a literature-bridging exercise and is meant to address the isolation of business law scholarship by explaining that there is already a robust body of knowledge concerning family businesses in disciplines such as management, organizational psychology, and behavioral science that should inform legal analysis. Moreover, business law scholars have much to learn from family law scholars who have studied how households function as economic institutions.

Extrapolating guiding principles, Chapter 3 offers a theoretical account of how the law can accommodate the intimacy that is a defining feature of family businesses, defending a broad articulation of private ordering that encompasses the parties' expectations and values in full context. To be workable, any such approach must *integrate* the business system and the family system. In a family business, for example, status relationships continue to exert influence over business arrangements. Instead of perceiving contract law as a formalistic tool for addressing discrete business or family matters, I argue that contract law concepts should be used to reinforce the parties' relationships across traditional legal categories.

1

Why Corporate Law Excludes Family Relationships

The "study of family business is still relatively new" and too often neglected by legal academics.[1] This lack of attention impacts not only scholarship but the training of new attorneys: "[C]orporate law casebooks are astonishingly devoid of any systematic consideration of family dynamics."[2] The most straightforward explanation for the oversight is doctrinal. As a matter of business enterprise law, affective ties among shareholders are irrelevant. A family business may be organized as a partnership, corporation, or limited liability company (LLC). There is no separate business entity form reserved for use by families. Thus, despite burgeoning research in other disciplines, the study of family businesses by US legal scholars has until recently remained the specialized province of estate planners and tax lawyers.[3]

The lack of legal scholarship concerning family business governance may also signal deeper methodological limitations. Modern corporate law

[1] Kelin E. Gersick et al., Generation to Generation: Life Cycles of the Family Business 4 (1997); *see also* Susan Clark Muntean, *Analyzing the Dearth in Family Enterprise Research*, *in* Theoretical Developments and Future Research in Family Business 3, 4 (Phillip H. Phan & John E. Butler eds., 2008) ("Given the dominance of family business enterprise, it is a puzzle that the study of family is rare in theoretical and empirical studies of corporations.").

[2] Eric A. Chiappinelli, *Stories from Camp Automotive: Communicating the Importance of Family Dynamics to Corporation Law Students*, 34 Ga. L. Rev. 699, 710 (2000). Professor Chiappinelli found this neglect "surprising, in that many small businesses, and a few (though atypical) large ones, are owned and managed by a single family." *Id.* at 700. Almost twenty-five years later, Professor Chiappinelli does not believe the situation has changed.

[3] *See, e.g.*, Dwight Drake, *Transitioning the Family Business*, 83 Wash. L. Rev. 123 (2008). For an argument that family businesses need more holistic advice, see Steven H. Hobbs & Fay Wilson Hobbs, *Family Businesses and the Business of Families: A Consideration of the Role of the Lawyer*, 4 Tex. Wesleyan L. Rev. 154 (1998) (describing "family business law as a unique specialty with emerging practice parameters").

scholarship reflects the profound influence of law and economics.[4] Among its advantages, economic analysis offers a sophisticated model for analyzing and predicting behavior and can inform the design of legal rules and institutions.[5] Corporate law scholars often begin by asking how economically rational, autonomous investors would select appropriate default governance rules and bargain to protect their individual interests.[6] From this perspective, business entities are fundamentally contractual.[7] To the extent that family relationships intrude, they are perceived in economic terms as a trust mechanism that may substitute for *ex ante* bargaining, lowering the transaction costs of investment.[8]

1.1 AN ECONOMIC THEORY OF THE FIRM

For an economist, regardless of whether a business is organized as a partnership, corporation, or LLC, it is a "firm" if it organizes the factors of production – land, labor, and capital – to manufacture and sell products and services.[9] The economic theory of firms assumes that participants seek to maximize their profits. With that goal in mind, economists must answer a basic question: *Why* are there firms? Until relatively recently, most economists took firms for granted, treating them as little more than a "black box" that transforms inputs into outputs.[10] But, when pressed, they could not explain why the "black box" existed in the first place. If individuals can contract with one another to exchange goods and services at mutually agreed prices in an undistorted market, no further organizing mechanism is needed.[11]

4 *See generally* STEPHEN BAINBRIDGE, CORPORATION LAW AND ECONOMICS (2002).

5 *See, e.g.*, Ronald H. Coase, *The Problem of Social Cost*, 3 J. LAW & ECON. 1, 13 (1960) ("Judges have to decide on legal liability but this should not confuse economists about the nature of the economic problem involved.").

6 *See* FRANK H. EASTERBROOK & DANIEL R. FISCHEL, THE ECONOMIC STRUCTURE OF CORPORATE LAW 232 (1991); GARY S. BECKER & KEVIN M. MURPHY, SOCIAL ECONOMICS: MARKET BEHAVIOR IN A SOCIAL ENVIRONMENT (2003).

7 *See* Michael D. Klausner, *The Contractarian Theory of Corporate Law: A Generation Later*, 31 J. CORP. L. 779 (2005–2006).

8 *See* EASTERBROOK & FISCHEL, *supra* note 6, at 232 ("If family-owned ventures reduce the agency costs of management, there will be gains for all to share.").

9 More specifically, firms acquire capital, use that capital to produce goods or services, and seek to sell those goods and services for more than the cost of production. *See* DENNIS W. CARLTON & JEFFREY M. PERLOFF, MODERN INDUSTRIAL ORGANIZATION 14 (1st ed. 1990); George S. Geis, *The Space Between Markets and Hierarchies*, 95 VA. L. REV. 99, 106 (2009).

10 *See* Ronald H. Coase, *The Nature of the Firm*, 4 ECONOMICA 386, 389 (1937).

11 *Id.* at 387 ("An economist thinks of the economic system as being co-ordinated by the price mechanism."); *see also* Henry N. Butler, *The Contractual Theory of the Corporation*, 11 GEO.

Indeed, as a matter of economic efficiency, the widespread use of firms to coordinate productive activity seems counterintuitive. Centrally planned allocations of resources are more expensive and, therefore, less efficient than open-market contracts.[12] For example, when a business decides to make items in-house rather than buying them from an external source, the lack of competitive pressure may lead to a decline in quality.[13] Also, firm owners must monitor the performance of employee agents and the sheer cost of creating and maintaining the hierarchical structure of the firm.[14] The problem, then, is to explain the phenomenon of firms without rejecting either the price mechanism as a means of allocating scarce societal resources or the assumption that individuals will rationally pursue the course of action best calculated to maximize their wealth.[15]

In work for which he later received the Nobel Prize in Economics, Ronald Coase hypothesized that organizing production through firms can be cheaper than relying upon open-market contracts.[16] That is because, in the real world, the contracts that govern performance must be negotiated, written, monitored, and, if necessary, enforced.[17] These are transaction costs to be subtracted from the expected benefit of the transaction. In longer-term relationships that do not involve a discrete exchange of goods and services, it becomes quite difficult to negotiate all issues satisfactorily and there remains a considerable risk that market actors will exploit power and information disparities to their advantage. When transaction costs are significant, rational market actors may decline to enter into trades that would generate value for all participants.

MASON L. REV. 99, 103 (1989) ("In theory, all possible gains from specialization could be realized through market coordination in the absence of transaction costs.").

12 *See, e.g.*, F. A. Hayek, *The Use of Knowledge in Society*, 35 AM. ECON. REV. 519, 524 (1945) (arguing that market prices contain information and send signals that lead to more rapid and accurate allocations of resources than could be replicated by even the wisest central planner).

13 *See* Geis, *supra* note 9, at 107 ("Essentially, the argument is that sourcing any given activity internally shields production from the pressures of the marketplace."); Coase, *supra* note 10, at 389 ("[T]he distinguishing mark of the firm is the suppression of the price mechanism.").

14 *See* Geis, *supra* note 9, at 108 ("Anyone who has tried to navigate the shoals of a large corporate bureaucracy" will understand the costs of coordinating internal activity); KENNETH J. ARROW, THE LIMITS OF ORGANIZATION 25 (1974) (noting that a firm's "internal organization is … hierarchical and bureaucratic").

15 *See* Coase, *supra* note 10, at 390 ("Our task is to attempt to discover why a firm emerges at all in a specialised exchange economy."). Alternatively, one could offer a political rationale for firms, rather than justifying firms as a matter of market efficiency. *See* PAUL MILGROM & JOHN ROBERTS, ECONOMICS, ORGANIZATION & MANAGEMENT 73 (1992).

16 Coase, *supra* note 10, at 390 ("The main reason why it is profitable to establish a firm would seem to be that there is a cost of using the price mechanism.").

17 *Id.* at 390–91.

Rational actors endeavor to minimize *all* costs. Therefore, if transaction costs burden market transactions, it may be cheaper to organize production within a firm instead.[18] A crucial implication of Coase's work is that the solution to contract problems that make markets inefficient is, well, contracts. For example, an entrepreneur can use employment contracts to establish a right to direct the manner in which work is performed. Although the relationship between employer and employee is hierarchical, it is defined by the employment contract; the employer has "no power of fiat, no authority, no disciplinary" power beyond what would be available through "ordinary market contracting."[19] According to this view, the firm is just a label that stands for the set of contracts that organize economic production.[20]

Because the firm is the aggregate of a set of contractual relationships, its boundaries are loosely defined. Contracts exist inside and outside the firm and pertain to the same economic substance – the development and sale of goods and services. Thus, whether a particular contractual relationship falls within or crosses over the boundaries of the firm requires functional analysis.[21] There is no categorical difference. What we see when we open up the black box is identical to what we find outside the black box: contracts among various parties organizing the factors of production.

Moreover, from an economist's perspective, the nexus-of-contracts conception of the firm includes agreements even if they would not satisfy the basic legal elements of a contract. Economic contracts include, more broadly, "compacts among people, who recognize their mutual interests and agree to modify their behavior in ways that are mutually beneficial."[22] Such agreements are considered contractual in this broader sense "regardless of whether they have the legal status of contracts."[23] By focusing on the functional role of contract, rather than the formal indicia that lawyers

18 *See* Butler, *supra* note 11, at 103 ("[O]nce transactions costs are added, the least costly, or most efficient, form of coordination of certain economic activities may be through the firm.").

19 Armen A. Alchian & Harold Demsetz, *Production, Information Costs, and Economic Organization*, 62 AM. ECON. REV. 777, 777 (1972).

20 Michael C. Jensen & William H. Meckling, *Theory of the Firm: Managerial Behavior, Agency Costs and Ownership Structure*, 3 J. FIN. ECON. 305, 311 (1976) ("The private corporation or firm is simply one form of legal fiction which serves as a nexus for contracting relationships.").

21 *Id.* at 311. ("Viewed this way, it makes little or no sense to try to distinguish those things which are 'inside' the firm … from those things that are 'outside' of it. There is in a very real sense only a multitude of complex relationships (i.e., contracts) between the legal fiction (the firm) and the owners of labor, material and capital inputs and the consumers of output.").

22 MILGROM & ROBERTS, *supra* note 15, at 127; *see also* John H. Langbein, *The Contractarian Basis of the Law of Trusts*, 105 YALE L.J. 625, 629 (1995) ("The bedrock elements of contract are consensual formation and consensual terms.").

23 MILGROM & ROBERTS, *supra* note 15, at 127.

use to separate enforceable from unenforceable agreements, economists can extend contractual analysis to explain the economic logic underpinning a wide variety of voluntary human associations.[24]

1.2 CORPORATE LAW AND ECONOMICS

The economist's theory of the firm as a contractual response to transaction costs has had a remarkable influence on legal scholarship. Before the advent of law and economics, the prevailing theory of corporate law characterized the corporation as a legal person authorized and defined by the state, operated by private individuals as a concession from the state, and subject to extensive regulation. Although the corporation was deemed a legal person, its metaphysical characteristics remained uncertain.[25] In a famous article, Professor Felix Cohen ridiculed "as transcendental nonsense" the notion that one could, for example, sensibly ask where a corporation is located.[26] A jurisprudence that takes such "supernatural" concepts seriously becomes an empty, "autonomous system of legal concepts, rules, and arguments."[27] Corporate law, Cohen argued, does not stand apart from "ethics and … such positive sciences as economics or psychology."[28]

Whatever the limitations of the underlying corporation-as-person metaphor, most corporate law scholarship focused on practical concerns regarding the managerial power resulting from the separation of ownership and control in large public corporations.[29] Deeper reflections on the nature of the corporation, let alone theories of economic firms in general, were an afterthought until, borrowing from Michael C. Jensen and William H. Meckling's work in economics, legal academics in the late 1970s and early 1980s reframed the debate in corporate law.[30] The signature work encapsulating

[24] *See* JON ELSTER, EXPLAINING SOCIAL BEHAVIOR: MORE NUTS AND BOLTS FOR THE SOCIAL SCIENCES 20 (2007) (stating that one measure of the credibility of a social science hypothesis is whether it has "excess explanatory power" with "implications that are novel, counterintuitive, and as different from the original explanandum as possible").

[25] *See* William W. Bratton, Jr., *The New Economic Theory of the Firm: Critical Perspectives from History*, 41 STAN. L. REV. 1471, 1482, 1489 (1989).

[26] *See* Felix S. Cohen, *Transcendental Nonsense and the Functional Approach*, 35 COLUM. L. REV. 809, 810 (1935).

[27] *Id.* at 821.

[28] *Id.*

[29] *See* Bratton, *supra* note 25, at 1486; *see also* ADOLF A. BERLE, JR. & GARDINER C. MEANS, THE MODERN CORPORATION AND PRIVATE PROPERTY 119 (1932).

[30] *See, e.g.*, Lucian Arye Bebchuk, *Limiting Contractual Freedom in Corporate Law: The Desirable Constraints on Charter Amendments*, 102 HARV. L. REV. 1820, 1820–21 (1989); Frank H. Easterbrook & Daniel R. Fischel, *Corporate Control Transactions*, 91 YALE L.J. 698, 701

the law and economics contribution remains Frank H. Easterbrook and Daniel R. Fischel's *The Economic Structure of Corporate Law*.[31]

Law and economics largely abandon the personhood metaphor and proceed instead from the assumption that corporations and other forms of business organization are best understood as a nexus of contracts organizing production within the firm, as well as with external suppliers and customers.[32] The arrangements are presumed to be voluntary and, at least in an economic sense, contractual.[33] The contractual bargain contains two basic elements. First, there is the choice of form. State laws provide a variety of different entity choices, each with its own coherent set of (mostly) default rules.[34] Investors are not locked into a single template and can choose the default structure they prefer as the starting point for further contractual modification. Second, having selected the entity form, rational individuals seeking to maximize the value of their investment will negotiate modifications to the default rules.[35] Corporate law rules, then, are mostly "trivial" because they either track what the parties would have negotiated or are discarded in favor of the parties' actual preferences.[36]

If business organizations are contracts entered into by economically rational individuals seeking to maximize their own advantage, it follows that family

(1982); Daniel R. Fischel, *The Corporate Governance Movement*, 35 VAND. L. REV. 1259, 1261–62 (1982); Ronald J. Gilson, *Evaluating Dual Class Common Stock: The Relevance of Substitutes*, 73 VA. L. REV. 807, 808–11 (1987).

31 EASTERBROOK & FISCHEL, *supra* note 6. For a survey of contemporary work in corporate law and economics, see generally RESEARCH HANDBOOK ON THE ECONOMICS OF CORPORATE LAW (Claire A. Hill & Brett H. McDonnell eds., 2012).

32 *See* BAINBRIDGE, *supra* note 4, at 8; Jonathan R. Macey, *Fiduciary Duties as Residual Claims: Obligations to Nonshareholder Constituencies from a Theory of the Firm Perspective*, 84 CORNELL L. REV. 1266 (1999) ("[A]ccording to the law and economics perspective that the nexus-of-contracts approach to corporate law exemplifies, one should view the corporation as a 'complex set of explicit and implicit contracts.'") (citation omitted); Lewis A. Kornhauser, *The Nexus of Contracts Approach to Corporations: A Comment on Easterbrook and Fischel*, 89 COLUM. L. REV. 1449 (1989); Steven N. S. Cheung, *The Contractual Nature of the Firm*, 26 J.L. & ECON. 1 (1983).

33 *See* Jean Braucher, *Contract Versus Contractarianism: The Regulatory Role of Contract Law*, 47 WASH. & LEE L. REV. 697, 698 (1990) ("[D]ifficulty is presented by the fact that contractarian theorists to some extent use the idea of contract metaphorically.").

34 *See* Larry Ribstein, *Why Corporations?*, 1 BERKELEY BUS. L.J. 185 (2004).

35 *See* EASTERBROOK & FISCHEL, *supra* note 6, at 229 ("[I]t is essential to use contractual devices to keep people in a position to receive the return on their investment."); David Charney, *Hypothetical Bargains: The Normative Structure of Contract Interpretation*, 89 MICH. L. REV. 1815, 1871 (1991) (observing that "it is generally feasible for the small number of shareholders in a close corporation to bargain among themselves").

36 *See* Bernard S. Black, *Is Corporate Law Trivial?: A Political and Economic Analysis*, 84 NW. U. L. REV. 542 (1990).

relationships that may exist among investors are not relevant to the corporate contract and should not affect the legal outcome in the event of a dispute. That is to say, the law largely ignores social connections among investors because, as in a classic economic market, "[t]he parties have no pre-contractual obligations to provide each other with the goods they exchange."[37] The impersonal nature of "market relations … defines a sphere of freedom from personal ties and obligations."[38] As such, "[t]he market leaves its participants free to pursue their individual interests without considering others' interests. Each party to a market transaction is expected to take care of herself."[39]

The value of the contractarian model depends upon its underlying assumption that individuals are economically rational in that they consult only their own preferences and then pick the best strategy to advance those preferences.[40] Therefore, according to standard law and economics, "[r]ational individuals invest their human and money capital with a view to maximizing the value of such resources."[41] In selecting an investment, a rational actor "engages in an ongoing comparative search for the … investments that promise the most attractive return on invested capital given the investor's taste for risk."[42]

Although presented as a single concept, the elements of rational choice can be disaggregated. First, there is the proposition that individuals are capable of perfectly gathering and processing information so that their market interactions are the best evidence of their preferences and also the best avenue for securing the things that they value. Individuals neither overestimate nor underestimate risk and avoid mental shortcuts in favor of full analysis of each decision. Much criticism of rational-choice economics involves the presentation of evidence that human beings are not rational in the same way that a thinking machine would be and, in fact, are systematically irrational.[43]

[37] Elizabeth Anderson, Value in Ethics and Economics 145 (1993) (identifying the moral values associated with market exchange).

[38] *Id.*

[39] *Id.*

[40] *See* Bainbridge, *supra* note 4, at 23 (stating that "neoclassical economics is premised on rational choice theory, which posits an autonomous individual who makes rational choices that maximize his satisfactions"). A perfectly rational actor would gather the optimal amount of information and pick the course of action best designed to achieve the ends that they have selected. *See* Elster, *supra* note 24, at 191; Eric Posner, *Economic Analysis of Contract Law after Three Decades: Success or Failure?*, 112 Yale L.J. 829, 865 (2003).

[41] Charles R. O'Kelley, Jr., *Filling Gaps in the Close Corporation Contract: A Transaction Cost Analysis*, 87 Nw. U. L. Rev. 216, 220 (1992).

[42] *Id.*

[43] *See* Choices, Values, and Frames (Daniel Kahneman & Amos Tversky eds., 2000); Jon D. Hanson & Douglas A. Kysar, *Taking Behavioralism Seriously: The Problem of Market Manipulation*, 74 N.Y.U. L. Rev. 630, 673 (1999); Melvin A. Eisenberg, *The Limits of Cognition and the Limits of Contract*, 47 Stan. L. Rev. 211 (1995).

For example, business owners may systematically overestimate the ability of their children when deciding whether to sell a business at its current value or transfer it to the next generation.

A second, distinct assumption is that individuals evaluate information and proceed to the best of their ability to maximize their own advantage.[44] The claim that individuals always act to further their own interests is the more interesting, broadly influential, and largely nonfalsifiable aspect of rational-choice theory. Even if individuals make predictable mistakes in the calculation of their own advantage, in other words, it could still be the case that they are motivated to pursue their own interests. If so, the market's normative framework still pertains and family relationships only have significance if a rational individual can use them to lower contracting costs.[45] When business dealings involve family members, this perspective requires us to ignore the prospect that someone might rationally accept a smaller economic outcome in order to benefit other family members. Thus, economic assumptions can get in the way of understanding the motivations of family business participants.

1.3 APPLYING THE ECONOMIC PERSPECTIVE

One unfortunate consequence of the economic perspective is that it counsels a narrow approach to dispute resolution and will often miss the nature of the underlying conflict that would be needed for a fair resolution. Assuming that the rational-choice economic perspective is correct, that is, and that corporations consist of a network of contracts meant to lower overall transaction costs, it follows that the proper function of courts is largely to resolve business disputes by identifying and enforcing the parties' economic bargain.[46] In light of this priority, status-based family relationships would be excluded from consideration, even in a family business. Courts adhering to rational-choice economic principles should not adjust the parties' rights in the name of fairness, fiduciary duty, or any other concept external to the economic

[44] *See* John Ferejohn, *Rationality and Interpretation: Parliamentary Elections in Early Stuart England, in* The Economic Approach to Politics 279, 281 (Kristin Renwick Monroe ed., 1991) ("[R]ational choice theorists are committed to a principle of universality: (all) agents act always to maximize their well-being as they understand it.").

[45] *See* Easterbrook & Fischel, *supra* note 6, at 229 (observing that the "[p]articipants in closely held corporations frequently have familial or other personal relations in addition to their business dealings" and that "[t]he continuous and nonpecuniary nature of these relationships reduces agency problems").

[46] *See* Larry E. Ribstein, *From Efficiency to Politics in Contractual Choice of Law*, 37 Ga. L. Rev. 363, 395 (2003).

fundamentals of the parties' contractual relationship. Thus, a key question for law and economics is whether a court can go beyond the literal terms of the parties' agreement, as memorialized in various corporate documents, and, if so, what additional evidence or arguments might properly sway the court.

For example, minority shareholders in close corporations are vulnerable to the risk that the majority owners will abuse their control to take disproportionate value from the business, sometimes freezing out minority shareholders from any economic benefit. The nature of the problem is clear: In a close corporation, there are relatively few shareholders, no publicly traded shares, and, typically, direct shareholder management.[47] Although many close corporations operate by consensus, and family norms may drive ordinary decisions, majority owners retain the formal power to appoint the board of directors. Mistreated minority shareholders cannot exit and recover the value of their investment because the shares are not publicly traded and no rational investor would pay for a frozen-out minority's shares.[48] With no market protections readily available, minority investors who have not negotiated employment agreements, buy-sell provisions, or other contractual alternatives must depend upon the willingness of courts to intervene to remedy oppression.

Yet, in cases of shareholder oppression, courts are asked to protect minority shareholders who failed to negotiate adequately to protect their own interests. At first blush, intervention to provide special relief for minority shareholders who could have bargained for protection against majority opportunism appears inconsistent with a rational choice, economic model of corporate governance, and some courts and scholars reject it on precisely this ground.[49] Nevertheless, the judicial role may often be reconcilable with a strictly economic approach to contract. For example, negotiating a long-term business contract involves significant costs. Therefore, when a dispute arises, the right question to ask is

47 *See* 1 F. Hodge O'Neal & Robert B. Thompson, Close Corporations and LLCs: Law and Practice §§ 1:2, 1:9 (rev. 3rd ed. 2010).

48 *See* Nixon v. Blackwell, 626 A.2d 1366, 1379 (Del. 1993) (noting that "there is no market and no market valuation"); Donahue v. Rodd Electrotype Co. of New England, Inc., 328 N.E.2d 505, 514 (Mass. 1975) (same).

49 *See* Edward B. Rock & Michael L. Wachter, *Waiting for the Omelet to Set: Match-Specific Assets and Minority Oppression in Close Corporations*, 24 J. Corp. L. 913, 915 (1999) (asking "what, if anything, the courts should do for the minority shareholders in cases where the parties have not provided for the problem by contract" and stating as a "basic answer … that courts should not do anything except enforce the participants' contracts"); *Nixon*, 626 A.2d at 1380 ("It would do violence to normal corporate practice … to fashion an ad hoc ruling which would result in a court-imposed stockholder buy-out for which the parties had not contracted.").

not whether private bargaining could have anticipated and resolved the dispute but whether the cost of such bargaining would have exceeded its likely benefit.

Rational actors take transaction costs into account and will proceed without a fully specified bargain when the anticipated length and complexity of the relationship makes a complete contract unrealistic.[50] At the same time, rational actors expect others to act opportunistically and would not invest in a venture unless some alternative form of protection existed.[51] If the cost of negotiating protections is too high, the individually rational decision might be to walk away from otherwise viable investment opportunities. Thus, corporate law rules that constrain majority shareholders may be economically efficient apart from any equitable goals they serve.[52] Judicial monitoring is not necessarily an exception to principles of contractual ordering but only a further recognition that in a market "[e]ach party values the other only instrumentally, not intrinsically."[53]

As one scholar explains, judicial monitoring may further the parties' own intentions even though it involves intervention in the governance rules that would otherwise apply by default:

> The strategy is consistent with courts' behavior faced with long-term contracts in which it is prohibitively costly to specify the parties' required actions in all states. Legal scholars often call these transactions relational contracts. Close corporations fit the paradigm because the parties' failure to build in specific protections against the majority appropriating wealth from the minority is plausibly a result, not of their desire to permit such appropriation, but rather of the prohibitive cost of writing a contract to achieve that result. To the extent that courts can supply implicit contract terms that are consistent with the parties' preferences, they can reduce the cost of forming close corporations.[54]

50 Even strict defenders of law and economics admit that complete bargains are often impossible. *See* EASTERBROOK & FISCHEL, *supra* note 6, at 34 ("Even when they work through all the issues they expect to arise, [venturers] are apt to miss something. All sorts of complexities will arise later."); George G. Triantis, *Financial Contract Design in the World of Venture Capital*, 68 U. CHI. L. REV. 305, 307 (2001) (identifying information and agency problems that prevent parties from reaching complete financial contracts).

51 *See* GARY S. BECKER, THE ECONOMIC APPROACH TO HUMAN BEHAVIOR 14 (1976) (contending that individuals "maximize their utility from a stable set of preferences and accumulate an optimal amount of information and other inputs in a variety of markets").

52 *See* JONATHAN R. MACEY, CORPORATE GOVERNANCE: PROMISES KEPT, PROMISES BROKEN 22 (2008) ("Fiduciary duties are part of the contractual nature of the corporation and exist to fill in the blanks and inevitable oversights in the actual contracts used by business organizations.").

53 ANDERSON, *supra* note 37, at 154 (distinguishing intimate sexual relationships from prostitution on the basis of reciprocity, a norm that cannot be fully commodified).

54 Paul G. Mahoney, *Trust and Opportunism in Close Corporations*, *in* CONCENTRATED CORPORATE OWNERSHIP 193 (Randall K. Morck ed., 2000).

This is not, however, an open-ended invitation to courts to rewrite the parties' bargain – after all, most matters not specifically addressed in shareholder agreements are committed to the default majoritarian rules of corporate law.[55] Only in an exceptional case involving apparent abuse of control would a court supply a term that the parties chose not to include.

At bottom, the law and economics approach assumes that each party is focused on their own wealth maximization. To that end, family-owned businesses are just one possible choice among others, all of which can be measured and compared along the same economic metric.[56] Furthermore, because the focus is on individual wealth maximization, the relationships among family members are not relevant to their rights and responsibilities as business co-owners. Accordingly, the methodological influence of rational-choice economics produces a sophisticated, but limited vision of how corporations are formed, how they are governed, and how disputes among their co-owners should be resolved. Noneconomic investment motivations have mostly fallen by the wayside.

[55] *See* O'Kelley, *supra* note 41, at 220.

[56] *See* Easterbrook & Fischel, *supra* note 6, at 231:

> [I]t is a mistake to conclude that shareholders in closely held corporations face unique risks of oppression, just as it is wrong to argue that shareholders in publicly held corporations face unique risks of exploitation because of the separation of ownership and control. Each organizational form presents its own problems, for which people have designed different mechanisms of control. At the margin the problems must be equally severe, the mechanisms equally effective – were it otherwise, investors would transfer their money from one form to the other until the marginal equality condition were satisfied. Because the world contains so many different investment vehicles, none will offer distinctively better chances of return when people can select and shift among them.

2

Distinctive Features of Family Businesses

To understand family firms – what makes them function, and what causes them to break down – we need to consider the influence of family life and the role identifications that can motivate participation in a family business.[1] The standard law-and-economics account summarized in the previous chapter is not sufficient. Even a broader economic analysis that acknowledges that trust among participants can lower transaction costs retains the assumption that individuals join collective associations to advance their own ends.[2] This reductive account treats family intimacy as a means to an end. Thus, there is little reason to expect that a more careful assessment of transaction costs will produce an optimal solution to problems of shareholder oppression or other conflicts in family businesses.

Family business governance is challenging because it includes family relationships and business relationships.[3] In this context, ignoring nonmarket

[1] Note that this analysis does not assume that "family" is itself a stable category, unaffected by business ventures undertaken by family members. Rather, the point is that family and business institutions interact. *See* MARTHA ALBERTSON FINEMAN, THE AUTONOMY MYTH: A THEORY OF DEPENDENCY 61 (2004).

[2] Methodological individualism may go unnoticed because it is analogous to the construction of the individual that forms the basis for the modern liberal state. As communitarian scholars have observed, however, a vulnerable assumption of liberal theory is that "[w]e are distinct individuals first, and *then* we form relationships and engage in co-operative arrangements with others." MICHAEL J. SANDEL, LIBERALISM AND THE LIMITS OF JUSTICE 133 (2d ed. Cambridge University Press, 1998) (1982). Yet, in our family relationships we may consider ourselves to be members of a group first and individuals second. *See* MICHAEL WALZER, SPHERES OF JUSTICE: A DEFENSE OF PLURALISM AND EQUALITY 126 (1983).

[3] *See* Ivan Lansberg, *Managing Human Resources in Family Firms: The Problem of Institutional Overlap*, 12 ORGANIZATIONAL DYNAMICS 39, 40 (Summer 1983) (describing families and businesses as "two qualitatively different social institutions"). However, the sharp segregation of working life and family life is culturally specific and relatively recent. *See* Frances Olsen, *The Family and the Market: A Study of Ideology and Legal Reform*, 96 HARV. L. REV. 1497, 1499 (1983) ("In the early nineteenth century, as men's work was largely removed to the factory

motivations means missing at least half the picture. Most families distribute roughly equal resources to their children,[4] offer special protection to their most vulnerable members,[5] and seek to preserve their identity over time.[6] Moreover, family relationships are considered valuable for their own sake and not principally for their economic or other instrumental advantages.[7] By contrast, a traditional business relies on contracts negotiated at arm's length, aims to make a profit, and seeks to identify and reward merit on an objective basis.[8] For investors, the business serves as a means to an end.[9]

In a family business, however, the values associated with family life must coexist with the values of the marketplace.[10] For instance, when the junior employees in a business venture are also the children of the founders, family concerns become work concerns and vice versa.[11] Individuals cannot negotiate the distinct expectations associated with each environment simply by adopting one social identity when in the workplace with colleagues and another when at home with family.[12] Thus, a successful family business must find ways to mediate the tension between expectations rooted in family life and expectations inherent to the marketplace.[13]

while women's work remained primarily in the home, there came to be a sharp dichotomy between 'the home' and 'the [workaday] world.'") (citation omitted).

4 Lansberg, *supra* note 3, at 42 ("In horizontal family relationships, such as the relationships among siblings, equality is the dominant fairness norm.").

5 *See id.* at 40 ("[S]ocial relations in the family are structured to satisfy family members' various developmental needs.").

6 *See* Teresa J. Rothausen, *Management Work – Family Research and Work – Family Fit: Implications for Building Family Capital in Family Business*, 22 FAM. BUS. REV. 220, 226 (2009) (stating that "shared vision" is part of what constitutes a family) (citation omitted).

7 *See* ELIZABETH ANDERSON, VALUE IN ETHICS AND ECONOMICS 157 (1993) (reprinted 1995).

8 Lansberg, *supra* note 3, at 42 (observing that "the norm of fairness that operates in the firm is based on the concept of merit").

9 *See* Daniel J. H. Greenwood, *Fictional Shareholders: For Whom Are Corporate Managers Trustees, Revisited*, 69 S. CAL. L. REV. 1021, 1023 (1996) ("[W]hatever else shareholders may or may not want, every shareholder wants to make a profit and this is all that is really important for the operation of corporate law and, indeed, the corporation itself.").

10 *See, e.g.*, MANFRED F. R. KETS DE VRIES ET AL., FAMILY BUSINESS ON THE COUCH: A PSYCHOLOGICAL PERSPECTIVE 9 (2007) ("[I]n a business family, normal family goals may come into conflict with the business's economic goals because an important theme within the family system is to meet the human and psychological needs of its members rather than to arrive at the best economic return.").

11 *See, e.g.*, Keating v. Keating, No. 00-749, 2003 WL 23213143 (Mass. Super. Ct. 2003); Orchard v. Covelli, 590 F. Supp. 1548 (W.D. Pa. 1984).

12 KELIN E. GERSICK ET AL., GENERATION TO GENERATION: LIFE CYCLES OF THE FAMILY BUSINESS 5 (1997).

13 *See* TORSTEN M. PIEPER, MECHANISMS TO ASSURE LONG-TERM FAMILY BUSINESS SURVIVAL 7 (2007); GERSICK ET AL., *supra* note 12, at 5; Lansberg, *supra* note 3, at 39; DOUG

When expectations align, the business and family both stand to benefit.[14] The strength and durability of family relationships can be harnessed to solve business problems. For example, family members might create or modify business roles without formal contracts and managers generally have the flexibility to pursue longer-term opportunities at the expense of short-term profits.[15] In a pinch, family members will sometimes loan money to the business or agree to work without compensation.[16] Moreover, business ownership can provide nonmonetary benefits to family members such as stable employment, status in the community, and agreeable working conditions. Indeed, some commentators celebrate family business as a model for creative, humane capitalism.[17]

However, the strengths of a family business are also potential weaknesses. Over time, "conflicts manifest themselves in the form of normative contradictions whereby what is expected from individuals in terms of family principles often violates what is expected from them according to business principles."[18] For example, the transfer of control from one generation to the next invites tension between the family norm of equal treatment and the business norm of meritocracy. In a crisis, the close emotional bonds that once supported a family

Baumoel & Blair Trippe, Deconstructing Conflict: Understanding Family Business, Shared Wealth and Power (2016).

14 For a discussion of value creation in family firms, see Michael Carney, *Corporate Governance and Competitive Advantage in Family-Controlled Firms*, 29 Entrepreneurship Theory & Prac. 249 (2005).

15 *See* Amy Schuman et al., Family Business as Paradox 2 (2010) (stating that family businesses "have a longer time horizon than most non-family firms"); *see also* Andrew Martin, *In Company Town, Cuts but No Layoffs*, N.Y. Times, Sept. 25, 2011, at BU1 (describing efforts by a family business to retain employees despite lower product demand and quoting the company's president, a granddaughter of the founder: "'You can't cut your way to prosperity. You can't grow if you are cutting your lifeblood.'").

16 *See, e.g.*, Emily Chamlee-Wright & Virgil Henry Storr, *Community Resilience in New Orleans East: Deploying the Cultural Toolkit Within a Vietnamese American Community*, *in* Community Disaster Recovery and Resiliency: Exploring Global Opportunities and Challenges 101, 116 (DeMond Shondell Miller & Jason David Rivera eds., 2011) (describing how a woman was able to restore her seafood processing business after Hurricane Katrina by living with her daughter and obtaining a "$300,000 loan from another of her daughters and son-in-law, which was enough to buy cooling and freezing equipment to store the seafood").

17 *See* Steven H. Hobbs & Fay Wilson Hobbs, *Family Businesses and the Business of Families: A Consideration of the Role of the Lawyer*, 4 Tex. Wesleyan L. Rev. 153, 158 (1998) ("Socially and culturally, the family business offers the opportunity to unify work and family concerns for the benefit of succeeding generations."); *see also* Andrea Colli, The History of Family Business, 1850–2000 23 (2003) (describing without endorsing a view that the family firm "held out the prospect of a new production model – one much more creative and less impersonal, moulded by elements like friendship and kinship").

18 Lansberg, *supra* note 3, at 40; Schuman et al., *supra* note 15, at 21.

business can become obstacles to rational action.[19] Siblings sue siblings;[20] children sue parents;[21] spouses divorce;[22] families and businesses fall apart.

If family businesses in the United States were relatively rare or economically unimportant, legal scholars understandably might pay scant attention to whether the current corporate-law framework is sufficient. In fact, family businesses are a vital part of the economy: They are approximately one-third of all businesses, employ about half the nation's workforce, and contribute a substantial amount to the nation's gross domestic product.[23] Small businesses often begin as entrepreneurial family ventures and some of the United States' largest corporations remain family controlled.[24]

The rational-actor model relied upon in standard law-and-economics analysis and discussed in Chapter 1 excludes an entire dimension of moral concern – family values – that is integral to many family businesses and no less important than wealth maximization for the long-term health of society. To be sure, family relationships can lower transaction costs, but this is not the whole story. The rational-actor model of standard law and economics lacks the conceptual resources necessary to fully appreciate the nature of private ordering within a family business. That is the case, because, in addition to their economic function, family businesses are an extension of family relationships in which the participants find intrinsic and not merely instrumental value.[25] Whether organized as partnerships, corporations, or limited liability

[19] *See, e.g.*, Lansberg, *supra* note 3, at 41 ("Founders often find themselves in the difficult situation of having to choose between either hiring (or firing) an incompetent relative or breaking up their relationship with some part of the family.").

[20] Morrison v. Gugle, 755 N.E.2d 404 (Ohio Ct. App. 2001) (shareholder oppression dispute between twin sisters); Meiselman v. Meiselman, 307 S.E.2d 551 (N.C. 1983) (finding shareholder oppression where one brother, the majority shareholder, had excluded his brother from participation in the business venture).

[21] Keating v. Keating, No. 00-749, 2003 WL 23213143, at *1 (Mass. Super. Ct. 2003) (noting that the dispute "pits father and daughter against son and vice versa in a lengthy internecine struggle for control of the administration of the family-run closely held food distribution business").

[22] Thrasher v. Thrasher, 103 Cal. Rptr. 618, 621 (Cal. Ct. App. 1972) (withholding of dividends motivated by marital dispute).

[23] The numbers vary, of course, depending on how we define family business. Also, although the typical family business operates on a small scale, some of the United States' and the world's largest enterprises are family dominated.

[24] Internationally, family businesses are even more prevalent. *See, e.g.*, Teemu Ruskola, *Conceptualizing Corporations and Kinship: Comparative Law and Development Theory in a Chinese Perspective*, 52 Stan. L. Rev. 1599 (2000).

[25] The family is, among other things, a system that connects individuals and structures their experiences. *See, e.g.*, David Bork, Family Business, Risky Business: How to Make It Work 26 (1986) ("A systems concept sees what is going on in the individual as inseparable from the family network of relationships in which the individual is embedded, the emotional processes in that system, and the way the system was balanced before symptoms appeared.").

companies, family firms are economic institutions embedded in a context of family social roles and values.[26] In interpreting the parties' business contract, social context has explanatory power and deserves normative weight. In short, family status matters.

2.1 DEFINING FAMILY BUSINESS

The traditional corporate model assumes diffuse share ownership with centralized management,[27] and yet, according to one commentator, "[f]amily dominated businesses comprise more than 80 percent of U.S. enterprises, employ more than 50 percent of the nation's workforce, and account for the bulk … of America's gross domestic product."[28] However, the precise economic impact of family business depends upon what we mean by family business and no single definition has been established.[29]

That is, before evaluating whether family businesses merit separate legal analysis, logic would suggest that we must first clarify the meaning of family business – thereby providing a stable referent for analysis.[30] To this end, we might begin with a simple requirement that effective control of the business rests in family hands and that at least two family members be involved as owners or managers.[31] In the finance and management literatures, other definitions variously require an intention to maintain family ownership over

26 For a general discussion of how economic institutions are embedded in social context, see Neil Fligstein, The Architecture of Markets: An Economic Sociology of Twenty-First-Century Capitalist Societies (2001). Of course, families are themselves a way of structuring the use of economic resources. *See* Jill Elaine Hasday, *Intimacy and Economic Exchange*, 119 Harv. L. Rev. 491, 493 (2005) ("Economic exchange is not foreign to intimate relations, either as a matter of first principles or as a positive matter of legal regulation.").

27 *See* Adolf A. Berle, Jr. & Gardiner C. Means, The Modern Corporation and Private Property (1932); Lucian A. Bebchuk & Mark J. Roe, *A Theory of Path Dependence in Corporate Ownership and Governance*, 52 Stan. L. Rev. 127 (1999).

28 Dwight Drake, Business Planning: Closely Held Enterprises 314 (5th ed. 2018); Ernesto J. Poza, Family Business (2004).

29 *See* Colli, *supra* note 17, at 8 ("Contrary to the relatively easy definition of big business and of the modern managerial corporation, it is not as simple to delineate the boundaries and features of the family business, even from a 'residual' perspective."); Melissa Carey Shanker & Joseph H. Astrachan, *Myths and Realities: Family Businesses' Contribution to the U.S. Economy – A Framework for Assessing Family Business Statistics*, 9 Fam. Bus. Rev. 107 (1996).

30 *See* Jon Elster, Explaining Social Behavior: More Nuts and Bolts for the Social Sciences 15 (2007) (emphasizing that the first, and "easily overlooked" step in social science explanation is "to establish that the fact *is* a fact").

31 *See* Danny Miller & Isabelle Le Breton-Miller, *Challenge Versus Advantage in Family Business*, Strategic Org. 127 (Feb. 2003) (stating the requirement that "a family has enough ownership to determine the composition of the board, where the CEO and at least one other top executive is a family member, and where the intent is to pass the firm on to the next generation").

time, the involvement of more than a single generation of family owners, or high-level managerial involvement.[32]

Any broad definition involves simplification, however, and may be difficult to apply in particular cases. For instance, what is the proper characterization of a business formed by a married couple who divorce but continue to work together?[33] Or surviving spouses who share no connection other than the sibling bond of their deceased partners? Or a business founded by unrelated individuals whose children later fall in love and marry? In these cases, and others that might be imagined, family connections exist but are difficult to define. It is even possible to create a family relationship to satisfy a business requirement, rather than the other way around.[34] Moreover, any definition of family business presupposes a definition of family.[35] Adding to the complexity of the task, the scope of recognized kinship ties varies across cultures.[36] In the United States, immigration has led to a proliferation of different family cultures, which may explain differences in family business organization.[37] At the margin, the tally of family businesses could vary depending on what types of relationships are considered sufficiently familial.

Differences in business scale may require further diversification of the family business model. For example, in a small, family-owned entity, the external consequences of a business dispute may be limited to the family relationships among owners.[38] In larger organizations, destabilizing family disputes affect

[32] *Id.*

[33] *See* William M. Long & Scott A. Sissel, *Divorce and the Family Business – What Are the Options?*, 9 BUS. ENTITIES 30, 35 (2007).

[34] *See* Vikas Mehrotra et al., *Adoptive Expectations: Rising Sons in Japanese Family Firms*, 108 J. FIN. ECON. 840, 841 (2013) (examining "two unique practices of Japanese business families: marriages arranged to inject talent into business families and adoptions of promising adults as principal heirs").

[35] According to one scholar, a family is a "patterned system to distribute the obligations for dependent individuals (children and the elderly)." Steven L. Nock, *Time and Gender in Marriage*, 86 VA. L. REV. 1971, 1972 (2000). Whereas "[a] century ago, 'family' was culturally confined to persons related by marriage and blood; today, family is defined by relations of affinity, love, and commitment." William N. Eskridge, Jr., *Family Law Pluralism: The Guided-Choice Regime of Menus, Default Rules, and Override Rules*, 100 GEO. L.J. 1881, 1883 (2012). Thus, the boundaries of family life can be difficult to ascertain. *See* Laura A. Rosenbury, *Between Home and School*, 155 U. PA. L. REV. 833 (2007); Martha Minow, *Redefining Families: Who's In and Who's Out?*, 62 U. COLO. L. REV. 269 (1991).

[36] *See* FINEMAN, *supra* note 1, at 63 ("[I]f the family is constructed through interaction with the state and society, the family cannot be posited as a 'natural' entity with a form that is constant over time and culture.").

[37] I am grateful to Moss Blachman for this observation.

[38] *See, e.g.*, Meiselman v. Meiselman, 307 S.E.2d 551 (N.C. 1983) (involving a dispute over ownership of family-owned close corporations).

hundreds of employees and may even have civic implications. To cite one case in point, the Los Angeles Dodgers organization was thrown into turmoil when the owner's divorce created uncertainty about who would gain control of the team, while the sheer cost of the divorce allegedly siphoned away funds needed to sustain operations.[39] A more detailed typology could also distinguish vertical and horizontal family ties, designate the generation of family ownership, and account for other significant ethnic or religious affiliations.[40]

For simplicity's sake, and following broad conventions in family business analysis, I will use a relatively broad definition of family business comprised of two elements. First, the family must have the ability to control or substantially influence business decisions. Typically, this would mean the ability to appoint top management. Depending upon the governance structure, a family might have control even without a majority ownership stake. For example, through the use of different classes of stock, a family business could retain control in family hands while allowing public investment.[41] Further, while direct participation of family in management or on the board of directors is the more usual situation, a family business could retain professional managers without losing its distinctive status – those managers still need to account for the special requirements of family owners and, ultimately, serve at the pleasure of family owners.

Second, there must be at least two family members who own a stake in the business or participate in its operation. Without this qualification, all sole proprietorships would count as family businesses, which may explain why some commentators estimate that family businesses are the vast majority of all businesses. Yet, from a lawyer's perspective, any reasonable understanding of family business requires something more than the fact that a business owner is also a member of a family. For example, governance conflicts in family businesses turn on a failure to integrate family and work values – when what

[39] When the Dodgers' owner, Frank McCourt, sought refuge in a bankruptcy proceeding, the Commissioner of Major League Baseball filed papers indicating the possibility of terminating the franchise. *See* Lester Munson, *The "Death Penalty" and the Dodgers*, ESPN (Sept. 30, 2011), https://bit.ly/4mhaM32 [http://perma.cc/U95D-RMUJ] ("Paying his personal expenses with Dodgers money, baseball says, prevents McCourt from 'acquiring new players,' meeting 'future payroll obligations' and 'improving the Dodgers fan experience.'").

[40] *See, e.g.*, Hobby Lobby Stores, Inc. v. Sebelius, 723 F.3d 1114, 1120 (10th Cir. 2013), *cert. granted* 134 S. Ct. 678 (2013) (asserting corporation's right to free exercise of religion based upon the family owners' religious beliefs); Conestoga Wood Specialties Corp. v. Sec'y of U.S. Dep't of Health & Human Servs., 724 F.3d 377, 380 (3d Cir. 2013), *cert. granted* 134 S. Ct. 678 (2013) (same).

[41] For an article addressing issues of family control in the context of publicly held corporations, see Deborah A. DeMott, *Guests at the Table?: Independent Directors in Family-Influenced Public Companies*, 33 J. CORP. L. 819 (2008).

is owed depends upon whether one stands in a family or business relation. If only one family member were involved in the business, other family members would have no greater or lesser an expectancy in the business than in any other valuable asset held by that family member.[42]

Stricter definitions of family business sometimes require either the involvement of more than one generation or an intention to pass the business to succeeding generations.[43] These factors can cement the identification of a family business but are not essential. For instance, if multiple generations were deemed necessary, a business owned and operated jointly by a married couple would not qualify as a family business, even though the co-owners have overlapping business and family obligations to one another. The definition based on an intention to maintain family ownership captures something important but may be difficult to assess. Also, even assuming perfect information, the test seems too restrictive – a business might be run with substantial family involvement, consistent with family values, and for the benefit of family, and yet the founder might reserve judgment as to whether it would best serve the interests of the family to sell the business or pass it down to a next generation of family owners.[44]

In sum, any single definition of family business will struggle to account for a wide variety of family and business contexts. Even worse, the leading indication of whether a business should qualify as a family business may be whether the participants believe that they are in a family business. For rigorous empirical analysis, these definitional hurdles are daunting if not insurmountable. Yet, the difficulties in determining, on a case-by-case basis, how to categorize businesses are no impediment to identifying recurring challenges involving the combination of business and family interests.[45]

Accordingly, when assessing the role of law in structuring and monitoring governance arrangements, what matters is not the formal definition, but

[42] Notably, a family member may be involved in a family business without any formal ownership stake. For instance, a spouse or child may assist in the development of a business venture without receiving any shares.

[43] *See* Miller & Le Breton-Miller, *supra* note 31, at 127 (defining family firm as "one in which a family has enough ownership to determine the composition of the board, where the CEO and at least one other executive is a family member, and where the intent is to pass the firm on to the next generation").

[44] For example, after establishing a transition plan for the benefit of his son, one business owner made a deathbed decision to revoke his son's inheritance of a car-dealership business. *In re* Estate of Richard C. Poe, Deceased, 648 S.W.3d 277 (Tex. 2022).

[45] *See, e.g.*, Kets de Vries, *supra* note 10, at 9 ("[I]n a business family, normal family goals may come into conflict with the business's economic goals because an important theme within the family system is to meet the human and psychological needs of its members rather than to arrive at the best economic return.").

whether the participants understand themselves to be involved in a family business. Ordinarily, family business status will not be at issue. In the first generation, the key individuals will typically consider themselves part of the same immediate family. If the business survives to a second generation, there will often be an association of siblings. By the third generation, many family businesses are owned by a consortium of cousins.[46] Thus, for present purposes, there is no need to consider the boundaries of family life, and we may assume only that it is possible to identify a distinct group of family businesses.[47] Indeed, although family relationships are distinctive, it may be that some of the same concerns would apply to fiduciary-like bonds among friends.[48]

2.2 OVERLAPPING VALUES

Family businesses present a governance challenge because they combine the values and expectations of the workplace with more intimate family bonds. When parents and children are also coworkers, for example, connections rooted in family life must be adjusted to meet the obligations of the workplace.[49] Before industrialization, when many people worked where they lived, whether that was on a family farm or in a small business such as a blacksmith's shop, there was usually little distance between home and work, literally and figuratively.[50] This was my grandmother's experience, too, growing up above her parents' delicatessen. The modern workplace, however, refers not only to a physical location but also a distinct culture with its own language, expected

[46] *See* IVAN LANSBERG, SUCCEEDING GENERATIONS: REALIZING THE DREAM OF FAMILIES IN BUSINESS (1999).

[47] Professor Muntean concludes that many definitions of family business seem to be "unnecessarily strict." Susan Clark Muntean, *Analyzing the Dearth in Family Enterprise Research, in* THEORETICAL DEVELOPMENTS AND FUTURE RESEARCH IN FAMILY BUSINESS 13 (Phillip H. Phan & John E. Bulter eds., 2008). For instance, one survey of family business only lists "those firms in which a single family has members actively engaged in the management of operations and are at least in the second generation of management." *Id.* at 14. But the definition leaves out "corporations in which more than one family owns and controls the firm," "firms in the first generation," and "family owned and controlled firms in which family members are no longer managing the daily operations of the firm." *Id.*

[48] *See* ETHAN J. LEIB, FRIEND V. FRIEND: THE TRANSFORMATION OF FRIENDSHIP – AND WHAT THE LAW HAS TO DO WITH IT (2011); Laura A. Rosenbury, *Friends with Benefits?*, 106 MICH. L. REV. 189 (2007).

[49] *See* ANDERSON, *supra* note 7, at 25.

[50] *See* NANCY F. COTT, THE BONDS OF WOMANHOOD: "WOMAN'S SPHERE" IN NEW ENGLAND, 1780–1835 22 (2d ed. Yale University Press, 1997) (1977).

behaviors, and value system.[51] In the context of family businesses, wherever they may be physically located, workplace values and family values interact in complex ways, and an analysis of the law's application to such businesses should take this interaction into account.

2.2.1 *Social Identity Theory*

According to social identity theory, people use social roles to "categorize themselves and others as a means of ordering the social environment and locating themselves and others within it."[52] Thus, "[s]ocial role differentiation, in enabling people to occupy different roles at different times and places, enables them to establish different priorities in different parts of their lives."[53] These roles are not casually adopted: "Experiences are constrained and filtered through institutionalized structures such that the very sense of self in many situations is derived largely from the role one is enacting."[54] For example, "when individuals are asked 'Who are you?', they typically respond in terms of social categories (e.g. female, wife, French, lawyer)."[55]

A role, taken by itself, may be clear and well defined. Family roles follow a script that most people know by heart:

> The most obvious and well-established examples of standardized relationships in western culture are those that exist within the family .... To be sure, the specific understanding of particular roles has changed drastically in the last thirty years. But it is safe to say that it is generally assumed that parents will provide their children with love, financial support and some degree of

[51] Blake E. Ashforth, Role Transitions in Organizational Life: An Identity-Based Perspective 1 (2001) (stating that individuals "must often enter organizations and adopt more or less formal roles" in order to accomplish tasks that were once handled more informally at home or in the community). Even where remote work has become normalized in many industries, cultural norms remain distinct from familial norms. Modern remote work in the digital age is distinct from the interrelatedness of the family farms of old. *See* Julia Guerrein, *Work-Life Balance in the Digital Age*, 50 Vt. B.J. 20 (Spring 2024). The reality of distinct and sometimes conflicting responsibilities in modern remote work is evidenced by recommendations to remote employees to manufacture formalities including some physical boundaries to mimic the "natural boundaries between homelife and work life." H. Nicole Werkmeister, *The Evolution of Hybrid Work in a Post-COVID World: Navigating the New Norm*, 40 GPSolo 65 (Sept./Oct. 2023).

[52] Ashforth, *supra* note 51, at 25 (stating that "[b]y identifying, individuals perceive themselves as psychologically intertwined with the fate of the social category or role, sharing its common destiny, and experiencing its successes and failures").

[53] *See* Anderson, *supra* note 7, at 25.

[54] *See* Ashforth, *supra* note 51, at 27.

[55] *Id.*

> education … that children will strive to be respectful to their parents and act in a way that pleases them; that older children will care for aging parents; that husbands and wives will be each other's primary source of emotional support; and that family members will act to benefit the whole – or at least refrain from causing harm to other members.[56]

Social roles, however, pose two related challenges for participants in family businesses. First, although "roles are typically associated with differentiated social domains" and "differentiated audiences," family businesses conflate family and workplace categories.[57] An employer–employee relationship may also be a parent–child relationship.[58] Thus, it may be unclear which role should take precedence in any given situation.[59] The expectations that we have of members of our family – that we will put the family's interests first, that we will take care of each other – may conflict with the goal of maximizing economic return in a business.[60] To the extent the social roles are incompatible, family business has a built-in conflict.

Second, individuals must be able to transition effectively between roles. When role identities make different demands, everyday transitions may be difficult to accomplish. Role transitions over longer periods can also be difficult. Most important for family business, it can be very hard for one generation to cede control to the next – because work and family are linked, stepping down as CEO may feel like a surrender of status as a family patriarch or matriarch.[61] Or, alternatively, the power structure of the family system may work at odds with any changes of control contemplated in the business.[62] (I return to these issues in Chapter 6 and explain how role conflict can destroy a family business.)

56 Melanie B. Leslie, *Enforcing Family Promises: Reliance, Reciprocity, and Relational Contract*, 77 N.C. L. Rev. 551, 585 (1999).

57 Ashforth, *supra* note 51, at 27.

58 *Id.* at 26 ("When interacting with another person, one necessarily occupies a particular role such as friend, spouse, or coworker.").

59 Anderson, *supra* note 7, at 25 (observing that a parent's choice whether to focus on a "child's demands for attention" or a "client's needs" may depend upon whether the parent is "at home or at work"). Professor Anderson further observes that these decision frames are not typically gender neutral since society "assigns different meanings to mothers and fathers making the same tradeoffs of work and parental responsibilities." *Id.*

60 *See, e.g.*, Lansberg, *supra* note 3, at 2 (noting that, regardless of merit, "it is assumed that in allocations among siblings, each individual is entitled to an equal share of resources and opportunities").

61 Ashforth, *supra* note 51, at 3 ("How does a newly retired chief executive officer (CEO) cope with the loss of identity and status?").

62 *See* F. Hodge O'Neal & Robert B. Thompson, Oppression of Minority Shareholders and LLC Members § 3:1, at 3–2 (rev. 2d ed. 2005).

Social identity theory helps us to appreciate that the interconnection of family and business value systems can create conflict in family businesses. Individuals may find themselves torn between advancing the interests of the business and upholding their obligations as members of a family.[63] Even if these social identities seem to align, or can be made to do so, the possibility of conflict always exists, especially during periods of business transition. Thus, "[a] better understanding of how family relationships influence behavior more generally promises to improve our understanding of the organizational and strategic choices made in the family-controlled firm."[64]

2.2.2 *The Three-Circle Model*

The problem of reconciling social roles requires more than just an understanding of the general values and expectations in each sphere. A further complexity arises because not all family business participants are similarly situated. Notably, some family members may participate in the management of the business while others become passive investors.[65] Moreover, the business may retain professional, nonfamily managers and board members.

The management literature represents these dynamics visually with a Venn diagram.[66] The three-circle model includes family business conflict and extends the analysis to include "a critical distinction between the ownership and management subsystems within the business circle."[67] The three-circle model is shown at Figure 2.1.

According to the diagram, individuals can be placed into one of seven possible positions: (1) family membership with share ownership and active participation in company management; (2) family membership with active participation in management but no share ownership; (3) share ownership and management but no family membership; (4) family membership with share ownership but no management participation; (5) family membership only; (6) management only; and (7) share ownership only. The three-circle model illustrates the variety of distinct roles in a family business, each with its own set of expectations and responsibilities.

[63] *See* SCHUMAN ET AL., *supra* note 15, at 76 ("A fundamentally paradoxical feature of family business is that families tend to be socialistic, while businesses are firmly capitalistic.").

[64] Muntean, *supra* note 47, at 18.

[65] *See id.*

[66] *See id.*; GERSICK ET AL., *supra* note 12, at 6. The three-circle model was first developed by Renato Taiguri & John A. Davis, *Bivalent Attitudes of the Family Firm*, 9 FAM. BUS. REV. 199 (1996).

[67] GERSICK ET AL., *supra* note 12, at 5 ("That is, some individuals are owners but not involved in the operation of the business; others are managers but do not control shares.").

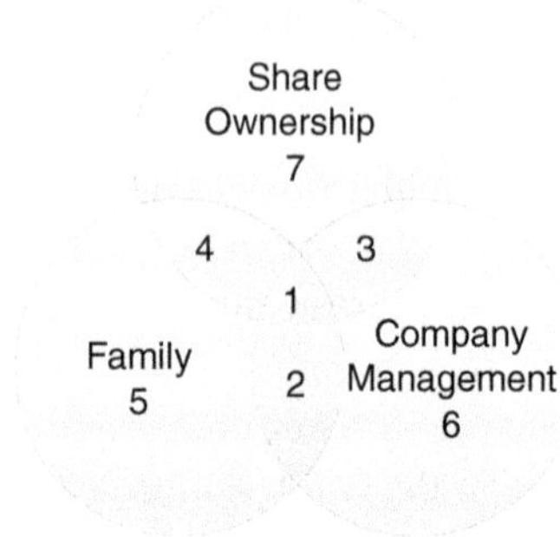

FIGURE 2.1 Three-circle model. Based on Renato Taiguri & John A. Davis, *Bivalent Attitudes of the Family Firm*, 9 FAM. BUS. REV. 199 (1996).

As the diagram illustrates, family relationships are central to our understanding of family businesses – a person's rights and responsibilities depend upon where they are in the family and the business hierarchy.[68] Although business relationships turn on productivity and merit, "[t]he standing of an individual in a family is determined more by who the individual 'is' than by what the individual 'does.'"[69] In order to design effective legal principles for evaluating and remedying business conflict, it is important to first understand the institutional context to which they will be applied. For family businesses, that means appreciating the overlapping demands of family and business values and the ways that individuals, depending on their position within the family, ownership, and management structure, may interpret their obligations to the business and to their family.

In the next section, I review this chapter's themes concerning the nature of family business ownership by telling the story of Chase Oil, a South Carolina fuel distribution company. Now in its third generation, Chase Oil benefits from the strength of the sibling bond between its two co-owners, Charles Howard and Chase Howard. In this respect, Chase Oil provides a useful counterpoint to the sibling conflict described in the book's preface. The story of Chase Oil also illustrates the importance of integrating informal family norms with more formalized business procedures – to hire and mentor employees, to

68 Indeed, economic action is always "embedded" in social context and "takes place within the networks of social relations that make up the social structure." Neil J. Smelser & Richard Swedberg, *The Sociological Perspective on the Economy*, *in* THE HANDBOOK OF ECONOMIC SOCIOLOGY 3, 18 (Neil J. Smelser & Richard Swedberg eds., 1994).

69 Lansberg, *supra* note 3, at 43. Thus, "[a]pplying a set of objectively derived criteria to evaluate a family member's performance goes against the very principles that regulate and define social behavior in the family." *Id.*

ensure compliance with legal regulations, and to establish financial controls sufficient to protect the business from internal and external risks.

2.3 CASE STUDY: CHASE OIL

Founded in 1946, Chase Oil has served the greater Florence (SC) area as a gasoline distributor for more than seventy-five years. Now in its third generation of family ownership, Chase Oil supplies approximately seventy-seven sites affiliated with industry giants such as AMOCO, BP, and Shell. In addition, the company recently diversified its portfolio by launching Scrubby's Car Wash. Chase Oil's success in each generation can be attributed to an entrepreneurial mindset, a willingness to revise core business procedures, and, equally important, a cooperative partnership among family owners.

The First and Second Generations. In 1945, while enjoying breakfast at a local diner in Florence, Maitland Chase struck up a conversation with a representative from AMOCO. The representative invited Maitland to establish a local distribution hub for AMOCO. Although Maitland already had a stable job in the heating and air conditioning industry, he saw a once-in-a-lifetime chance to join a high-growth industry and invested his life savings to start his own business.

Chase Oil opened in 1946 as a full-service AMOCO gas station where "bowtie-wearing, rag-in-the-back-pocket" attendants not only pumped gas but also cleaned windows, checked oil levels, and performed basic vehicle maintenance. Under Maitland's leadership, Chase Oil quickly expanded, growing to nearly twenty full-service gas stations.

Many entrepreneurs view day-to-day profitability as a step toward the ultimate goal: a large financial return on their investment. To that end, Maitland might have sought to sell Chase Oil to a larger competitor. When it came time to consider the future of the business, however, Maitland chose to keep Chase Oil in the family. By the 1960s, his son Maitland Jr. and son-in-law Charles Howard Sr. had become deeply involved in the company. Their close work with Maitland over the years ensured a smooth leadership transition when he passed away in 1970.

The transition from sole ownership to co-ownership in the second generation reflects a common pattern in family businesses, where the founding owner hands over control to a sibling partnership. This structure introduces additional governance complexities, however, and founders should consider whether it would be preferable to appoint a single successor. A parent's desire to treat children equally is not the same thing as a judgment concerning their merit to run a business. But the partnership model can be successful if children earn their place in the business and collaborate effectively, as Maitland Jr. and Charles Sr. did.

In the late 1970s, the brothers led Chase Oil through a significant transformation, steering the company away from the traditional full-service model and toward the emerging trend of combining gas stations with convenience stores. This shift not only diversified their revenue but also improved profit margins by reducing operational costs, as it eliminated the need for attendants to pump gas and provide mechanical services. Their willingness to reinvent the business model demonstrated entrepreneurial initiative – a readiness to reinvent that is essential for family-owned businesses seeking to avoid the risk of stagnation and decline. Maitland Jr. and Charles Sr. understood that long-term success required preserving the company's core values without being constrained by specific business practices.

Transition to the Third Generation. The transition of a family business from one generation to the next often presents financial and leadership challenges. The business may need to draw heavily on cash reserves or to take on debt to address the financial needs of the retiring generation. Also, the younger family members may lack the passion and work ethic necessary to lead the business. If those qualities are lacking, the current owners would be well advised to consider selling the business to someone outside the family or investing in professional management to handle day-to-day decision-making.

In the late 1990s, as Maitland Jr. prepared to retire, Charles Sr. offered his sons, Charles Jr. and Chase, the chance to join the family business. Both had strong professional backgrounds – Charles Jr. in finance and Chase in sales – which equipped them to contribute meaningfully to Chase Oil. Because Maitland Jr. did not have children, it was natural for Chase Oil to continue the sibling-partnership structure into the third generation. However, Charles and Chase were informed that it was not a gift; they would first have to purchase their uncle's shares. To avoid taking on external debt obligations, the parties agreed to an owner-financed deal. This approach allowed the brothers to "buy in" over time, earning their ownership stake through labor.

After their uncle retired, Charles and Chase worked alongside their father, Charles Sr., who maintained his status as president. As Charles remarked, "Dad literally worked until the day he died." The sudden loss of both parents within six months in 2021 presented the brothers with the dual challenge of grieving while also restructuring the business and managing their parents' estate. The transition required careful attention to both the company's operations and the broader financial reorganization of family assets. For more than a year, it was a full-time endeavor. Had their parents engaged in more complete estate planning, many of the issues that arose could have been avoided.

The brothers have since taken steps to put their own affairs in order so that history does not repeat itself.

As they took on leadership responsibilities, Charles and Chase made two significant changes. First, they streamlined Chase Oil's operations, shifting from day-to-day operations, such as running convenience stores and managing inventory, to wholesale gasoline distribution. By relying upon independent contractors to manage the convenience stores, Chase Oil has been able to expand the number of convenience stores from eleven to seventy-seven. Second, the brothers diversified Chase Oil's investment portfolio by entering the car wash business. Scrubby's Car Wash is a separate company that operates as a division of Chase Oil.

Sibling Partnership. Chase Oil's success across generations demonstrates the potential strength of sibling partnerships in family businesses. While Maitland started the company and ran it for decades as the sole owner, the second and third generations successfully embraced a co-ownership governance model. (As used here, the term "partnership" refers to the equal sharing of ownership responsibilities; from a legal standpoint, Chase Oil is organized as a corporation, which means that those who hold an equity stake in the business are shareholders.)

The partnership was not always easy for Charles and Chase, the third-generation owners. Until they learned how to work together, they were "constantly bumping into each other and stepping on each other's toes." Charles described running a business with a family member as an experience akin to marriage: "In a marriage, there's a lot of give and take and there's things that you both have to give on … You just have to let it go for the greater good."

The key to the brothers' successful business partnership is a strong bond of trust. As Charles says of Chase, "I trust him immensely with everything he works on, and I think he would say the same for me, and that's our secret sauce." Each brother focuses on his strengths – Charles in finance and Chase in sales – and they rely on each other to manage different aspects of the business. This complementary approach, combined with mutual respect, has allowed them to avoid sibling conflicts that often undermine family businesses.

Scrubby's Car Wash. In 1999, Charles Sr., Charles Jr., and Chase established Scrubby's Car Wash as a limited liability company. According to a bare-bones operating agreement that has apparently never been updated, Charles Sr. held 90 percent of the equity, although the idea for the business came from his sons. Charles Jr. and Chase thought that Chase Oil needed to develop another source of revenue. Also, they judged that the car wash industry was not able to meet existing customer demand, so that early entrepreneurs would have an opportunity to grab market share. The brothers' decision to deploy business capital to pursue a high-growth opportunity showed the same entrepreneurial mindset as their grandfather, Maitland Chase, who tapped his life savings in the 1940s to join the fast-growing oil industry.

However, it took some time to develop the necessary expertise, identify a suitable location, and acquire the property and equipment for a car wash. The first Scrubby's Car Wash opened in 2012, using in-bay wash technology, where vehicles remained stationary while cleaning equipment worked around them. Later, keeping up with technological advances in the industry, Scrubby's transitioned to tunnel express washes, where vehicles move through a tunnel system, creating a more immersive experience for customers. Today, Scrubby's operates at seven locations in the Carolinas, with another location under construction. The business serves over 20,000 club members and has been recognized as one of the top 100 car washes nationally.

The rapid growth of the car wash business in the past decade has presented its own set of challenges. According to Charles, "It's like the gold rush – there's a race to claim market share, and we're competing with regional and national companies." Each location costs around 5 million dollars to build, and securing the necessary capital is a major hurdle. One option the brothers are considering is bringing in a silent partner to provide equity for expansion. Although the potential investor is a friend, each side has retained counsel to develop operating agreements and other formal structures to ensure that everyone's expectations are fully aligned.

Improving Operational Efficiency. As the brothers sought to grow Chase Oil and Scrubby's Car Wash, which, among other things, meant hiring more employees, they recognized a need for greater formality in their business practices. Previously, the company operated with a high level of informality typical of many family businesses. For example, raises were often given without formal reviews, and team meetings were infrequent. All significant decisions were made either by Charles or Chase.

To establish a better foundation for growth, Charles and Chase brought in a business consultant to help them implement employee management practices, such as regular team meetings and a systematic employee training process. They also learned from painful experiences. For example, a trusted long-term bookkeeper defrauded the company by issuing unauthorized checks. This incident prompted the brothers to put stronger financial safeguards in place, including separating financial responsibilities across multiple employees to prevent fraud. The company also relies on legal and financial advisors to navigate complex challenges in the oil and car wash industries, such as environmental regulations and property disputes.

However, despite the added layers of formality, Charles and Chase continue to emphasize the value of maintaining the personal connections that make family businesses unique, particularly their relationships with customers, suppliers, and employees. For example, the son of an employee who had worked with the company for more than thirty years became the first college graduate in his family with the support of Charles and Chase. Today, the son is also part of the company, serving as a manager. Chase remarked, "And those are the little victories we get in the family business atmosphere." Chase also makes a point of getting to know the managers who run Chase Oil's convenience stores. He has been invited to attend family dinners and weddings and takes satisfaction in having built relationships founded on something more durable than mutual economic advantage.

Cybersecurity. Like many small businesses, Chase Oil has had to confront the growing threat of cyberattacks. In 2019, the company fell victim to a phishing scam that resulted in the fraudulent issuance of checks totaling nearly 400,000 dollars. The hackers manipulated emails to deceive the bookkeeper into issuing unauthorized checks, going as far as exploiting Charles's absence during work travel to avoid detection. The scheme went undetected for nearly four months, until the company's chief operating officer identified a suspicious invoice. Fortunately, a recently purchased cyber insurance policy helped mitigate the financial loss, but the incident was a wake-up call.

Since then, Charles and Chase have invested heavily in cybersecurity, working with outside experts to improve network security and conducting regular employee training sessions. The brothers begin each monthly team meeting by discussing recent developments in cybersecurity and potential new threats, emphasizing the importance of staying vigilant. They have also implemented measures such as Positive Pay and Automated Clearing House verification to protect financial transactions. Reflecting on the experience, Charles notes, "I'll be honest with you, I just didn't understand the importance of it until it was in our face."

Charles is now a vocal advocate for greater cybersecurity awareness among small business owners, using his platform within the South Carolina Petroleum Marketers Association to share his experience and educate others on the risks. During a panel discussion at a convention addressing petroleum-related issues, Charles shared his firsthand experience as a victim of cybercrime, emphasizing the widespread misconception among small business owners that they are immune to such attacks. "It's the single biggest issue facing small businesses today," he warned.

Conclusion. The story of Chase Oil and Scrubby's Car Wash highlights the entrepreneurial spirit, adaptability, and resilience that are key components of successful multigenerational family businesses. From its origins as a single AMOCO gas station in the 1940s to its current status as a diversified enterprise that spans wholesale gasoline distribution and a thriving car wash chain, Chase Oil has sustained growth across three generations of family ownership. In 2024, Charles and Chase were recognized as businesspersons of the year by the Greater Florence Chamber of Commerce. Thanks to their leadership, Chase Oil is likely to remain a cornerstone of the Florence business community for years to come.

3

Integrating Family and Business Values

Progress in modern life, whether economic or social, has sometimes been described as a move from preordained status relations to voluntary contractual ordering.[1] Over time, restrictive castes tend to give way to flexible private ordering based on consent. The freedom to make our own choices, often enhanced by contract, is a crucial feature of modern life. Thus, in a family business, we might conclude that contractual freedom is the key to reconciling family and business expectations. Indeed, one of this book's central arguments is that contractual principles offer an important resource for developing a family business law that respects the participants' values and expectations. In its account of the development of human societies,[2] however, the status to contract thesis overstates its case and wrongly assumes that status relationships are inflexible while contracts can readily accommodate flexible, sometimes idiosyncratic preferences.

Family businesses illustrate the problem. First, the status-to-contract thesis assumes a radical distinction between "status" and "contract" that ignores the larger sense in which both are culturally constructed and deeply interrelated: The traditional rights and duties of marriage, for instance, are cast

1 *See* HENRY SUMNER MAINE, ANCIENT LAW 140 (Dorset Press, 1986) (1861) ("Nor is it difficult to see what is the tie between man and man which replaces by degrees those forms of reciprocity in rights and duties which have their origin in the Family. It is contract."); Lawrence E. Mitchell, *The Age of Aquarius or, How I (Almost) Learned to Stop Worrying and Love Free Markets*, 88 MINN. L. REV. 921, 944 (2004) ("In little more than a generation, the structure of American society has changed, as an age of hierarchy has given way to an age of markets.").

2 MAINE, *supra* note 1, at 140–41:

> Starting, as from one terminus of history, from a condition of society in which all the relations of Persons are summed up in the relations of Family, we seem to have moved steadily toward a phase of social order in which all these relations arise from the free agreement of individuals .... [W]e may say that the movement of the progressive societies has hitherto been a movement from Status to Contract.

in the form of a contractual covenant. Second, a classic problem in family businesses is that the legal governing documents have become outdated and no longer reflect the needs of the family. Making "progress" in a family business may require less attention to what the contracts say and more reliance on fostering an open dialogue among the participants. To give contractual bargains the necessary flexibility to accommodate family and business goals, they should be given effect across the family–business divide and with sensitivity for status-based relationships among participants.

3.1 THE BENEFITS OF VOICE

The overlap of status-based and contractual relationships in family businesses suggests the need for a different approach to governance. As Alfred Hirschman observed, members of an organization may respond to problems through "exit" or "voice" – leaving the organization altogether or stating their concerns and seeking improvement.[3] Often, exit may be the simpler solution. In publicly traded corporations, this is known as the "Wall Street Walk." A disappointed shareholder can sell their stock and move on. The sale involves a simple transaction, mediated by a stock exchange, between an anonymous seller and an anonymous buyer. In closely held businesses, and especially in family businesses, exit can be more difficult. Consequently, the ability for a shareholder to be heard takes on greater importance as a mechanism for addressing problems, and it can offer significant benefits. Notably, corporate decisions based on open discussion will more often serve the interests of all shareholders, and the minority will more likely accept the results of an inclusive, deliberative process as fair.

The minority's participation in governance – its voice – enables the minority to advance its interests and to be heard on important issues, a process protection lost when close corporations fail to hold shareholder meetings and lacking when the minority has no active role in management. Enhanced minority participation can improve close corporation governance, especially in family businesses, by increasing the range of perspectives brought to bear on any given problem.[4]

[3] Albert O. Hirschman, Exit, Voice, and Loyalty: Responses to Decline in Firms, Organizations and States (1970).

[4] *See* Stephen M. Bainbridge, *Why a Board? Group Decisionmaking in Corporate Governance*, 55 Vand. L. Rev. 1 (2002) (arguing for director primacy based on studies of cognitive advantages of group decision-making). Professor Bainbridge opposes enhanced shareholder participation in public corporations. *See* Stephen M. Bainbridge, *Director Primacy and Shareholder Disempowerment*, 119 Harv. L. Rev. 1735 (2006). However, in close corporations, the

Formal studies indicate that groups have important cognitive advantages over sole decision-makers,[5] a finding consistent with arguments at least as old as Aristotle.[6] When minority shareholders participate in decision-making, the majority may benefit from the presentation of opposing arguments and will be pressed to defend its own preferences.[7] If, for instance, payment of dividends depends upon the corporation's expected need for cash in the coming year, reviewing the corporation's financial outlook together with minority shareholders will make it more likely that a reasonable consensus will emerge. If the corporation does not truly need to retain earnings, controlling shareholders will find it harder to withhold or reduce dividends.

Conversely, where the majority can articulate an objective basis for its own view, the minority may disagree but will see that there are countervailing considerations and will more likely accept the outcome as fair.[8] In a family business, concerns about fairness can be paramount. Sometimes, it is valuable to be heard on an issue, even when ultimate authority to make the decision rests elsewhere. For example, shareholders in public corporations have demanded the ability to cast nonbinding votes concerning executive compensation.[9]

cognitive advantages of group decision-making he identifies would seem to support robust minority shareholder participation, especially when there is a single majority shareholder.

5 *See, e.g.*, Gary Charness, Edi Karni, & Dan Levin, *Individual and Group Decision Making under Risk: An Experimental Study of Bayesian Updating and Violations of First-Order Stochastic Dominance*, 35 J. RISK UNCERTAINTY 129, 129 (2007) ("The violation rate when groups make decisions is substantially lower, and decreasing with group size, suggesting that social interaction improves the decision-making process.").

6 *See* ARISTOTLE, POLITICS, *reprinted in* THE POLITICS OF ARISTOTLE 1, 123 (Ernest Baker trans., 1962) ("Feasts to which many contribute may excel those provided at one man's expense. In the same way, when there are many who contribute to the process of deliberation each can bring his share of goodness and moral prudence.").

7 *See* RONALD M. MASON, PARTICIPATORY AND WORKPLACE DEMOCRACY: A THEORETICAL DEVELOPMENT IN CRITIQUE OF LIBERALISM 35 (1982) (observing that a crucial first step for effective governance is the identification of problems, and that "[p]articipation is thus an indispensable aid to improve input to government").

8 The difference between an opportunity to participate and total exclusion is well illustrated by the following testimony of a minority shareholder:

> My brother had the majority of stock … before this management contract. As to whether he had the final say in the control of [the corporation], that is the point. He might have been the final say, but when [the new corporation] started, I lost all say-so because he wouldn't listen to anybody.

Meiselman v. Meiselman, 307 S.E.2d 551, 555 (N.C. 1983). The connection between voice and legitimacy is that "participation increase[s] acceptance of decisions." MASON, *supra* note 7, at 38.

9 *See* Claudia H. Deutsch, *Say on Pay: A Whisper or a Shout for Shareholders?*, N.Y. TIMES, Apr. 6, 2008, at Bus. 9 ("Last year, investors filed 60 resolutions asking for a say on pay …. This year, there were more than 90 such resolutions filed.").

Although the board sets compensation, shareholders want a voice in the process. Among other things, they believe that compensation committees will act with greater deliberation if their work is subject to enhanced scrutiny and meaningful, if nonbinding, feedback from shareholders. In two foreign jurisdictions, "say on pay" appears to have had an impact on compensation.[10]

That deliberation is desirable and produces better, more legitimate outcomes than the alternative is a contestable claim but also one that is fundamental to our representative form of government.[11] Advocates of deliberative democracy argue for greater levels of participation and hold that legitimacy depends upon discussion, not just voting – and that we owe one another reasons.[12] On this view, the goal of deliberation is to improve collective understanding and to reach decisions that all can regard as fair.[13]

The argument that an inclusive deliberation is more legitimate and more likely to lead to a correct outcome need not be limited to the political realm.[14] In *Hoschett v. TSI International Software, Ltd.*,[15] Chancellor Allen cited the value of deliberation in holding that a corporation's annual shareholder meeting is mandatory, even when the majority has enough votes to elect a new slate of directors on written consent:

[10] *Id.* ("In one sense, American investors are coming late to the party. Say-on-pay resolutions have been common in Britain and Australia for several years, and governance experts say they have most likely reined in compensation in those countries.").

[11] *See* Cass R. Sunstein, Democracy and the Problem of Free Speech 241 (1993) (stating that the "American constitutional system" is designed "to ensure discussion and debate among people who are genuinely different in their perspectives and position, in the interest of creating a process through which reflection will encourage the emergence of general truths"). The alternative to deliberation is tallying existing preferences. *See* Amy Gutmann & Dennis Thompson, Why Deliberative Democracy? 13 (2004) (rejecting aggregative theories, which take preferences as given, and advocating a deliberative conception of governance, which assumes that preferences can be reexamined).

[12] *See* Gutmann & Thompson, *supra* note 11, at 4 ("The reasons are meant both to produce a justifiable decision and to express the value of mutual respect."). The importance of giving reasons may depend in part on whether we view the goals of participants as achieving self-interest, defined in terms of fixed preferences on a rational-choice model, or whether we believe that human behavior, viewed from a political perspective, can escape the reductive power of classical economic reasoning.

[13] *See id.* at 12 ("Through the give-and-take of argument, participants can learn from each other, come to recognize their individual and collective misapprehensions, and develop new views and policies that can more successfully withstand critical scrutiny.").

[14] *See* Brett H. McDonnell, *Employee Primacy, or Economics Meets Civic Republicanism at Work*, 13 Stan. J.L. Bus. & Fin. 334, 335 (2008) ("Writing on civic republicanism and on corporate law rarely overlaps, but republican ideas can offer a very useful perspective on corporate law."); Gutmann & Thompson, *supra* note 11, at 34 ("Corporations are another … example of an institution that should be subject to more deliberation.").

[15] Hoschett v. TSI International Software, Ltd., 683 A.2d 43 (Del. Ch. 1996).

> The theory of the annual meeting includes the idea that a deliberative component of the meeting may occur. Shareholders' meetings are mandated and shareholders authorized by statute to transact proper business because we assume that at such meetings something said may matter. Obviously these meetings are very far from deliberative convocations, but a keen realization of the reality of the degree of deliberation that is possible, should make the preservation of residual mechanisms of corporate democracy more, not less, important.[16]

Chancellor Allen observed that "while the model of democratic forms should not too strictly be applied to the economic institution of a business corporation," the shareholders' meeting facilitates "a form of discourse (i.e., oral reports, questions and answers and in rare instances proxy contests) among investors and between shareholders and managers."[17]

Arguably the mere ability to vote may be of little consequence for a minority shareholder if the controlling shareholders are in the majority.[18] Yet, a person's ability to participate and to be heard on issues important to a shared enterprise, whether family, business organization, or nation state, does not turn on the final tally of votes.[19] Voice is not as crude a mechanism as the decision whether to exit; its value lies in its nuance as a means of shaping the goals of a close corporation to better accommodate the interests of all shareholders.[20]

Of course, to the extent that the majority still controls the outcome, the participants are not substantively equal, even if there is formal equality of

[16] *Id.* at 46.

[17] *Id.* at 45–46. In a closely held corporation with relatively few shareholders, Chancellor Allen's vision of a deliberative process is more feasible and more usual.

[18] *See* Robert B. Thompson, *Exit, Liquidity, and Majority Rule: Appraisal's Role in Corporate Law*, 84 GEO. L.J. 1, 8 (1995) ("[I]f those in control already have a majority, voting becomes an empty vessel."). For an exploration of the value of voting in the corporate context, see Robert B. Thompson & Paul H. Edelman, *Corporate Voting*, 62 VAND. L. REV. 129 (2009). The authors observe, correctly, that "[v]oting within close corporations or by controlling shareholders is the mechanism to implement the property rights that follow from acquiring the controlling interest" and so "[t]he likelihood of the correct decision when there is a vote with a majority shareholder is exactly the likelihood of the majority shareholder alone getting the right answer; voting does not improve accuracy." *Id.* at 151. What follows, however, is not that minority shareholder participation is useless, but that voice must mean more than voting for it to matter.

[19] Indeed, the imbalance of power makes participation all the more important, if we are to reduce the frequency of shareholder litigation. *Cf.* GUTMANN & THOMPSON, *supra* note 11, at 6–7 (noting that full consensus may be impossible to achieve but that those who "disagreed with the original decision are more likely to accept it if they believe they have a chance to reverse or modify it in the future").

[20] *See* MASON, *supra* note 7, at 39 ("That participation can even transform an individual's conceptualization of his interests indicates that participation is a potent agent as well as medium of socialization. Through participation in any system, support will develop for that system.").

participation.[21] In addition, there will not always be a "right" decision, since the majority and minority may have different interests, neither one of which impacts the efficient operation of the business. Although voice is not a panacea for conflict in family business, it is nonetheless reasonable to expect that enhanced participation will improve close corporation governance overall and that close corporations that invite minority participation will be less likely to behave oppressively toward the minority.

For example, in a 2012 lawsuit concerning closely held family businesses that owned resort properties on Kiawah Island and other assets, the minority-owner plaintiffs argued that they were suffering oppression at the hands of their cousin, the controlling owner, Charles P. "Buddy" Darby, III.[22] According to Matthew T. Richardson, who represented the plaintiffs, the fundamental problem was that Buddy believed that the business was his to run as he saw fit, and he was not willing to share information about the business or to include the other owners in any dialogue. Buddy's plan involved a risky offshore, multi-year development project that, if successful, would lead to greater profits in the long run. In the meantime, however, the plaintiffs would not receive dividends. And there was a chance that the project could fail, destroying the value of the existing business. Unlike Buddy, the plaintiffs did not draw salary from the business, and they were not independently wealthy. Despite the misalignment of owner perspectives, Mr. Richardson believes that litigation could have been avoided if Buddy had agreed to institute basic controls – such as a board of directors – to ensure that business decisions were more transparent and took into account the needs of all owners. Buddy's refusal to grant the minority owners any voice in the business led to a lawsuit and, ultimately, to a settlement in which all the businesses were sold to third parties.

3.2 FAMILY BUSINESS BARGAINS

For the reasons discussed in the previous section, shareholder voice is an important tool for reconciling family and business values. Accommodating status-based family relationships and values in a family business setting also

[21] *Hoschett*, 683 A.2d at 46 (noting that, unlike democracies, "votes are weighted by the size of the voter's investment"); Usha Rodrigues, *The Seductive Comparison of Shareholder and Civic Democracy*, 63 WASH. & LEE L. REV. 1389, 1391 (2006) ("By virtue of the one-vote-per-share principle, larger shareholders inevitably have a greater say in corporate governance than do smaller shareholders.").

[22] *See* David Slade, *Lawsuit Shows Rift in Kiawah Island Real Estate Dynasty*, POST & COURIER, Jun. 6, 2012; Long Family Assocs., L.P. v. Charles P. Darby, III, C.A. 2012 CP 10-3663 (June 6, 2012), filed in the South Carolina Court of Common Pleas.

requires a more flexible approach to contract interpretation. Yet, according to current orthodoxy in corporate law, cogently summarized by a former chief justice of the Delaware Supreme Court, "courts need to be mindful of the distinction between status relationships and contractual relationships."[23] In the event of a dispute, "the contractual relationships between parties … should be the analytical focus … not the status relationship of the parties."[24] Chief Justice Steele's recommended approach assumes that status and contract are distinct categories. The premise of his argument is flawed, at least when applied to family businesses, for several reasons.

First, acknowledging the significance of status relationships in family businesses does not diminish the importance of private ordering via contract. Family members' agreements regarding business and family matters interrelate and should not be read in isolation.[25] Trusts, wills, and other testamentary documents may be as constitutive of the family business as articles of incorporation, bylaws, and shareholder agreements. Likewise, because divorce can seriously disrupt a family business, married couples may use nuptial agreements to specify whether business assets count for purposes of equitable division in the event of divorce.[26] Thus, the contractual bargains that constitute a family business include not just business contracts, but all bargains among participants that affect the business.

Second, an insistence that the "analytical focus" should be on contracts, not status relationships, fails to appreciate that accounting for status relationships can provide helpful context for the interpretation of business contracts. For example, in a posttrial decision upholding a daughter's contractual claim based upon the termination of her employment with the family business, the court recognized that family considerations had motivated the parties' business bargain: "The parties' intent in entering into the Shareholders Agreement was not to establish an operational model for the Company, defining the individual shareholders' rights and responsibilities. Rather, the Shareholders Agreement was meant to be an estate-planning tool."[27]

[23] Myron T. Steele, *Judicial Scrutiny of Fiduciary Duties in Delaware Limited Partnerships and Limited Liability Companies*, 32 DEL. J. CORP. L. 1, 9 (2007).

[24] *Id.* at 25.

[25] *See* G. Mitu Gulati et al., *Connected Contracts*, 47 UCLA L. REV. 887, 894 (2000) (arguing for a conception of "connected contracts" in which the boundaries of a firm are constantly undermined by "a fluid, nonlinear, nonhierarchical set of interactions and interrelationships").

[26] *See* UNIF. PREMARITAL & MARITAL AGREEMENTS ACT § 9(c), 9C U.L.A. 22–23 (2012).

[27] Federico v. Brancato, No. 50902(U), slip op. at *7–8 (N.Y. Sup. Ct. June 9, 2014) (citing Peter Mahler, *Interview with Law Professor Benjamin Means on Conflict in Family-Owned Businesses: Part Two*, N.Y. BUS. DIVORCE (Feb. 4, 2013), http://bit.ly/4mzV9TO).

Once the context was understood, the plaintiff's contractual argument regarding the meaning of "executive duties" prevailed notwithstanding her limited role in the business. That is, because the parents intended to distribute assets to their daughter through the company, her level of participation was not material to the arrangement.[28]

Third, even if contracts should ordinarily take precedence over status relationships, the two concepts are not easily untangled. Notably, it would be a mistake to assume that business roles are inherently contractual and that family relationships are based on status.[29] Corporations, for example, create status relationships among participants as authorized by statute and assign mandatory fiduciary obligations to directors and officers. Status relationships are a starting point for analysis, even if courts have been willing to permit contractual modifications, especially in closely held businesses.[30]

Family roles likewise involve a mix of status and contract. For example, traditionally, the marriage contract represented the voluntary assumption of a state-determined status.[31] Increasingly, courts and legislatures have permitted individuals to strike bargains concerning their marital and family relationships.[32] In this regard, the Uniform Premarital Agreement Act, which was drafted to standardize practice across US jurisdictions, proposes that couples may contract regarding "any … matter, including their personal rights and

28 *Id.* at *8.

29 *See* Deborah A. DeMott, *Relationships of Trust and Confidence in the Workplace*, 100 Cornell L. Rev. 1255, 1261 (2015) (observing that fiduciary relationships are often status based).

30 *See, e.g.*, Stephen M. Bainbridge, Corporation Law and Economics 808 (2002) (describing the shift toward codification of the principle that shareholder bargains are valid in close corporations, even if they impinge upon the role of the board of directors); Benjamin Means, *Nonmarket Values in Family Businesses*, 54 Wm. & Mary L. Rev. 1185, 1220 (2013) ("In some respects, the gradual recognition of contractual bargaining within domestic relationships resembles the process by which courts became willing to enforce shareholder agreements in close corporations.").

31 *See* 1 William Blackstone, Commentaries on the Laws of England 154 (University of Chicago Press, 1979) (1765) (stating that because "husband and wife are one person in law" a contractual relationship is conceptually impossible); Lon L. Fuller, *The Forms and Limits of Adjudication*, 92 Harv. L. Rev. 353, 371 (1978) (arguing that courts "refused to enforce agreements between husband and wife affecting the internal organization of family life" because legal intervention is inconsistent with "successful human association [that] depends upon spontaneous and informal collaboration").

32 *See* Martha M. Ertman, *Marriage as a Trade: Bridging the Private/Private Distinction*, 36 Harv. C.R.-C.L. L. Rev. 79, 81–82 (2001) (listing "matters such as entry into marriage, contractual ordering of marriage, nonmarital relationships, divorce, adoption, the use of reproductive technologies, and the privatization of domestic relations dispute resolution").

obligations, not in violation of public policy."[33] Through contract, families can define their own boundaries and recognize new forms of intimacy.[34]

Therefore, rather than seeking to separate what is status based and what is contractual, a better approach would widen the contractual lens and take relationships as the starting point for an integrated analysis. In that regard, we should seek to establish appropriate default rules for the interpretation and enforcement of family business bargains that presuppose a relational context. The parties' intentions, which are otherwise unclear, may be informed by the communal aspects of family life.[35] Moreover, family members may not have addressed key issues in advance because actual bargaining can undermine trust.[36] Properly informed, contract law could serve as a resource for the parties, generating a set of preferred outcomes and facilitating more particular bargaining.[37] By overlaying simultaneously relevant business and family considerations, a contractual approach makes it possible to appreciate what is at stake in a family business.

Adhering to the economic perspective described in Chapter 1, however, some might counsel a narrower view of contractual private ordering in family-owned businesses, in order to respect the supposedly "separate spheres" of intimacy and markets.[38] According to this objection, family relationships are

[33] UNIF. PREMARITAL & MARITAL AGREEMENT ACT § 3, 9C U.L.A. 373 (1983).

[34] *See* Elizabeth Emens, *Monogamy's Law: Compulsory Monogamy and Polyamorous Existence*, 29 N.Y.U. REV. L. & SOC. CHANGE 277, 364 (2004). Even when family law rules remain mandatory, rational business participants will still take them into account. *See* Larry E. Ribstein, *The Important Role of Non-organization Law*, 40 WAKE FOREST L. REV. 751, 754 (2005) ("Federal tax, securities, bankruptcy laws, and some state non-organization laws are important because firms can minimize their impact only by complying or changing their transaction form.").

[35] *See* DAVID BORK, FAMILY BUSINESS, RISKY BUSINESS: HOW TO MAKE IT WORK 26 (1986) (arguing that "what is going on in the individual [is] inseparable from the family network of relationships in which the individual is embedded [and from] the emotional processes in that system"); *see generally* Ian Ayres & Robert Gertner, *Filling Gaps in Incomplete Contracts: An Economic Theory of Default Rules*, 99 YALE L.J. 87, 91–93 (1989) (exploring the role of courts in defining contractual obligations in the absence of explicit terms based on assumptions regarding the parties' intentions).

[36] *See* Margaret M. Blair & Lynn A. Stout, *Trust, Trustworthiness, and the Behavioral Foundations of Corporate Law*, 149 U. PA. L. REV. 1735, 1805–06 (2001) (noting that parties may avoid explicit bargains in order to preserve trust).

[37] *See* Adam J. Hirsch, *Default Rules in Inheritance Law: A Problem in Search of Its Context*, 73 FORDHAM L. REV. 1031, 1045 n.52 (2004) ("The tendency of parties to accede to default rules in order to avoid the cost of contracting around them renders them 'sticky[.]'") (citing Ian Ayres & Robert Gertner, *Majoritarian vs. Minoritarian Defaults*, 51 STAN. L. REV. 1591, 1598 (1999)).

[38] *See* VIVIANA A. ZELIZER, THE PURCHASE OF INTIMACY 23 (2005) (noting that "worries about the incompatibility, incommensurability, or contradiction between intimate and impersonal relations are long-standing and persistent").

extraneous to the nexus of business contracts because firms are economic institutions and economic actors will rationally pursue their own advantage.[39] By contrast, family is an institution that protects a sphere of intimacy apart from competitive market relationships.[40] Even if families could be redescribed in the language of economics,[41] the typical range of family concerns may seem far removed from the narrower economic objectives of a business corporation.[42] Thus, according to some scholars, the residual role of family relationships is to establish a background of trust that can reduce the transaction costs of forming and operating a firm.[43]

In truth, families cannot be excluded from the economic sphere, because no family can avoid economic considerations.[44] The household is the original unit of economic analysis and the source of the word *economics*.[45] Consider, for example, one successful author's account of marital problems caused by a changed economic dynamic:

39 *See* Charles R. O'Kelley, Jr., *Filling Gaps in the Close Corporation Contract: A Transaction Cost Analysis*, 87 Nw. U. L. Rev. 216, 220 (1992) ("Rational individuals invest their human and money capital with a view to maximizing the value of such resources."); Henry N. Butler, *The Contractual Theory of the Corporation*, 11 Geo. Mason L. Rev. 99, 109 (1989) (noting that the contractual theory of corporate law is "based in part on the assumption that the shareholders' primary interest is in the maximization of the value of their investments").

40 Jana B. Singer, *The Privatization of Family Law*, 1992 Wis. L. Rev. 1443, 1522 ("[T]he values associated with a 'successful' family – altruism, sympathy, mutualism – were precisely those that were viewed as incompatible with success in the economic sphere."). Also, some aspects of family life may not be commodities, or ought not to be treated as such. *See* Margaret Jane Radin, *Market-Inalienability*, 100 Harv. L. Rev. 1849, 1923–28 (1987).

41 *See* Richard A. Posner, The Economics of Justice 237 (1981) (extending the assumption of rationality to choices regarding marriage, children, and friendships); Gary S. Becker, The Economic Approach to Human Behavior 169–94 (1976).

42 *See* Blake E. Ashforth, Role Transitions in Organizational Life: An Identity-Based Perspective 139 (2001) ("Work and home are often stereotypically perceived as opposites on many dimensions.").

43 For instance, "if family-owned ventures reduce the agency costs of management, there will be gains for all to share." Frank H. Easterbrook & Daniel R. Fischel, The Economic Structure of Corporate Law 232 (1991).

44 *See* Zelizer, *supra* note 38, at 13 ("Economic transactions include all social interactions involving consumption, production, and distribution of goods, services, or the means of acquiring them – for example, when one sibling buys a car from another, an immigrant father supervises his daughter's work in the family store, a salesman spreads free samples among his close friends, or parents lend their children money for purchase of a home."); Piper v. Hoard, 13 N.E. 626, 629 (N.Y. 1887) ("Marriage has its sentimental and its business sides.").

45 Robert C. Ellickson, *Unpacking the Household: Informal Property Rights Around the Hearth*, 116 Yale L.J. 226, 232 n.14 (2006) ("Although *oikos* [house] is the etymological root of 'economics,' until recent decades few economists have paid more than passing attention to home economics.").

> We expected that things would proceed one way – he'd be the primary breadwinner, a successful attorney, and I'd make less money, stay home with the kids, with fiction essentially a lucrative hobby .... When it didn't work out that way, I think we both had a hard time rewriting the contract of the marriage.[46]

Whether or not a family owns and operates a business, the family must address questions of economic production and exchange and reconcile economic activity with other expectations.[47]

Acknowledging the economic concerns that families and businesses share should not obscure differences in their respective values. The observation that family life has an economic component is not meant to be a reductive claim that families and businesses amount to the same thing – ways of organizing to accomplish collective, largely economic purposes. In this vein, one commentator defines marriage as "a written, oral, or customary long-term contract between a man and a woman to produce children, food, and other commodities in a common household."[48] If family and business were "nothing-but" economics and their only differences concerned the goods sought by the parties, the nature of transaction costs, and the terms of the default contract, then the goal of family business law would be to provide a single, coherent conception of value, largely consistent with the law-and-economics view of rational choice.[49]

However, invoking contractual principles to align family and business planning places no limits on the permissible interests of contracting parties and, therefore, does not require us to deny the distinctive values of families and businesses.[50] Recall that the economists' theory of the firm uses the building block of open-market transactions – contract – to construct an alternative to markets.[51] Contract should be seen as a means of expressing values and making them

[46] Rebecca Mead, *Written Off: Jennifer Weiner's Quest for Literary Respect*, NEW YORKER, Jan. 13, 2014, at 37, 40.

[47] *See* ZELIZER, *supra* note 38, at 13.

[48] BECKER, *supra* note 41, at 43.

[49] According to Professor Viviana Zelizer, "Impatient with stark dualisms, critics have sometimes countered separate spheres and hostile worlds accounts with reductionist nothing but arguments: the ostensibly separate world of intimate social relations, they argue, is nothing-but a special case of some general principle." ZELIZER, *supra* note 38, at 29.

[50] *See* Ivan S. Lansberg, *Managing Human Resources in Family Firms: The Problem of Institutional Overlap*, 12 ORGANIZATIONAL DYNAMICS 39, 42 (1983) ("The exchange of resources in the family is guided by implicit affective principles that focus ... on the needs and long-term well-being of the other, rather than on the specific value of the goods and services."). By contrast, "the norm of fairness that operates in the firm is based on the concept of merit." *Id.*

[51] *See* Michael C. Jensen & William H. Meckling, *Theory of the Firm: Managerial Behavior, Agency Costs and Ownership Structure*, 3 J. FIN. ECON. 305, 311 (1976).

legally enforceable, rather than a concept that imposes values.[52] Accordingly, the fact that businesses and families engage in private ordering tells us little about what it is they value and have reason to value. In a family business, the ability to choose among different plausible options is particularly important.

Even if doubts remain concerning the introduction of contractual principles into supposedly nonmarket family institutions, expanding the range of available choices in the domestic sphere is not the same thing as treating family relationships as fungible, market commodities. For instance, family law scholars have explored contract as a potential mechanism for enhancing individual autonomy and for counteracting issues of gender or other social inequality.[53] Depending on their situation, individuals might "use private agreements to reinforce their marital commitment"[54] or to create structures for intimate relationships that fall outside existing recognized categories.[55]

In some respects, the gradual recognition of contractual bargaining within domestic relationships resembles the process by which courts became willing to enforce shareholder agreements in close corporations, even when those agreements altered central features of corporate law such as the authority of the board of directors.[56] Families, like businesses, are entities comprised of individuals who seek to achieve joint purposes, and it seems logical to look to business law to find helpful models for contractual ordering in the family context.[57] As one family law scholar has observed:

[52] However, courts may still invoke public policy concerns and refuse to enforce a private bargain if the subject matter is perceived as inimical to "the public good." Kaiponanea T. Matsumura, *Public Policing of Intimate Agreements*, 25 Yale J.L. & Feminism 159, 163 (2013).

[53] *See* Ertman, *supra* note 32, at 82 ("Business models are free of the antiquated notions of status, morality, and biological relation that have hampered family law's ability to adapt with the times.").

[54] *See* Elizabeth S. Scott, *Social Norms and the Legal Regulation of Marriage*, 86 Va. L. Rev. 1901, 1903 (2000) (stating that such agreements face "continuing reluctance" and that "[f]ew courts, for example, would enforce a premarital agreement incorporating covenant marriage terms" (citing Theodore F. Haas, *The Rationality and Enforceability of Contractual Restrictions on Divorce*, 66 N.C. L. Rev. 879, 901–04 (1988)).

[55] *See* Emens, *supra* note 34, at 277. One issue that arises at the boundary of intimacy and commercial exchange is whether "sugar baby" relationships in which one partner provides financial resources in the form of gifts in exchange for an intimate connection that usually involves sexual activity should be classified as sex work. *See* Bridget Crawford, *Taxing Sugar Babies*, 109 Minn. L. Rev. 737, 747 (2024) (predicting that "taxing authorities are unlikely to become entangled in the gray area between romance and commercial sex that is propped up by the dominant refrain that sugar babies receive 'gifts,' not income").

[56] The enforceability of shareholder agreements in closely held corporations has now been codified but evolved through a process of common law interpretation of existing, apparently mandatory, corporate law rules. *See* Bainbridge, *supra* note 30.

[57] Adrienne D. Davis, *Regulating Polygamy: Intimacy, Default Rules, and Bargaining for Equality*, 110 Colum. L. Rev. 1955, 1955 (2010) (proposing partnership framework for

> The law governing intimate relationships would benefit from exploring the metaphorical and doctrinal analogies between business and intimate affiliations. These affiliations bridge the ... distinction by drawing connections between private business law and private family law. They also improve upon conventional family law's understanding of family. The exploration remedies long-standing inequities within current family law discourse that are fossilized artifacts of the naturalized construction of intimate relationships.[58]

There are several specific, structural similarities between close corporations and marriages. First, "close corporations and marriages are intended to be 'long-term, ongoing entities' that require 'stability and predictability to function properly.'"[59] Second, each form of social organization requires formal state recognition.[60] Third, the dissolution of a business "parallels divorce."[61] Moreover, "a close corporation often is a hybrid of family and business that bridges the private/private divide by its very existence."[62] Thus, families and businesses can be described as long-term, relational contracts, an analogy that extends to matters of formation, governance, distribution, and dissolution.[63]

Though their formal legal doctrines diverge, businesses and families are both institutions that facilitate cooperative relationships designed, in important part, to achieve economic objectives.[64] Business organization laws permit the entry of individuals into long-term relationships to achieve shared

intimate relationships among multiple partners); Mary Anne Case, *Marriage Licenses*, 89 MINN. L. REV. 1758, 1779 (2005) (noting reduction in mandatory regulation of marriages and business entities); Ertman, *supra* note 32, at 79–80; Singer, *supra* note 40, at 1443.

58 Ertman, *supra* note 32, at 79–80.

59 *Id.* at 112.

60 *See id.* at 112–13.

61 *Id.* at 118. Professor Ertman explains that "[l]ike a minority shareholder, a disadvantaged spouse (often a woman) takes a serious financial risk when exiting marriage." *Id.* at 115.

62 *Id.*

63 The analogy does not require us to ignore substantial differences that remain between family and business institutions. *See* MARGARET F. BRINIG, FROM CONTRACT TO COVENANT: BEYOND THE LAW AND ECONOMICS OF THE FAMILY (2000) (identifying limits of commodification-based analysis). We should not expect existing forms of business organization to provide an adequate template for all matters now covered by domestic relations law. *See* Larry E. Ribstein, *Incorporating the Hendricksons*, 35 WASH. U. J.L. & POL'Y 273, 276 (2011) ("[E]ven if a contractual model of the family is appropriate on policy grounds, the differences between business associations and domestic relationships likely would continue to demand qualitatively different standard forms.").

64 *See* Armen A. Alchian & Harold Demsetz, *Production, Information Costs, and Economic Organization*, 62 AM. ECON. REV. 777, 777 (1972) ("The mark of a capitalistic society is that resources are owned and allocated by such nongovernmental organizations as firms, households, and markets.").

purposes, partly defined by the state and subject to its regulation.[65] Similarly, the institution of marriage gives legal recognition to the voluntary union of two people, and, if needed, judicial monitoring of their rights and obligations.[66] In each context, the parties' relationship is said to be contractual,[67] even if some aspects are mandatory or subject to fiduciary constraint.[68]

Moreover, the contractual conception of the firm does not force family members to bargain at arm's length and to rethink all aspects of their mutual relationships. To the contrary, family business law informed by evidence of the choices families make, including common mistakes, could serve as a resource – a best-practices synthesis of business law and family law. In some cases, as when a child is given a beneficial interest in a trust or shares of a corporation, there is no literal bargain.[69] Nevertheless, envisioning a broad set of voluntary business and family relationships makes it possible to catalogue options so that default rules broadly match expectations. Indeed, "contract supposes and depends on a rich background of social norms to stabilize the parties' expectations and to guide legal interpretations of their obligations."[70] In the right circumstances, invoking contractual values can reinforce relationships, inducing family business participants to be more deliberative,

65 *See* A. A. Berle, Jr., *For Whom Corporate Managers Are Trustees: A Note*, 45 HARV. L. REV. 1365, 1365–66 (1932); E. Merrick Dodd, Jr., *For Whom Are Corporate Managers Trustees?*, 45 HARV. L. REV. 1145, 1147–48 (1932).

66 *See* MERRIAM-WEBSTER'S COLLEGIATE DICTIONARY 761 (11th ed. 2003) (defining traditional marriage as "the state of being united to a person of the opposite sex as husband or wife in a consensual and contractual relationship recognized by law"). Until relatively recently, "the state, and not individual marriage partners, determined many of the consequences of marital status." Singer, *supra* note 40, at 1446.

67 Courts treat questions of governance and distribution largely as default matters subject to modification by the parties. *See* Case, *supra* note 57, at 1779; Singer, *supra* note 40, at 1567 ("A preference for private over public ordering has characterized the development of family law over the past quarter century.").

68 *See* Shahar Lifshitz, *Married Against Their Will? Toward a Pluralist Regulation of Spousal Relationships*, 66 WASH. & LEE L. REV. 1565, 1597 (2009) ("Traditionally, legal regulation of marriage expressed and supported shared moral principles and interests of society as a whole, sometimes even at the cost of limiting the couple's freedoms."); Melvin Aron Eisenberg, *The Structure of Corporation Law*, 89 COLUM. L. REV. 1461, 1505 (1989) (observing that the characterization of corporate law as a series of default rules ignores important mandatory provisions that cannot be abrogated by the parties).

69 *See* Robert H. Sitkoff, *An Agency Costs Theory of Trust Law*, 89 CORNELL L. REV. 621, 639 (2004) (contending, in the context of trust law, that "even if the beneficiaries do not literally contract with the other principal parties, ... contractarian principal-agent modeling nonetheless illuminates the problems of governance relevant to the beneficiaries' welfare").

70 Ronald J. Gilson et al., *Braiding: The Interaction of Formal and Informal Contracting in Theory, Practice, and Doctrine*, 110 COLUM. L. REV. 1377, 1446 (2010) (citing EMILE DURKHEIM, THE DIVISION OF LABOR IN SOCIETY 211–12 (George Simpson trans., Macmillan Co. 1933) (1893)).

anticipating conflicts before they arise.[71] If done in a manner respectful of the relationships that exist among the parties, the process of tailoring default principles can be as beneficial as the agreed-upon substantive rules. In this regard, the formality inherent in operating a business might help family members to broach sensitive issues in the first place.

By studying how family businesses harness the shared commitment of family members to achieve both economic success and personal fulfillment, we might further question the dichotomy between market and nonmarket values in family and nonfamily businesses alike:

> We expect the market to achieve the efficient production of goods and services; it is not the arena in which we are supposed to develop our personalities or satisfy human relational wants …. The expression of the desires to develop personality and to interact with others is relegated to the family and simultaneously glorified and devalued. We see the market as a means to an end, whereas we see the family as an end in itself …. Dividing life between market and family compartmentalizes human experience in a way that prevents us from realizing the range of choices actually available to us.[72]

In this vein, developing a more nuanced understanding of family business could help us to consider a fuller range of options for the collective pursuit of shared purposes.[73] Families themselves are a locus for economic activity as well as intimacy, and the workplace can be a source of deep friendship and social networks of mutual support.[74] Indeed, the starting assumption that there are discrete sets of values may itself be problematic.[75]

[71] The constructive role of contract is one reason that family law scholars have argued in favor of private ordering as a strategy for organizing family life. *See, e.g.*, Ertman, *supra* note 32, at 79.

[72] Frances Olsen, *The Family and the Market: A Study of Ideology and Legal Reform*, 96 HARV. L. REV. 1497, 1564 (1983). However, to the extent that our more intimate choices routinely discriminate on the basis of gender and race, see Elizabeth F. Emens, *Intimate Discrimination: The State's Role in the Accidents of Sex and Love*, 122 HARV. L. REV. 1307 (2009), blending the neutral values of the workplace with closer affective ties may lead to discrimination, whether intentional or unintentional. *See* Katharine T. Bartlett, *Making Good on Good Intentions: The Critical Role of Motivation in Reducing Implicit Workplace Discrimination*, 95 VA. L. REV. 1893 (2009).

[73] *See* Vicki Schultz, *The Sanitized Workplace*, 112 YALE L.J. 2061 (2003).

[74] Laura A. Rosenbury, *Working Relationships*, 35 WASH. U. J.L. & POL'Y 117, 118 (2011) ("The legal assignment of intimacy to the home and production to the workplace masks various dynamics within the home, the workplace, and spaces in between."); Katharine Silbaugh, *Turning Labor into Love: Housework and the Law*, 91 NW. U. L. REV. 1 (1996).

[75] *See, e.g.*, Steven L. Winter, *Foreword: On Building Houses*, 69 TEX. L. REV. 1595, 1614 (1991) ("[O]nce the sophisticated liberal acknowledges that neither the market nor the family exist in a purely 'natural' state – that is, once she affirms that the purpose of the legal system is to contain and shape both – liberalism and its critique become one and the same.").

For instance, as one scholar observes, "most intimacy at work is neither simply an instrument of workplace success nor irrelevant to that success."[76] Thus, from the outset, the filtering of experience through separate legal and institutional structures implies a category difference that does not exist:

> [T]he economic and intimate spheres are simply not as distinct as the two models would suggest .... Neither model represents a truth about social and economic organization. While one biologizes the organization of a socio-economic unit by explaining its internal stratification as a function of the *natural* sexual division of labor, the other voluntarizes a socioeconomic unit by explaining its unequal functional differentiation in terms of *consensual* agreements.[77]

We can recognize the usefulness of maintaining different distributional principles in different contexts without insisting on an all-or-nothing approach. For example, although their relationships are rooted in intimacy, family members in a household must negotiate economic questions of production, distribution, and exchange.[78]

In a family business, the background economic concerns of family life are central, not ancillary, to the structure of the business and the parties' mutual expectations.[79] As extensions of family life, family businesses are defined by broader economic goals and more intimate associations. Because the economic concerns of business and family do not reside in separate spheres, contractual adjustments can help to clarify the parties' expectations. Indeed, the

[76] Rosenbury, *supra* note 74, at 132. The popular phenomenon known as the platonic "work spouse" reflects the influence that closeness and confidence can have on workplace synergies and satisfaction even without marital intimacies. *See* Jared Sandberg, *The Second Marriage: Workplace "Couples" Keep Each Other Sane*, WALL ST. J., Sept. 24, 2003.

[77] Teemu Ruskola, *Home Economics: What Is the Difference Between a Family and a Corporation?*, *in* RETHINKING COMMODIFICATION: CASES AND READINGS IN LAW AND CULTURE 335 (Martha Ertman & Joan Williams eds., 2005).

[78] *See* ZELIZER, *supra* note 38, at 241 ("Many households ... build commercial activity directly into their daily operations."). Professor Zelizer contends that "commercial relationships do not simply transect and influence household relationships; they *become* household relationships." *Id.*; *see also* Jill Elaine Hasday, *Intimacy and Economic Exchange*, 119 HARV. L. REV. 491, 493 (2005) (arguing that "[e]conomic exchange is not foreign to intimate relations, either as a matter of first principles or as a positive matter of legal regulation").

[79] Families are regulated by law but subject to further contractual agreements among members. *See* Elizabeth S. Scott & Robert E. Scott, *Marriage as Relational Contract*, 84 VA. L. REV. 1225, 1229 (1998) ("Like relational contracts in commercial contexts, a marital contract contemplates a long-term commitment to pursue shared goals, the fulfillment of which will enhance the joint welfare of the parties."); Singer, *supra* note 40, at 1444 (contending that private ordering has increasingly "supplanted state-imposed rules and structures for governing family-related behavior"); *see also* Marjorie Maguire Shultz, *Contractual Ordering of Marriage: A New Model for State Policy*, 70 CAL. L. REV. 204, 208 (1982).

parties may use contracts to establish a boundary between family and business, as when a prenuptial agreement defines business assets as nonmarital property. Regardless of the parties' objectives, if private ordering is accepted in the family-law context, and if the stakeholders in a business are also free to bargain among themselves, there seems to be little basis left for rejecting broader bargains that address real-world concerns in family businesses.[80]

[80] To be clear, this does not mean that family dynamics of power and status should be irrelevant to contract interpretation and enforcement. Rather, those concerns exist across different contractual subject matter and should be addressed in consistent fashion. *See, e.g.*, Melvin Aron Eisenberg, *The Bargain Principle and Its Limits*, 95 HARV. L. REV. 741, 801 (1982) (arguing that the administrative simplicity of strict enforcement of contractual bargains should be weighed against the possible injustices that can result).

PART II

APPLICATION

In Part I of the book, I contended that family values and expectations cannot be separated from business values and expectations. They exert a gravitational pull. Unless corporate law scholarship accounts for family businesses, it will fail to understand the disputes that can arise among family co-owners and will be unable to provide useful guidance for preventing and resolving those disputes. To make the case more concretely, the following chapters examine the overlap of family and business concerns in three contexts: marriages, especially when there is a divorce that puts stress on the identification of marital and personal assets; employment, especially in answering questions about whether kinship should be considered a relevant qualification; and succession, especially in identifying reasons why family owners tend to avoid or mishandle the planning process. In each area, business law concepts alone do not tell us what we need to know.

4

Marriage

To see how the overlap of family and business law, values, and expectations affects family-owned businesses, consider the complexities introduced by marriage. For married couples who co-own a business together, it can be challenging to navigate marital dynamics alongside the governance of a business. The two types of relationships do not always reinforce each other. For example, although a marriage is an equal partnership, one of the spouses may be the majority owner of the business. In that case, the two parties are, at the same time, equal and unequal. When there are serious disagreements, the intertwined nature of the marriage and the business can make them more difficult to resolve. In a divorce, the couple may struggle to distinguish business assets from the broader set of economic assets that belong to the household. These are, however, issues that can be anticipated and addressed.

4.1 MARITAL AGREEMENTS

Because marriage superimposes an economic partnership in which assets are shared equally on top of business arrangements that may contemplate a different allocation, marital agreements may be needed to align the parties' rights and expectations. Further, the terms and conditions of marital agreements may be part of a broader business bargain.[1] Consider, for instance, the Swigs,

[1] In fact, the absence of a marital agreement may be notable. *See* David F. Larcker et al., *Separation Anxiety: The Impact of CEO Divorce on Shareholders*, STAN. CLOSER LOOK SERIES, Oct. 1, 2013, at 1 ("[W]hen news leaked that Harold Hamm, Chairman and CEO of Continental Resources, was getting divorced from wife Sue Ann of 25 years, shares of the company fell 2.9 percent. The Hamms did not sign a premarital contract, making Harold's 68 percent ownership stake (worth $11.2 billion) subject to equitable distribution under Oklahoma family law."); Tom Fowler, *Divorce Clouds Billionaire's Stake in Oil-Drilling Giant*, WALL ST. J., Mar. 22, 2014, at B4.

whose marriage "united two of America's great real estate clans."[2] After suffering huge losses during the economic downturn of 2008, Mr. Swig obtained a business loan of 200,000 dollars from his in-laws, the Macklowes. In exchange, Mr. Swig entered into a postnuptial agreement providing that, "[i]n the event of a divorce, Ms. Swig would get both homes, while he would assume responsibility for the debts against the properties."[3]

The loan from the Macklowes might be described, in isolation, as establishing a debtor–creditor relationship with respect to a discrete business venture, but it can only be appreciated in the full context of the family relationship.[4] In particular, the Macklowes' help was conditioned upon a postnuptial agreement that protected the economic interests of Ms. Swig, their daughter. Functionally, the business loan and the marital agreement were connected, just as the Swigs' marriage mixed real estate and intimacy. A few months later, when the Swigs entered into divorce proceedings, the *New York Times* observed that the Swigs' divorce "ends more than a married life of galas at the Whitney and scenes in the Hamptons. It also represents the dissolution of the Macklowe-Swig business relationship."[5] A contractual model that includes family and business bargains helps us to perceive the Swigs' real-estate business as they themselves would have understood it: an economic partnership founded by marriage in which family and business interests were inseparable.

Marital agreements are not just a bargaining chip; they can play a crucial, independent role in family business planning by specifying whether business assets are to be treated as marital property.[6] While the Swigs' marital agreement

[2] Julie Creswell, *Breakup at 740 Park Avenue*, N.Y. TIMES, Feb. 2, 2014, at B1. Even before the marriage, each spouse had a stake in the real-estate world because of family connections. *See id.* at B4 ("Mr. Swig had reached this lofty perch the old-fashioned way: inheritance. He is the grandson of Benjamin Swig, who … began building a real estate dynasty.").

[3] *Id.* ("She would also get almost $12 million in artwork, including works by Jeff Koons and Takashi Murakami."). The business loan may not state that it is conditional upon the marital agreement, but both contracts were entered on the same day, and the timing cannot have been coincidental. *Id.*

[4] For instance, the loan contained "an unusual clause: The Macklowes agreed that they would not encourage or support any attempt to push Mr. Swig into involuntary bankruptcy." Although an unusual stipulation for an ordinary business creditor, it can be explained by the Macklowes' interest in the stability of their daughter's marriage. When the apparent rationale for the no-bankruptcy clause vanished, the Macklowes disregarded it: "Five months later, in March 2010, Kent Swig filed for divorce. And soon Harry Macklowe … began to break the promise he had made when he gave his son-in-law the loan." *Id.*

[5] *Id.*

[6] Carolyn J. Frantz, *Should the Rules of Marital Property Be Normative?*, 2004 U. CHI. LEGAL F. 265, 268 ("A large proportion of marital property rules are defaults: the law leaves some room for spouses to contract around provisions for the division of property on divorce and for the governance of marital property during marriage.").

seems to have been designed to protect Ms. Swig's interest in the nonbusiness assets of the marriage by allocating those assets to her, it also designated Mr. Swig as the owner of the real-estate businesses, including their debts. With his ownership rights clarified by contract, Mr. Swig is now in a position to resuscitate the business ventures, if he can.[7] Thus, setting aside the Macklowes' apparent ability to dictate terms, the parties used a contract to allocate their assets in accordance with the risk tolerances and preferences of each spouse.

In a contested divorce, the enforceability of a marital agreement may decide the fate of the family business.[8] A divorce involving the Los Angeles Dodgers provides a useful illustration. In 2004, Frank McCourt purchased the Dodgers team (including the stadium and surrounding real property) for 421 million dollars. Mr. McCourt had been very successful in Boston real estate and Jamie McCourt, his wife, after attending law school, served as General Counsel of the McCourt Companies – the family business. In early 2009, Ms. McCourt "became chief executive of the team and the highest-ranking woman in Major League Baseball."[9] In July 2009, however, the couple separated, and Ms. McCourt filed for divorce in October. The ensuing litigation concerned ownership of the Dodgers. Mr. McCourt claimed sole ownership, while Ms. McCourt alleged that she was a 50 percent owner.

As a matter of family law, this would have been an easy case. The Dodgers were acquired during the marriage and there was no question that Ms. McCourt contributed substantially to the effort. Therefore, the business would be subject to division as marital property. Even though the stock ownership was solely in Mr. McCourt's name, the default rules of family law determine the disposition of marital assets in a divorce. However, shortly after acquiring the Dodgers, the couple had entered into a marital property agreement and its enforceability controlled what the *Los Angeles Times* called "the central issue in the couple's divorce: Does he own the team or do they own it jointly?"[10]

7 Creswell, *supra* note 2, at B4 ("In the real estate game, fortunes are made, lost and, sometimes, remade. Mr. Swig, his spokesman said, is 'currently seeking real estate opportunities in which to invest and develop.'").

8 The consequences of divorce will be particularly harsh in so-called "'copreneurial businesses' – firms where husbands and wives jointly own or work in a business together." W. Gibb Dyer et al., *Should My Spouse Be My Partner? Preliminary Evidence from the Panel Study of Income Dynamics*, 26 Fam. Bus. Rev. 68, 68 (2012).

9 Bill Shaikin, *Jamie McCourt Wanted to "Renege" on Post-marital Agreement Involving Dodgers Because of Political Ambitions, Attorney Says*, L.A. Times (Aug. 30, 2010, 4:02 PM), http://bit.ly/40pX9jv [http://perma.cc/9CSE-RX6V].

10 Carlos Lozano & Bill Shaikin, *McCourt Divorce Trial Opens*, L.A. Times (Aug. 30, 2010, 9:03 AM), http://latimesblogs.latimes.com/lanow/2010/08/mccourt-divorce-trial-opens.html [http://perma.cc/S9TP-SFD4].

Ms. McCourt claimed that she signed the agreement without reading it, and that she believed the purpose of dividing assets was to separate the couple's business assets from their homes and other personal property.[11] In other words, she alleged that the goal was to protect the family's assets from possible creditors, not to allocate marital property in the event of a divorce. Mr. McCourt contended that Ms. McCourt wanted to insulate herself from the risks associated with the Dodgers – it had been losing 50 million dollars a year at the time of the McCourt investment, and Mr. McCourt had agreed to indemnify Major League Baseball for all losses going forward – and that the agreement accomplished its purpose.[12]

In December 2010, the court threw out the marital property agreement, in large part because the lawyer representing both parties had altered the provision at issue without notifying either party.[13] The court could not conclude whether either version of the agreement accurately reflected the parties' intentions. Accordingly, under the default rules of divorce, which now applied, Ms. McCourt was able to claim half-ownership of the Dodgers. In the end, Mr. McCourt had no choice but to sell his interest in the Dodgers in order to fund the divorce settlement.[14]

The narrow point is that poorly drafted agreements can have serious consequences. More broadly, though, the lesson to be drawn from the experience of the Swigs and the McCourts is that family business planning cannot rest at the formal boundaries of the firm but encompasses and organizes a wider set of "'[c]onnected contracts[,]' [which] may be thought of as shorthand for a fluid, nonlinear, nonhierarchical set of interactions and interrelationships."[15] Put plainly, no family business plan is complete unless it takes into account possible disruptions of family relationships, including divorce.[16]

11 Shaikin, *supra* note 9 ("Jamie McCourt has maintained she never would have knowingly signed away her right to the Dodgers. She says she signed the agreement without reading it, trusting her husband when he said the document was designed to protect the couple's homes from creditors.").

12 *Id.* ("Frank McCourt says the document did exactly what he said it did and that Jamie McCourt wanted it that way, that she insisted upon such an agreement so as not to risk losing the homes if the McCourts failed to reverse the Dodgers' financial losses.").

13 The lawyer had the parties sign a version of the agreement that included the Dodgers as marital property. He later substituted what he claimed was the correct language without notifying the parties. Bill Shaikin, *McCourt Divorce: Damaging Admission from Lawyer Who Negotiated Dodgers Agreement*, L.A. TIMES (Sept. 23, 2010, 2:30 PM), http://bit.ly/411FtjX [http://perma.cc/RMW4-DLFS].

14 *See* Bill Shaikin, *McCourts Agree on Dodgers*, L.A. TIMES, Oct. 17, 2011, at C1.

15 *See* G. Mitu Gulati et al., *Connected Contracts*, 47 UCLA L. REV. 887, 894 (2000).

16 In general, there are strong reasons to prefer private ordering concerning the consequences of a divorce to a state-imposed solution. *See* Robert H. Mnookin & Lewis Kornhauser,

Marital agreements that address the status of business assets are, therefore, an important part of the nexus of family business contracts.

4.2 ASSESSING SPOUSAL CONTRIBUTIONS

In a marriage that involves an equal sharing of economic resources, it may not appear necessary to define a spouse's role in a business entity owned by the other spouse. Yet, especially in smaller, unincorporated businesses, the nature of the business can turn on the characterization of spousal contributions.[17] No bright-line test will do, however, as the sharing of control, profits, and losses that define a business partnership also describe a marriage, and a spouse's involvement in a business might not fit neatly into either category.[18] According to a leading treatise, "The exercise of control by a spouse may be simply that of a helpmate in marriage rather than that of a partner; one spouse may share proceeds of the business in order to satisfy a support obligation."[19] Thus, disputes concerning alleged business partnerships turn on conceptions of business, family, and the appropriate relations between the two.

Consider, as an illustration, a family farm bankruptcy case in which each spouse sought to withhold 7,500 dollars in farming equipment under an

Bargaining in the Shadow of the Law: The Case of Divorce, 88 YALE L.J. 950, 956–57 (1979) ("[A] negotiated agreement allows the parties to avoid the risks and uncertainties of litigation, which may involve all-or-nothing consequences … [and] a consensual solution is by definition more likely to be consistent with the preferences of each spouse, and acceptable over time, than would a result imposed by a court.").

[17] If only one spouse has an ownership stake, the business enterprise may not count as a family business at all. Otherwise, the definition of family business would depend upon the marital status of the founder. Also, most people, married or not, have significant family ties, but, without more, those attachments cannot convert every sole proprietorship into a family business.

[18] *See* Larry E. Ribstein, *Incorporating the Hendricksons*, 35 WASH. U. J. L. & POL'Y 273, 296 (2011) ("Although the relationship may seem to have the usual partnership indicia of control and profit-sharing, these may actually be domestic arrangements."). Some feminist legal scholars cite unpaid labor in family business to ground "critiques of the market/family dichotomy, including the portrayal of market actors as self-sufficient individuals." Lisa Philipps, *Helping Out in the Family Firm: The Legal Treatment of Unpaid Market Labor*, 23 WIS. J.L. GENDER & SOC'Y 65, 66 (2008).

[19] ALAN R. BROMBERG ET AL., 1 BROMBERG & RIBSTEIN ON PARTNERSHIP § 2.10 (2d ed. 2014); *see also* LaRoque v. LaHood, 613 A.2d 1033, 1042 (Md. Ct. Spec. App. 1992) (holding that the fact both spouses "made management decisions for the business" did not, by itself, demonstrate the existence of a partnership); Cleland v. Thirion, 268 A.D.2d 842, 844 (N.Y. App. Div. 2000) (refusing to recognize partnership, despite the parties' apparent agreement, because "plaintiff's name was never placed on a certificate of doing business as partners, no partnership tax returns were ever filed and there never was any sharing of profits or losses").

exemption for "tools of the trade."[20] The bankruptcy trustee challenged the wife's claimed exemption on two grounds: Either the farm equipment was solely owned by the husband, consistent with tax records listing the farm as a sole proprietorship in his name; or, in the alternative, the farm had been operated as a partnership, in which case the personal equipment exemption was inapplicable. Accepting this logic, the bankruptcy court rejected the claimed exemption.[21]

On appeal, the Tenth Circuit held that both spouses could claim the exemption because the trustee had not met its burden of showing either a lack of ownership or the existence of partnership. Regarding the issue of joint ownership, the court noted that although Kansas does not treat all property within a marriage as community property,[22] there was both testimony and evidence that the farm had been operated jointly.[23] Also, "[a]ll proceeds from the farming operation were placed in a joint account, and funds to pay for the equipment came out of this account."[24] Both spouses signed the relevant loan documents in acquiring the farm equipment.[25]

However, the satisfactory resolution of the ownership issue threatened to confirm the disqualifying existence of a partnership, which is formed whenever two or more persons co-own a business for profit.[26] The prima facie case for partnership looked strong, as it was alleged by the debtors that they "co-owned the farm equipment, jointly participated in the work, and shared the profits."[27] Yet, the court further observed that the "usual indicia of a partnership are blurred by the marital relationship." For instance, "[t]he co-owning of property, sharing of profits, and the apparent authority for one spouse to act on behalf of the other are all common to the marital relationship even

[20] *In re* Lampe, 331 F.3d 750, 752 (10th Cir. 2003) ("Debtors Donald and Shelia Lampe are husband and wife farmers who filed for Chapter 7 bankruptcy.").

[21] *See In re* Lampe, 278 B.R. 205, 208 (B.A.P. 10th Cir. 2002) (citing and reversing unpublished bankruptcy court order that had concluded Mrs. Lampe lacked a separate "ownership interest" and, therefore, could not assert the tools-of-the-trade exemption).

[22] *See* Alvin E. Evans, *Primary Sources of Acquisition of Community Property*, 10 CAL. L. REV. 271, 271 (1922) ("Whatever is acquired by the joint efforts of the husband and wife shall be their community property." (internal quotation marks omitted)).

[23] *In re* Lampe, 331 F.3d at 756 ("Shelia Lampe worked on the farm and operated all equipment except the planter and combine.").

[24] *Id.*

[25] *Id.* ("Shelia Lampe co-signed on the notes and security agreements to obtain operating loans for which the farm equipment served as collateral.").

[26] Specifically, under Kansas law, "the association of two or more persons to carry on as co-owners a business for profit forms a partnership, whether or not the persons intend to form a partnership." KAN. STAT. ANN. § 56a-202 (West 1998).

[27] *In re* Lampe, 331 F.3d at 757.

absent a business." The "indicia" of partnership overlap with those of marriage, and the trustee could not sustain its burden of establishing the existence of a partnership separate from the marriage itself.[28] Thus, because of the family relationship, it was possible to conceive of the farm as occupying a space between the sole proprietorship and the general partnership, an unrecognized hybrid in which shared ownership is defined more by marriage than by business agreement.

Definitional disputes involving households and business ventures can arise even in more formally established business entities. For example, the Supreme Court of North Carolina concluded, in a divorce proceeding involving the ownership of a Kentucky Fried Chicken franchise, that the husband's ownership claim could be sustained as a contract claim based on a preexisting partnership even though it would not have merit under the North Carolina Business Law, which requires shareholder agreements to be in writing.[29] The intermediate appellate court, by contrast, had held that "any agreement [between] the husband and wife for the husband to join her in the business was not enforceable under contract law because [it was] not supported by valuable consideration, since plaintiff's interest in the business evolved from his status as a husband, and not as a business partner."[30] Thus, a broadly contractual view of the parties' relationship supplanted a status-based view of marriage, on the one hand, and a formalistic application of corporate law, on the other.[31]

28 *Id.* ("Although the Lampes deposited profits in a joint account, no evidence suggested this arrangement was required by an agreement to share profits as partners rather than the voluntary co-mingling of funds as spouses."). Accordingly, "[a]bsent a showing of some other indicia of a partnership beyond those incident to the marital relationship, the Trustee has not met its burden of proving a partnership existed, and Shelia Lampe therefore is entitled to claim the 'tools of the trade' exemption." *Id.*

29 Penley v. Penley, 332 S.E.2d 51, 64 (N.C. 1985) ("Plaintiff has properly chosen an alternate legal theory, premised primarily on defendant's oral agreement to convey an interest in the corporation – a question of simple contract law. Accordingly, we do not view the parties' agreement as an unenforceable shareholders' agreement.").

30 *Id.* at 56. According to the wife's testimony, there was no separate business agreement: "'[A]s far as him owning the franchise, he didn't own it. He knew he didn't own it, and it never was his. But being married to somebody, you more or less take him as a partner. I didn't take him as a partner in 1968 when he went to work over there; we were partners in marriage.'" *Penley*, 310 S.E.2d at 363.

31 *See Penley*, 332 S.E.2d at 62 (holding that "the jury could find that plaintiff reasonably premised his decision to render services on a full-time basis on promises made to him by defendant-wife, which led plaintiff to reasonably conclude and expect that his contributions would be rewarded by sharing in the business equally"). Although the jury could instead have found "that plaintiff joined the business ... solely because he was the husband of an ill wife, the jury was not *required* as a matter of law to so find." *Id.* at 61.

Likewise, another court held that the distribution restrictions in an antenuptial agreement did not preclude the wife from asserting a 50 percent partnership interest in a business enterprise that had grown "from approximately $430,000 at the date of marriage to over $12 million at the date of the dissolution judgment."[32] Under the antenuptial agreement, she was entitled to the home equity, 6,000 dollars, the family car, and household furniture.[33] However, she alleged successfully that she was a partner in the family business. Although she did not receive a salary, during the marriage she "began working full time in [the] husband's business."[34] As her role in the company expanded, she acted as "the head of the office when [the husband] was away on business" and the "business name registration" was later updated to reflect that the company was "a proprietorship of husband and wife."[35]

The court concluded that the wife's waiver of interest in the husband's property "does not preclude wife from asserting an interest in the company by virtue of her partnership with husband, but rather only precludes her from asserting an interest in husband's undivided one-half interest by virtue of the marriage."[36] Thus, because of the overlap of business law and family law, a claim to ownership that might have been waived by a marital agreement was sustained under an alternate theory of business partnership. In each of the cases discussed so far, the question of business ownership is complicated because the economic partnership of marriage coexists with any separate business arrangements that the parties may have made.

4.3 DIVORCE LAW

The impact of divorce law on family businesses co-owned by married couples further illustrates the entanglement of family law and business law. Not only must the parties exit the marital relationship, but also the change in marital status will, in most cases, involve the exit of one or both parties from the co-owned business. Just as a practical matter, the simultaneous winding up of two different legal entities creates problems of coordination.[37] If one

[32] *In re* Marriage of Leathers, 779 P.2d 619, 621 (Or. Ct. App. 1989).

[33] *See id.* at 620.

[34] *Id.*

[35] *Id.* at 621.

[36] *Id.* at 623.

[37] *See* Brandon Southward, *Double Trouble: When Spouses Who Share a Business Call It Quits*, FORTUNE (Apr. 9, 2014, 10:28 AM), https://tinyurl.com/yjky2jme [http://perma.cc/6Q3N-6Y8M].

spouse files a business-related dispute in one court, and the other spouse files for matrimonial divorce in a different court, a threshold issue to consider is which court has jurisdiction.[38] Further, the parties' rights are not identical in each context and equitable principles of divorce law often trump conflicting corporate law rules.

In a corporation, for instance, it is fundamental that the allocation of residual profits is determined by stock ownership.[39] Equally fundamental, the corporation is a legal person independent of any of its shareholders.[40] Thus, unlike a general partnership, a corporation cannot be dissolved by the express will of a shareholder. In order to exit the investment, a shareholder has to find a willing purchaser.[41] A family-owned business is subject to the same corporate law rules as any other business.[42]

Yet, when family business assets are at issue in a divorce proceeding, a narrow focus on corporate law rules can be misleading.[43] Once a petition for divorce invests a family law court with jurisdiction, the court has broad, equitable discretion to identify and divide marital assets.[44] For example, as discussed previously, Jamie McCourt did not own any stock in the Los Angeles Dodgers but was able to claim 50 percent in her divorce from Frank

38 *See, e.g.*, Raik v. Clindent Devs., LLC, 282 AD.2d 513 (N.Y. App. Div. 2001) (dismissing as duplicative a later-filed action for dissolution of a family business in favor of divorce proceeding without prejudice to refiling to address issues not adjudicated in the divorce action). For further discussion, including more recent case law reaching the same conclusion, see Franklin C. McRoberts, *Parallel Business and Matrimonial Divorce Proceedings*, N.Y. Bus. Divorce Blog (Jan. 8, 2024), https://tinyurl.com/3n57enn2.

39 *See* James D. Cox & Thomas Lee Hazen, Corporations § 13.01 (2d ed. 2003) ("A share of stock is primarily a profit-sharing contract, a unit of interest in the corporation based on a contribution to the corporate capital.").

40 *See id.* § 1.02 ("A business corporation is a legal device for carrying on a business enterprise for profit, a legal unit with a status or capacity of its own separate from the shareholders or members who own it.").

41 *See* Ian B. Lee, *Citizenship and the Corporation*, 34 Law & Soc. Inquiry 129, 153 (2009); Frederick Tung, *Confirmation and Claims Trading*, 90 Nw. U. L. Rev. 1684, 1701 (1996).

42 Analogous principles apply in LLCs. *See* Douglas K. Moll, *Minority Oppression & the Limited Liability Company: Learning (or Not) from Close Corporation History*, 40 Wake Forest L. Rev. 883, 928 (2005).

43 The same caution applies in cases involving partnerships or other forms of business organization. *See, e.g.*, Bobrow v. Bobrow, No. 29D01-0003-DR-166, 2002 WL 32001420, at *20 (Ind. Super. Sept. 20, 2002) ("Courts across the country agree with Indiana that a partnership agreement that governs the distribution of assets among partners upon withdrawal from the partnership cannot and does not control what constitutes 'property' under state law for purposes of marital dissolution.").

44 *See* Edwin T. Hood et al., Closely Held Businesses in Estate Planning § 8.10[G] (2d ed. 1998). Indeed, a spouse who held no stock and did not participate in a business may nevertheless argue that the business assets should be treated as marital assets.

McCourt, the team's sole owner.[45] Despite her role as Chief Executive to the Dodgers before the divorce, and her unofficial designation as the team's co-owner, she would not otherwise have had any legal claim to ownership. Yet, regardless of who owns the stock, the principle of equal division that governs exit from a marriage can dictate the terms of a business separation.[46]

Divorce law may crowd out corporate law, even if the parties have negotiated a shareholder agreement with tailored dispute-resolution provisions. For example, the Supreme Court of Oklahoma held in *Colclasure v. Colclasure* that the equitable principles of divorce law, rather than the terms of a buyout agreement, should control the "valuation of the marital business."[47] Before marriage, the wife was "the sole owner and operator" of a limited liability company (LLC), and she sold a 49 percent stake to her fiancé for a nominal sum. Approximately two years after getting married, the couple entered into an operating agreement that provided a number of triggers for dissolution or buyout, including divorce, and specified a valuation mechanism.[48]

By filing a petition for divorce, the wife triggered the dissolution provision of the LLC's operating agreement. However, the court observed that "[a] divorce suit is one of equitable cognizance in which the trial court has discretionary power to divide the marital estate."[49] Moreover, the court stated that, absent a valid antenuptial agreement, it was bound to follow Oklahoma's divorce statute, which mandates an equitable division of marital assets. Even assuming that the parties' operating agreement might count as a nuptial agreement, it had been signed after the marriage and was not cognizable under Oklahoma's divorce law.[50] Accordingly, the court rejected the husband's argument that the operating agreement's valuation

45 *See* Shaikin, *supra* note 14, at C1 (reporting that Jamie McCourt had agreed to relinquish her ownership claim in exchange for 130 million dollars).

46 *See* Carolyn J. Frantz & Hanoch Dagan, *Properties of Marriage*, 104 COLUM. L. REV. 75, 100 (2004) ("The cornerstone of the contemporary law of marital property … is the rule of equal division upon divorce."). Although mandatory "in only three jurisdictions[,]" the principle operates as a strong presumption elsewhere. *Id.* at 100–01.

47 Colclasure v. Colclasure, 295 P.3d 1123, 1125 (Okla. 2012). The valuation question was the sole issue before the court on appeal. *Id.* A trial court judge had taken the opposite tack, valuing the husband's share of the business according to the agreement. *Id.*

48 *Id.* at 1126 n.7. The agreement stated that the value was to be "determined as of the last day of the month immediately prior to the month in which the Event of Dissolution occurred." *Id.* at 1127.

49 *Id.* at 1128–29.

50 *Id.* at 1129 (holding that the trial court erred in failing "to ensure a fair and just division of the marital assets" because "the only mechanism permitted by statute to override that obligation is an antenuptial agreement between the parties").

mechanism should control.[51] The court emphasized that the issue to be resolved was one of divorce law, not business law.[52]

Whatever the merits of the *Colclasure* decision, the broader lesson is that family-law rules applicable to divorce have significant business implications. Moreover, the threat posed by divorce continues if a family business survives long enough to include children and grandchildren, as their spouses may also be entitled to a share of business assets as marital property. Indeed, since nearly half of all marriages fail, the legal complications of divorce should be seen as a predictable, recurring feature of family business ownership.[53]

[51] *Id.* at 1129 ("[A] mere valuation of [the company] as of a date certain … does not determine what portion of the value of the business was the result of the husband's efforts, the wife's efforts, or their joint efforts.").

[52] *Id.* at 1131 ("The question is not whether he may be sued for breach of fiduciary duty, but rather whether his actions lowered [the company's] value so that he received more money in the property settlement than he should have received."). In a strongly worded dissent, three justices accused the court of "re-writing the parties' contract for what appears to be the single purpose of increasing the wife's settlement award." *Id.* at 1132.

[53] *See* William M. Long & Scott A. Sissel, *Divorce and the Family Business – What Are the Options?*, 9 Bus. Entities 30, 30 (2007) ("In a mature family-owned business, one that has been in existence long before the marriage of one of its young shareholders, the founders should have engaged in business-succession planning that contemplates the possibility of a shareholder's divorce.").

5

Employment

Family businesses that intend to preserve family control over business strategy and operations use kinship as an important factor for the selection of key personnel. Family heirs benefit not only from inherited wealth but also from access to employment opportunities reserved for them. Their status within the family conditions their eligibility to enter a contractual relationship with the business. The inheritance of managerial responsibilities may seem to fit the classic definition of nepotism: unfair preferences based on kinship.[1] However, insider-favoring models of control need not conflict with appropriate standards of merit.

5.1 THE MERIT PARADIGM

If we are to avoid the absurdity of concluding that all kinship preferences are nepotism, even the care and affection that parents provide for children within the family, we must find some means of distinguishing nepotistic and non-nepotistic kinship preferences. Nepotism refers not just to the existence of a kinship preference, but the context in which it arises. Some goods are properly assigned using kinship as a factor; others are not.[2]

[1] *See* Joan G. Wexler, *Husbands and Wives: The Uneasy Case for Antinepotism Rules*, 62 B.U. L. Rev. 75, 75 (1982); *see also* Stephen J. McNamee & Robert K. Miller Jr., The Meritocracy Myth 49 (2004) ("[M]eritocracy strictly applies only to the poorest of the poor; everyone else has at least some advantage of inheritance that places them ahead at the start of the race.").

[2] *See* Adam Bellow, In Praise of Nepotism 23 (2003) ("I am very far from wanting to suggest that what we call nepotism is simply the operation of a normal and natural preference for kin. Nepotism is properly defined as 'undue preference for a relative' where fair and open competition should prevail.").

The philosopher Michael Walzer has argued that "there has never been a single criterion … for all distributions."[3] Instead, each kind of social good should be handled according to the procedures appropriate for it.[4] Intimate relationships, political choices, and impersonal market transactions take place in separate spheres and are governed by different rules. For instance, because they involve matters of intimacy some goods are not supposed to be exchanged for money.[5] In other circumstances, where market conventions apply, money is all that is expected to matter.[6] When we seek to ascertain whether a kinship preference should be considered nepotism, the particular context is crucial. We must ask, specifically, whether kinship preferences are permissible in that sphere.[7]

Yet, Walzer's proposed mode of analysis does not tell us whether kinship preferences in family-owned businesses are improper because the spheres of family and business overlap. An intention to pass control from generation to generation is a constitutive element of family businesses. The appropriateness of kinship preferences is, therefore, inseparable from broader questions about the role of family businesses in society.

Perhaps family ownership does not make a difference and kinship preferences should be considered improper in any business context. Even if participants have preexisting relationships that affect their goals and their mutual expectations, they are still joined in a for-profit venture. Further, by selecting a corporate, limited liability company, or partnership form, a family business could be said to have accepted the market principles applicable to that form of business.[8] There is no separate, family-business-entity form available.

[3] MICHAEL WALZER, SPHERES OF JUSTICE: A DEFENSE OF PLURALISM AND EQUALITY 4 (1983) ("Desert, qualification, birth and blood, friendship, need, free exchange, political loyalty, democratic decision; each has its place, along with many others, uneasily coexisting, invoked by competing groups, confused with one another."); *see also* MARGARET JANE RADIN, CONTESTED COMMODITIES (1996); ELIZABETH ANDERSON, VALUE IN ETHICS AND ECONOMICS (1993); Bernard A. O. Williams, *The Idea of Equality*, *in* PHILOSOPHY, POLITICS, AND SOCIETY 110 (Peter Laslett & W. G. Runciman eds., 2d series 1962).

[4] WALZER, *supra* note 3, at 10 ("Every social good or set of goods constitutes, as it were, a distributive sphere within which only certain criteria and arrangements are appropriate.").

[5] *Id.* at 9 ("[T]he words prostitution and bribery … describe the sale and purchase of goods that, given certain understandings of their meaning, ought never to be sold or purchased.").

[6] *Id.* at 10 ("Whatever can rightly be sold ought to be sold to pious men and women and also to profane, heretical, and sinful men and women.").

[7] In arguing for distinctive spheres, Walzer recognizes that "[w]hat happens in one distributive sphere affects what happens in the others; we can look, at most, for relative autonomy." *Id.* at 10.

[8] *See* LARRY E. RIBSTEIN, THE RISE OF THE UNCORPORATION 26 (2009).

Across all forms of business associations, merit is the accepted principle for the distribution of opportunities in the workplace.[9]

Kinship preferences in family businesses may be problematic because they appear to violate the principle of distribution according to merit. That is, family businesses involve the preferential transmission of direct economic advantage to insiders as to employment matters – such as hiring and promotion – that would ordinarily depend on formally neutral criteria.[10] The fact that a family owns a business does not prove that kinship preferences in the workplace are inevitable or appropriate. Although family owners may pretend that the question is which heir is best qualified to take over management, the limitation is artificial. If they wished to do so, the family owners could hire professional managers to run the business and remove themselves from day-to-day operational decision-making.

On the other hand, we might ask who has grounds to complain about kinship preferences. If a business does not sell its stock to the general public and is held by a single family, the business is, effectively, the family's property.[11] In this regard, one scholar suggests that public affirmative action policies elicit greater concern because they involve the allocation of resources that are open to all members of society, whereas, "in the case of a family-owned business in which nepotistic hiring is a stage in a process that will end with intergenerational transfer of the business itself, we see nepotism as completely legitimate."[12] Why, after all, should a family have an obligation to distribute its assets to strangers? In some respects, employment in a family business is no less a family asset than any other kind of wealth.

As long as families are permitted to raise children, it is unrealistic to insist that families will convey certain benefits while withholding others. In fact, family members are expected, and in some respects legally obligated, to care for one another.[13] One commentator argues that "[w]e have a *duty* to

[9] Opportunities in this context should be broadly understood to include not only hiring and promotion but also performance evaluation. Failure to discipline or fire an employee because of kinship might also qualify as nepotism. *See* Bridget K. Mulder, *A Model of Organizational Nepotism*, *in* NEPOTISM IN ORGANIZATIONS 219, 220 (Robert G. Jones ed., 2012).

[10] *See* BELLOW, *supra* note 2, at 11 (observing that the practice of nepotism "violates our basic sense of fairness and elicits strong reactions of revulsion and distaste").

[11] By contrast, the managers of a publicly traded corporation take on a fiduciary responsibility to widely dispersed investors who have entrusted their capital to the enterprise without any direct ability to control its use. *See* D. Gordon Smith, *The Critical Resource Theory of Fiduciary Duty*, 55 VAND. L. REV. 1399 (2002).

[12] Deborah C. Malamud, *Values, Symbols and Facts in the Affirmative Action Debate*, 95 MICH. L. REV. 1668, 1699 (1997) (reviewing several books on affirmative action).

[13] *See* Martha Albertson Fineman, *The Vulnerable Subject and the Responsive State*, 60 EMORY L.J. 251, 263 (2010) ("The family is the mechanism by which we privatize … dependency and

be nepotistic, and if we fail to put our families first we may destroy the very sources of altruism on which society depends."[14] Thus, if nepotism is the "*unfair* preferment of nephews or relatives to other qualified persons,"[15] kinship-based preferences in family businesses may not qualify.[16]

Moreover, concerns about kinship preferences may be misplaced when kinship ties are marital in nature. In such cases, it is debatable whether there has been a distribution, let alone a preference. Within a marriage, business assets are hard to distinguish "from the broader economic life of a household."[17] That is, each spouse would likely be entitled to half the value of the family's business investment regardless of the formal ownership records, because the business assets are treated as part of the economic partnership of marriage.[18] A spouse's involvement in a business may be seen as a feature of the marriage rather than an example of nepotism.[19]

To summarize, even if business and family constitute separate spheres as a matter of conceptual logic, invoking those spheres does not guide the use of kinship preferences in family businesses. Neither sphere controls the outcome because family businesses (and families, more generally) involve an intermingling of economics and intimacy. Indeed, the conspicuous lack of an answer in this setting suggests that Walzer's spheres are unlikely to provide clear guidance regarding the distribution of resources in most

its implications."); Bellow, *supra* note 2, at 476 ("[M]any Americans agree with Robert Frost in defining home as the place where, when you have nowhere else to go, 'they have to take you in.'").

14 Bellow, *supra* note 2, at 476 (emphasis in original).

15 10 Oxford English Dictionary 327 (2d ed. 1989) (emphasis added).

16 In businesses that are family controlled but involve other owners, the situation is more complex, as nonfamily investors might reasonably view family preferences as self-dealing. *See, e.g.*, Donahue v. Rodd Electrotype Co. of New Eng., 328 N.E.2d 505 (Mass. 1975) (children caused the corporation to repurchase shares from a retiring parent, who had been the controlling shareholder, but refused to provide similar liquidity for an unrelated minority investor).

17 Benjamin Means, *The Contractual Foundation of Family-Business Law*, 75 Ohio St. L.J. 675, 693 (2014). Note that "[i]n its pristine form, coverture treated husband and wife as indistinguishable legal actors from the perspective of the outside world." Viviana A. Zelizer, The Purchase of Intimacy 33, 67 (2005).

18 Allison Anna Tait, *Corporate Family Law*, 112 Nw. U. L. Rev. 1, 5 (2017) (citing Andrea Colli, The History of Family Business 1850–2000 8 (2003)).

19 A spouse's involvement looks more like nepotism when the spouse takes on a role in the business that would ordinarily have an independent merit qualification – as when the director Roman Polanski cast his wife, Emmanuelle Seigner, as a co-lead in the movie *Venus in Fur* (2014). Favorable reviews, including observations that the plot resembles the Polanski marriage in certain respects, indicate that the casting decision may nonetheless have been well considered. *Cf.* Bayer v. Beran, 49 N.Y.S.2d 2 (N.Y. Sup. Ct. 1944) (opera singer hired to promote company was wife of the chair of the board of directors but had appropriate qualifications).

disputed cases.[20] Rather than seeking categorical answers, perhaps it would be more fruitful for us to inquire whether particular insider-favoring decisions are well supported or represent a departure from minimum standards. Section 5.2 argues that the continuation of insider control can reflect merit-based judgments. In this regard, while kinship preferences in family businesses may be motivated in part by other considerations, family owners are likely to take steps to ensure that heirs are properly qualified and to insist upon the satisfaction of objective criteria.

5.2 KINSHIP AS QUALIFICATION

Insider preferences would be improper if invoked as the sole basis for decision-making in a business setting. Perhaps most objectionably, a powerful benefactor might confer business opportunities – office, title, salary – regardless of qualifications. To ignore merit and to prefer insiders in all circumstances is cronyism in its most barefaced incarnation. Yet, rarely will the case be so clear. In a family business, a child might spend summers working for the business and, over time, develop the competence to run it. As one commentator observes, "Growing up around a business or vocation – learning how it works, getting to know the people in it – creates a powerful advantage that is tantamount to nepotism."[21] Such indirect advantages elude easy categorization.[22]

5.2.1 *The Boss's Nephew*

The term nepotism was first used to describe the improper practice of Renaissance-era popes who appointed nephews (perhaps actually illegitimate sons) to important ecclesiastical positions, thereby cementing family power and prestige.[23] This was a danger the Church had hoped to forestall by forbidding clergy from marriage: "Since it was one of the purposes of clerical

[20] *See* ZELIZER, *supra* note 17, at 33 ("In any particular social setting – not only households, but also workplaces, schools, churches, and clubs – multiple ties of different kinds coexist and often extend across the setting's boundary into other settings."); Frances Olsen, *The Family and the Market: A Study of Ideology and Legal Reform*, 96 HARV. L. REV. 1497 (1983).

[21] BELLOW, *supra* note 2, at 10.

[22] Harvey S. James, Jr., *What Can the Family Contribute to Business? Examining Contractual Relationships*, 12 FAM. BUS. REV. 61, 61 (1999) ("To the extent that family processes contribute to the efficient and effective functioning of the company, family businesses will survive and thrive.").

[23] BELLOW, *supra* note 2, at 11 ("The term *nepotismo* was coined sometime in the fourteenth or fifteenth century to describe the corrupt practice of appointing papal relatives to office – usually illegitimate sons described as 'nephews.'").

celibacy to cut the church loose from the feudal system and to ensure a succession of qualified individuals, the practice was identified as sinful early on."[24]

Nepotism continues to conjure an unpleasant image of patronage and of incompetent or lazy heirs trading on their family connections, eclipsing the career prospects of more qualified but less connected peers. We might call this the problem of the meritorious outsider.[25] As one commentator puts it, "From the workingman's perspective nepotism means hiring or promoting the boss's son-in-law, nephew, or girlfriend over the heads of more qualified candidates."[26] Yet, some version of "nepotism is often the rule in family businesses, and it is usually accepted as 'the way things are' by everyone involved."[27] Successful family businesses seem to rise above accusations of nepotism, perhaps because the heirs are not often so dismally qualified.

In family businesses, merit remains an important factor in hiring and promotion. Therefore, the concept of nepotism is potentially misleading because it obscures the manner in which kinship preferences normally function. Although the formal definition of nepotism – favoritism based on kinship – does not specify any central or less central examples, it is a feature of human reasoning that we organize concepts according to prototypes.[28] For example, robins are more central to our understanding of the concept "bird" than chickens, ostriches, or penguins.[29] Prototype "categories are structured by means of *idealized cognitive models* – culturally shared 'theories' of how to organize some portion of our experience."[30] When the concept is nepotism, we are likely to picture the polo-playing, feckless heir rather than a well-qualified understudy who receives special opportunities but makes the most of them.[31]

24 WALZER, *supra* note 3, at 147; BELLOW, *supra* note 2, at 191 ("The Renaissance papacy is one of the greatest monuments to nepotism in Western history.").

25 My thanks to Professor Kenneth Rosen who proposed the terminology.

26 BELLOW, *supra* note 2, at 11.

27 *Id.*

28 Nepotism's definition establishes a category and all examples that meet the definition fall within the category. *See* Steven L. Winter, *The Metaphor of Standing and the Problem of Self-Governance*, 40 STAN. L. REV. 1371, 1385 (1988) ("In the classical theory of categorization, all objects having the same relevant criteria are classed together. In this view, no category member is any more 'representative' of a category than another.").

29 GEORGE LAKOFF & MARK JOHNSON, METAPHORS WE LIVE BY 123 (1980).

30 Winter, *supra* note 28, at 1385.

31 Admittedly, polo-playing heirs are not entirely mythical creatures. *See The Checkered Past of August Busch IV*, CBS NEWS (Dec. 28, 2010), www.cbsnews.com/news/the-checkered-past-of-august-busch-iv/ (reporting legal travails of August Busch IV, aka the Fourth, "heir to his family's beer fortune" and CEO of the company before it was sold). For detailed reporting concerning the mismanagement that led to the company's forced sale to an international conglomerate, see JULIE MACINTOSH, DETHRONING THE KING: THE HOSTILE TAKEOVER OF ANHEUSER-BUSCH, AN AMERICAN ICON (2011).

Consequently, hiring decisions involving relatives with outstanding credentials look like outliers and may be difficult to reconcile with our basic understanding of nepotism. That is, "[b]ecause 'prototypes act as cognitive reference points of various sorts and form the basis for inferences,' they tend to play an important role in reasoning about categories."[32] We might paint with too broad a brush and treat kinship preferences as an affront to meritocratic principles, even if those kinship preferences do not involve the preservation of unearned privileges or the elevation of the incompetent.[33] For this reason, the position of the heir can carry with it a stigma, which "arises from the belief that nepotism is not just favoring a relative, but also favoring someone who is unqualified or incompetent compared to other applicants."[34] Customers and colleagues alike may be quick to conclude that the heir is lacking.[35]

Equally important, the distorting influence of the "nepotism" concept can leave us without a language to talk about family business hiring and promotion practices in which the beneficiaries of kinship preferences are qualified and capable of handling the responsibility entrusted to them.[36] Section 5.2.2 explores a variety of real-world situations involving kinship preferences.

5.2.2 *Access and Apprenticeship*

The advantages of insider connections are inescapable in almost any field of endeavor, infamously so in the world of entertainment. Hence, the term "nepotism baby" or "nepo baby." As one journalist put it, "In 2022, the internet uncovered a vast conspiracy: Hollywood was run on an invisible network

[32] Winter, *supra* note 28, at 1385.

[33] *Id.* ("Sometimes, we may not distinguish the variants from the prototype of the idealized cognitive model. An extreme example is when a child thinks that the teacher or daycare worker is the mother of the other children. In that case, we have a radical prototype effect in which the prototype overshadows the rest of the category.").

[34] Mulder, *supra* note 9, at 224. Similar perceptions regarding unfairness can stigmatize the beneficiaries of affirmative action policies, even though the basis and justification for such preferences may be quite different. *Id.*

[35] *See* Mark Russ Federman, Russ & Daughters: Reflections and Recipes from the House that Herring Built 5 (2013) ("'I am Mr. Russ.' I expected my pronouncement to end any further challenges. It took less than a second for her response. 'I know you. You're not Mistar Russ. Your grandfadder vas Mistar Russ.'").

[36] Winter, *supra* note 28, at 1385 ("One consequence of these extreme prototype effects is that the variants may be left unexpressed by the linguistic conventions of the culture. Because they have no name, these variants become suppressed aspects of our social consciousness."). In this vein, one commentator asserts that "[t]he reason we have tied ourselves in knots around this question [the meaning of nepotism] is really quite simple: there is a missing distinction in our lexicon between good nepotism and bad." Bellow, *supra* note 2, at 15.

of family ties – *and everybody was in on it!*"[37] For example, "At 16, the model and actress Lily-Rose Depp landed her first campaign with Chanel, the same house her mother, Vanessa Paradis, worked with; the year before, she'd made her film debut alongside her father, Johnny Depp."[38] When she later denied that she had it easier than anyone else, or that she was successful because of her connections, "[h]er fellow models castigated her on Instagram."[39] The denial was implausible because, "In an industry built on reboots, a famous last name can be valuable intellectual property."[40] So, is it fair to conclude that "a nepo baby is physical proof that meritocracy is a lie"?[41]

Not necessarily. Such connections, however helpful, are at most an indirect form of nepotism.[42] Willie Nelson, for example, cannot hand down hit singles to his son Lukas like a family heirloom. The children of successful celebrities have had to choose a career path and work for their own success. On the other hand, it would be naïve to overlook the value of industry connections, access to voice lessons, the right acting coaches, and the like. Whatever the native talent of Lukas Nelson, he has enjoyed opportunities not equally available to meritorious outsiders, the talented children of less well-connected parents.

In family businesses, in the entertainment industry and elsewhere, kinship affords access to a reservoir of information about a business and associated relationships. Nevertheless, as is true in other professional contexts, the entry of a younger generation into a family business does not necessarily signify that kinship has taken precedence over merit. Rather, it may be the case that the younger generation has developed a sincere interest in the business, learned the ropes, and, by the time control passes, qualified for the opportunity.

37 Nate Jones, *An All but Definitive Guide to the Hollywood Nepo Verse*, VULTURE (Dec. 19, 2022), www.vulture.com/article/hollywood-nepotism-babies-list-taxonomy.html.

38 *Id.*

39 *Id.* ("'i have many nepo baby friends whom i respect,' the top model Vittoria Ceretti wrote in an Instagram Story, 'but i can't stand listening to you compare yourself to me. i was not born on a comfy sexy pillow with a view.'").

40 *Id.*

41 *Id.* For an argument that "nepo babies" are an inevitable feature of human societies, see Maya Jasanoff, *The History of Nepo Babies Is the History of Humanity*, NEW YORKER (May 22, 2023), https://tinyurl.com/mryrxjds (*reviewing* SIMON SEBAG MONTEFIORE, THE WORLD: A FAMILY HISTORY OF HUMANITY (2023)).

42 BELLOW, *supra* note 2, at 10 ("No one can pick up the phone these days and get their kid a high-paying job, a record deal, or a spot on the national ticket."). Yet, "[w]hile not nepotism in the classic sense, it is rightly called nepotism because it involves exploiting the family name, connections, or wealth. The method may be different, but the result is much the same." *Id.* at 14–15.

For example, Arthur Gregg Sulzberger was well suited for the role of publisher of the *New York Times*, which he assumed on January 1, 2018, when his father stepped down after a quarter century in the position.[43] Mr. Sulzberger is the sixth member of the Ochs-Sulzberger family to serve as publisher since the Ochs-Sulzberger family acquired the paper in 1896. The Ochs-Sulzberger family continues to own approximately 91 percent of the paper's stock and controls the board. However, his appointment was not a foregone conclusion; Mr. Sulzberger was one of several candidates in contention, and the *Times* established an independent committee to make the decision.

Although Mr. Sulzberger stated in an interview that he "'wasn't someone who grew up aspiring to become publisher of the *New York Times*,'"[44] it is clear that he had been prepared for the role. He worked as a journalist beginning in 2003 and became a reporter for the *Times* in 2009, moving up to bureau chief and then deputy publisher. Perhaps most notably, Mr. Sulzberger took on important responsibility "heading the team that produced the *Times*'s 'innovation report' in 2014."[45] The innovation report recommended far-reaching changes to the paper's digital offerings. As evidenced by Mr. Sulzberger's leadership in reviewing the *Times*'s digital strategy, when changes are needed, family members may have the ability to force difficult conversations that outsiders might avoid. To this extent, Mr. Sulzberger's family status may enhance his qualifications for the role.

The advantages of upbringing do not always bespeak favoritism. An older generation may not even intend for younger family members to join the business.[46] In this regard, the third-generation owner of the Russ & Daughters delicatessen in New York recalls that his early education in the business may have been intended in some ways to *discourage* his eventual participation:

> Shouting and cursing were the accepted forms of communication, and there was no attempt to tone it down at all, even in the presence of a ten-year-old boy. Looking back now, I suspect that part of the show was for my benefit, with the underlying message being, "Look, kid, every day is a battle. We enjoy our battles; it's all we know. But you don't need to do this for a living. You'll get a good education and won't have to sell fish."[47]

43 *See* Sydney Ember, *A.G. Sulzberger, 37, to Take Over as New York Times Publisher*, N.Y. Times, Dec. 14, 2017.

44 *Id.*

45 *Id.*

46 According to one commentator, the modern version of nepotism is "not so much a matter of parents hiring or getting jobs for children as of children choosing to follow in their parents' footsteps." Bellow, *supra* note 2, at 10.

47 Federman, *supra* note 35, at 61–62.

Whether or not they are encouraged to do so, of course, children may still gravitate toward the family business.

The following case study shows how a business may benefit from the knowledge that parents pass to their children, as well as the desire of children to help their parents. When the process works well, the next generation preserves what is worth keeping but is unafraid to make bold changes.

5.3 CASE STUDY: BURNS DANCE STUDIO

When Rhoda Burns and her family relocated to Aiken, South Carolina, in 1982, she struggled to find work. Rhoda was an experienced dancer and had a background in dance instruction, but none of the existing dance studios would hire her. She was perceived as an outsider and treated accordingly. Then a former boss intervened, offering Rhoda 500 dollars and a variable-speed record player. He told her to "take the music, take your records, and go start your own business." Rhoda opened Burns Dance Studio with a clear vision – to share the joy of dance with the local community. One of her first students was her nine-year-old son, Corey.

Forty-two years later, Corey is the second-generation owner, and Burns Dance Studio has become a local institution. The studio offers classes for ages three and up in various dance styles, including ballet, tap, jazz, hip hop, tumbling, and contemporary. In addition to Corey, who teaches many of the classes, Burns Dance Studio employs a staff of experienced teachers and frequently wins the "Best Dance Studio" award as voted by the readers of the *Aiken Standard*. Rhoda and Corey take satisfaction from their work that goes beyond earning a living. Rhoda founded the business to share the joy of dance with others, and that same passion is why Corey has chosen to make Burns Dance Studio his life's work, too.

The formal transition of ownership from mother to son began in 2013. Although he had not planned to take over the business, Corey was well qualified for the role. He had continued to train and perform as a dancer, and he knew the Burns Dance Studio business well. Even as he focused on a career in public school administration, he continued to assist his mother with studio tasks on the side. By 2013, Corey was serving as a school principal. He realized that Rhoda needed more help to keep the studio on track, and he increased his hours accordingly. It became impossible to do both jobs properly. By June 2013, Corey had left the school district to focus on the studio full time.

Corey believed that the business had incredible potential value, but that it was in dire need of a revamp if it was to survive. Since taking over, Corey has been responsible for all aspects of the business, including registering for conventions and competitions, assembling music, preparing for classes, managing staff, and handling the finances. Under Corey's leadership, Burns Dance Studio has also adapted its culture. Moving away from Rhoda's more traditional methods of dance instruction, Corey has worked tirelessly to create an environment of calm where children learn not only a love for dance but also discipline, time management, and other life skills. The studio's motto is "Dance Training to Reinforce Life Training."

Corey's most significant decision was to expand and update Burns Dance Studio by building a new studio. Before incurring the debt, which could have jeopardized the business if expected revenues failed to materialize, Corey conducted due diligence. He met with a succession planning group and with lawyers to make sure that he had the necessary authority and that the project was consistent with his fiduciary obligations. He hired an accountant to review the company's financial situation. And, not without difficulty, he found a bank willing to provide financing. During the underwriting process, the bank investigated not only the studio, but also Corey and his personal life. For a small, family-owned business, credit worthiness is a holistic inquiry. Rhoda continued to help in any way she could, including using her own home as a line of credit to support the construction cost for the new studio. Construction began in 2015, was completed by 2016, and, as Corey hoped, facilitated an expansion of the business.

Rhoda has officially retired, but she remains very much involved with Burns Dance Studio. She teaches two to three classes a week, handles all the apparel, and helps to maintain the studio spaces. Not surprisingly, Corey and Rhoda sometimes disagree on how things should be run. As the founder, Rhoda feels a continuing obligation to provide guidance and believes that she should have the prerogative to make decisions. It is not uncommon in a family business for the older generation to have difficulty letting go. (In a nonfamily business, once the business is sold, the previous owners typically have little involvement with the business going forward.) Still, Corey understands his mother's passion for the studio and tries not to let philosophical differences negatively impact their relationship. For her part, while leaving the business to Corey was difficult, Rhoda respects his judgment and trusts him to maintain the legacy that she built.

There have been external challenges, too. Corey described the COVID-19 pandemic as a "train wreck." Although the studio survived, it struggled to return to pre-COVID numbers. Not only did the pandemic result in three months' worth of lost profits, it also required significant effort after reopening to make parents comfortable putting their children back into classes. To rebuild numbers, Corey has focused on learning new marketing techniques, especially via social media. Like other small businesses, Burns Dance Studio has begun to use popular media platforms to target the desired audience. As the current owner, Corey understands that he must innovate and that the business model he inherited is an adaptable foundation, not a fixed firmament.

In sum, Burns Dance Studio illustrates why a child is often the best choice to take over a business. Corey grew up in the business, and he is fully invested in its future. Few if any outside owners could have brought that same passion to the role. Corey readily admits that navigating the parent–child dynamic has been challenging at times but Burns Dance Studio's continued success is a testament to the perseverance of Corey and Rhoda and their shared entrepreneurial spirit.

6

Succession

At their best, family businesses exhibit a long-term commitment to generating value for the benefit of family owners and other stakeholders.[1] In order for a family business to outlast its current owners, however, there must be an effective transfer of power.[2] This is easier said than done.[3] Lawsuits concerning family business succession have impacted well-known businesses, including Koch Industries, the E&J Gallo Winery, Hyatt Hotels, and U-Haul.[4] Indeed, for family businesses, "leadership succession ... [is] the crucial issue."[5] As one commentator observes, "succession law is characterized by a need to manage multiple sets of legal rules from different subject matter areas that converge

1 *See* Nicholas Kachaner et al., *What You Can Learn from Family Business*, HARV. BUS. REV. (Nov. 2012), https://hbr.org/2012/11/what-you-can-learn-from-family-business ("Executives of family businesses often invest with a 10- or 20-year horizon, concentrating on what they can do now to benefit the next generation."); Danny Miller et al., *Stewardship vs. Stagnation: An Empirical Comparison of Small Family and Non-Family Businesses*, 45 J. MGMT. STUD. 51, 73 (2008) (noting that family business owners "exhibit much care about continuity, community and connection: specifically, about the long term preservation and nurturing of their business and its markets"); Benjamin Means, *The Value of Insider Control*, 60 WM. & MARY L. REV. 891, 935 (2019) (focusing on family control of public corporations and arguing that "controlled companies can soften the harder edges of capitalism by bringing the values of controlling owners into the marketplace").

2 *See* THE ENDURANCE OF FAMILY BUSINESSES: A GLOBAL OVERVIEW (Paloma Fernandez Perez & Andrea Colli eds., 2013); Benjamin Means, *Wealth Inequality and Family Businesses*, 65 EMORY L.J. 937, 939 (2016) ("Typically, owners seek to increase family wealth, to provide employment for family members, and, ultimately, to transfer control to a new generation of family owners.").

3 *See* Means, *supra* note 1, at 1191 (observing that "the transfer of control from one generation to the next invites tension between the family norm of equal treatment and the business norm of meritocracy").

4 For an account of these and many disputes involving family business succession, see GRANT GORDON & NIGEL NICHOLSON, FAMILY WARS: STORIES AND INSIGHTS FROM FAMOUS FAMILY BUSINESS FEUDS (2010).

5 ANDREA COLLI, THE HISTORY OF FAMILY BUSINESS: 1850–2000 66 (2003).

on the nexus of a business succession."[6] For example, the family owners might create a trust to effectuate a transition or might consider drafting an inheritance contract. Regardless of the legal mechanism chosen, there is an issue of timing – the older generation may hesitate to transfer power, and that hesitation can prove costly.

6.1 TRUST LAW

Lawyers who advise family businesses often recommend the use of trusts because, among other advantages, it is possible to allocate company stock and managerial control to one or more members of the family without depriving other family members of business profits.[7] Technically, the trust owns the stock and the children, who are beneficiaries of the trust, are not themselves owners.[8] Thus, a more capable child or an outside manager could be selected to serve as trustee while the remaining offspring receive some measure of economic security through their beneficial trust interest.[9] Alternatively, parents might give children a stake in a business, even a majority share, without relinquishing their own control.[10]

Trust instruments that control family business assets should be considered part of the business governance scheme, because the trust agreement defines the trustee's authority as business manager.[11] Any characterization of

6 Kenneth M. Rosen, *Company Law and the Law of Succession Droit Commercial/Commercial Law*, 62 AM. J. COMP. L. 387, 405 (Supp. 2014).

7 *See* DAVID BORK, FAMILY BUSINESS, RISKY BUSINESS: HOW TO MAKE IT WORK 129 (1986) ("As a general principle, countless problems can be avoided if family members who do not intend to be active in the business are not left stock in it.").

8 The trust creates "a fiduciary relationship with respect to property, subjecting the person by whom the title to the property is held to equitable duties to deal with the property for the benefit of another person." RESTATEMENT (SECOND) OF TRUSTS § 2 (1959).

9 *See, e.g.*, Karen E. Boxx, *Too Many Tiaras: Conflicting Fiduciary Duties in the Family-Owned Business Context*, 49 HOUS. L. REV. 233, 234–35 (2012) (describing the estate plan of jeweler Harry Winston). As Professor Boxx notes, "Mr. Winston had the same instincts as most parents in this situation: he wanted to treat his sons equally financially but also wanted his business-oriented son in charge of the company." *Id.* at 235.

10 *See* Jeffrey G. Sherman, *Posthumous Meddling: An Instrumentalist Theory of Testamentary Restraints on Conjugal and Religious Choices*, 1999 U. ILL. L. REV. 1273, 1275; Robert H. Sitkoff, *An Agency Costs Theory of Trust Law*, 89 CORNELL L. REV. 621, 646 n.122 (2004) (observing that this control can, in some cases, become oppressive when settlors seek "to maintain dominance over their family after death").

11 In one case, for instance, the settlor "'treated [the trust] and [the corporation] as a coordinated operation … intend[ing] the Trustees to work with and through the [corporation] … to make coordinated investments and gain control of businesses.'" Bartlett v. Dumaine, 523 A.2d 1, 8 (N.H. 1986) (quoting master's report). Families often use trusts to effectuate the transfer of property and other assets, including family-owned businesses. *See* Thomas P. Gallanis, *The*

the family business that failed to acknowledge the controlling trust would be misleading.[12] Rather, when trust law overlaps with business-organization law, the vital question is whether there is some appropriate mechanism for coordinating the parties' rights and obligations.[13]

For example, the applicable fiduciary standards differ significantly.[14] Unless modified, the default duty of loyalty owed by a trustee requires disgorgement of all profits, even if the dealings were fair.[15] A controlling shareholder, by contrast, is entitled to benefit from the share ownership as long as any self-interested transactions are fair to the other shareholders.[16] The trustee who manages a trust-controlled business appears to owe fiduciary duties in both capacities.

The inconsistency of fiduciary obligations becomes especially problematic when a family member is empowered as trustee to manage a family business for the benefit of other members of the family.[17] This arrangement involves a plain conflict of interest if the trustee is a beneficiary of the trust or a controlling shareholder of the family business.[18] For example, consider Rupert Murdoch's estate plan for transferring control of his multibillion dollar stake in News Corp, the company he founded, to his children. A principal means to that end includes, reportedly, a family trust to be run by the children from his first two marriages for their own benefit and the benefit of the children of his third marriage.[19] Rupert Murdoch later tried to amend

New Direction of American Trust Law, 97 IOWA L. REV. 215, 217 (2011); *see also* John H. Langbein, *The Secret Life of the Trust: The Trust as an Instrument of Commerce*, 107 YALE L.J. 165, 165 (1997) ("The trust originated at the end of the Middle Ages as a means of transferring wealth within the family, and the trust remains our characteristic device for organizing intergenerational wealth transmission.").

12 *See* Frank T. Becker, *Control of Trust-Held Companies by Trustees*, 19 J. CORP. L. 41, 41 (1993) ("Trusts often hold sufficient voting interest in business entities to effectively control them.").

13 *See* Boxx, *supra* note 9, at 235–36.

14 The duties may also apply to different parties. *See id.* at 235 (noting "complex dilemma" when trustee "must act both as corporate fiduciary, running the business in the best interests of all the stakeholders in the business, and as trustee to her sibling, owing undivided loyalty to this one shareholder").

15 *See* Langbein, *supra* note 11, at 656 ("The trustee who deals with trust property for the trustee's own account is liable to disgorge the profits to the trust even if the trustee paid fair value for the property.").

16 *See* Pepper v. Litton, 308 U.S. 295, 306 (1939).

17 *See* Boxx, *supra* note 9, at 233 (noting that trusts are a "popular solution" to the problem posed by multiple heirs, not all of whom are capable or interested in assuming a leadership position in the family business).

18 *See id.*

19 According to news accounts, Mr. Murdoch's disclosure of the unequal control arrangement during a television interview several years ago nearly caused the breakup of his third marriage. *See* Peter Lattman & Amy Chozick, *Wendi Murdoch Hires a New Lawyer, Suggesting*

the trust to repose full control in one designated heir.[20] A Nevada probate court ruled against Murdoch, concluding that the proposed changes were a "carefully crafted charade."[21]

Even for families that lack the complexity of the Murdoch clan, the trustee's role remains an issue. As one commentator explains:

> Low-grade conflicts of interest are especially endemic in family trusteeships. We see constantly in real-world practice some version of the case in which my father names me trustee for my mother for life, remainder to a group including me, with a power in the trustee to invade the corpus of the trust for the benefit of my mother in the event the life interest becomes inadequate for her comfort and support. My father has insisted on choosing a conflict-tainted trustee, making the judgment that I am to be trusted not to pauperize my mother to enrich myself. These situations are especially dangerous when the trust is given a controlling interest in a close corporation, and I am an officer of that firm.[22]

From the standpoint of the family member who is appointed trustee, the challenge is to discharge the trustee's obligations faithfully while also sharing in the benefits of the family business, both as beneficiary of the trust and as a controlling shareholder.[23]

When there is uncertainty or conflict, it may help to clarify the trustee's role by focusing attention on the family business bargain in its entirety.[24] Thus, whether or not the settlor defines the trustee's obligations explicitly, those obligations should be interpreted according to the overall context in which the trust was created:

a Divorce May Turn Messy, N.Y. Times, July 30, 2013, at B3 ("The slip almost created a separation, and prompted Mrs. Murdoch to negotiate more favorable terms for her daughters, according to people close to the couple.").

20 *See* Jonathan Mahler & Jim Rutenberg, *Rupert Murdoch Fails in Bid to Change Family Trust*, N.Y. Times, Dec. 9, 2024.

21 For in-depth reporting concerning the Murdoch family trust and the litigation, see Jonathan Mahler & Jim Rutenberg, *"You've Blown a Hole in the Family": Inside the Murdochs' Succession Drama*, N.Y. Times Mag. (Feb. 13, 2025), https://tinyurl.com/2sbmddey.

22 *See* Langbein, *supra* note 11, at 667.

23 *See* Boxx, *supra* note 9, at 235 (noting that the "[d]uties of a corporate fiduciary are much more lenient than that of a trustee").

24 *See* Langbein, *supra* note 11, at 630 ("In fields ranging from corporations and partnership, to landlord and tenant, to servitudes, to the law of marriage, scholars have come to understand our legal rules as resting mainly on imputed bargains that are susceptible to alteration by actual bargains."). Context should also factor into the interpretation: "Family and personal trustees often have interests adverse to the trust. The settlor's determination to ask these conflicted persons to serve bears materially on the standard of fiduciary duty that the trust deal embodies." *Id.* at 666.

> If he is well counseled, my father spells out broad authority for me as trustee, expressly trumping the default standards of the duty of loyalty. But when he neglects that step, contractarian analysis encourages us to look at the real nature of the trust deal, that is, what he and I understood, or what we would have understood about the purposes of the trust and the standard for my trusteeship.[25]

Such assessments of intent require a "sympathetic reading of the [trust instrument] as an entirety and in view of all the facts and circumstances under which the provisions … were framed."[26]

Trust agreements can also align the goals of the business organization with the values of the family owners. For example, the Green family that owns Hobby Lobby operates it "through a management trust (of which each Green is a trustee), … governed by religious principles."[27] Although Hobby Lobby is a for-profit business, the trust instrument designates a religious purpose – "to create, support, and leverage the efforts of Christian ministries" – and every beneficiary is required to affirm that religious purpose as a condition of membership in the trust.[28] By imposing religious conditions in the context of a family transfer of wealth, rather than as part of the governance structure of the underlying business, the Green family seeks to avoid the possibility that its religious mission might be stymied someday by a dissenting shareholder insistent upon the pursuit of profits.[29]

It might be objected that trusts are not corporate governance, properly understood, because "a trust is 'essentially a gift, projected on the plane of

[25] *Id.* at 667; *see also* Bartlett v. Dumaine, 523 A.2d 1, 11 (N.H. 1986) (applying corporate business judgment rule deference rather than enhanced scrutiny under trust law's prudent-investor rule: "Where, as in this case, a trust instrument allows the trustees to operate trust-controlled corporations, the trustees have wide discretion in running the corporate enterprises.").

[26] *In re* Estate of Winston, 205 A.D.2d 922, 923 (N.Y. App. Div. 1994) (internal quotation marks omitted) (analyzing a trust created by a will). According to one commentator, the "answer cannot be as simple as choosing one standard over the other but rather requires fashioning a distinct standard that both protects the beneficiary and allows sufficient management autonomy to allow the business to prosper." Boxx, *supra* note 9, at 236.

[27] Hobby Lobby Stores, Inc. v. Sebelius, 723 F.3d 1114, 1122 (10th Cir. 2013).

[28] *Id.* Each Green family member is bound to this mission, which encompasses Hobby Lobby, by a required signature joining a "Trust Commitment." *Id.* The use of a trust to require religious commitments is not an aberration. In another case, for instance, a son "transferred the control of his stock in the family corporations to his father in trust, a trust [that the son] could revoke without his father's consent only if he married a Jewish woman." Meiselman v. Meiselman, 307 S.E.2d 551, 553 (N.C. 1983).

[29] *See* Restatement (Third) of Prop.: Wills & Other Donative Transfers § 10.1 (2003) (stating that the "donor's intention is given effect to the maximum extent allowed by law").

time and so subjected to a management regime.'"[30] However, even if the trust organizes a transfer of property,[31] the rules by which the trust operates are set by mutual agreement between the settlor and the trustee – a relationship that resembles a third-party beneficiary contract in that it is a voluntary, legally enforceable commitment undertaken for the benefit of another party.[32] In short, like shareholder agreements, "trusts are contracts."[33] More important, whether trusts ought to be classified formally as property or contract,[34] the trustee's role is enmeshed in corporate governance, and, like other permitted modifications to the default rules, it is an economic relationship defined by voluntary agreement.

This is not to suggest that trustees are subject to the same rules as other corporate managers. In trust-controlled businesses, the law of trusts supplements and can even supersede otherwise applicable business law.[35] As settlors of the trust, parents appoint the trustee and have the power to ensure that their preferences are respected regarding the manner in which assets are disbursed. For instance, the settlors can direct a trustee to increase a beneficiary's share based on need.[36] No analogous mechanism would permit a corporate manager to distribute assets to a particular shareholder simply because

30 Gallanis, *supra* note 11, at 217. To effectuate the gift over time, "[l]egal title to the trust assets is transferred from the settlor to the trustee; equitable title is transferred from the settlor to the trust's beneficiaries." *Id.*

31 Traditionally, the trust has been viewed as a means of conveying property. *See* Langbein, *supra* note 11, at 644 (citing RESTATEMENT (SECOND) OF TRUSTS § 197 cmt. b (1959)). Professor Langbein further contends that "our doctrinal account of the trust remains inimical to recognizing the contractarian basis of the trust." *Id.*

32 Although the trust provides a mechanism for transferring property from a settlor to certain beneficiaries, "[t]he distinguishing feature of the trust is … the trust deal that defines the powers and responsibilities of the trustee in managing the property." *Id.* at 627. Whether the trust specifies particular obligations or relies upon default rules, "the deal between settlor and trustee is functionally indistinguishable from the modern third-party-beneficiary contract." *Id.*

33 *Id.*

34 *See id.* at 628 (arguing that the contractual features of trust law involve more "than mere labeling" and that "greater attention to the contractarian character of the trust would improve outcomes").

35 This may be true even for governance issues involving the settlors. *See* Scott Cacciola, *Plan B Eased Clippers Deal: Sterling's Diagnosis*, N.Y. TIMES, June 10, 2014, at A1, B12 (reporting that Rochelle Sterling invoked a trust provision to force the sale of the Los Angeles Clippers over the objection of her husband, and team co-owner, Donald Sterling). Apparently, the relevant "provision in the trust that controlled the Clippers … stipulated that if Mr. or Mrs. Sterling was found to have a cognitive impairment, the other had a fiduciary responsibility to become sole trustee." *Id.* at B12. At his wife's behest, Mr. Sterling had agreed to undertake a neurological examination, and her lawyers used the results of that examination as "the weapon they needed to strip the team from Mr. Sterling." *Id.*

36 *See* Sitkoff, *supra* note 10, at 654. In this regard, the settlors might define medical and educational expenses as needs justifying an increased share or even invasion of the trust corpus.

the shareholder had unrelated educational or medical expenses. Separating assets from the beneficial interest conveyed via trust may also insulate a family business should a child (or grandchild) divorce, and the trust structure can minimize taxes by limiting control and marketability with respect to the beneficial interest.

In addition, although trustees and corporate managers owe fiduciary duties to beneficiaries and shareholders, respectively, the fiduciary standards are distinct. To the extent the fiduciary duties of a trustee are stronger than those of a corporate manager, this state of affairs may provide more protection to trust beneficiaries than they would have as minority shareholders.[37] For instance, while corporate managers can claim the protection of the business judgment rule for anything short of gross negligence, "the trustee's default duty of care is set at the more restrictive reasonable person standard."[38] On the other hand, if the fiduciary standard is too exacting, trustees may fail to maximize business profits for fear of personal liability.[39]

The overlap of trust law and business law is also significant if a beneficiary would have grounds to object to the management of the business under the relevant business statute but faces obstacles to asserting those objections as a matter of trust law. When trust beneficiaries lack the ability to seek corporate records in order to monitor their investment or to pursue lawsuits against those in control of the corporation, they are more vulnerable to predatory misconduct. As a threshold matter, in order to bring an action that belongs to shareholders, a beneficiary must establish standing despite the lack of stock ownership.

In one case, a plaintiff sued his parents and petitioned for corporate dissolution alleging that the parents had abused the trust set up for his benefit because of their disapproval of his marriage.[40] The parents each held a 1 percent stake in the business that the father had founded, and the remaining 98 percent was owned by the son as the beneficiary of a family trust managed by the parents. Thus, as a result of their gifts to him, the son held an overwhelming economic interest in the family business but had no control rights and

[37] *Cf.* Boxx, *supra* note 9, at 235–36 (expressing concern that when both duties may apply, neither is entirely satisfactory to protecting the beneficiary's interests while also providing managers with the discretion necessary to manage a business).

[38] Sitkoff, *supra* note 10, at 657.

[39] *See* Frank H. Easterbrook & Daniel R. Fischel, The Economic Structure of Corporate Law 100 (1991) ("Exposure to liability causes managers' incentives to diverge from the path of wealth maximization.").

[40] Berger v. Berger, 592 A.2d 321, 322 (N.J. Super. Ct. 1991) (noting that plaintiff's marriage "affected the family's operations of its business and resulted in … litigation").

no direct stock ownership. The court concluded that the son was, in effect, a minority shareholder as he lacked control of the investment and permitted him to petition for dissolution.[41]

Of course, even if a beneficiary has the right to seek judicial intervention, additional hurdles may limit a plaintiff beneficiary's practical ability to challenge trust distributions. First, distributions need not be made on a pro rata basis, unless the trust agreement so specifies.[42] Thus, subject to a general obligation of impartiality, the trustee can exercise discretion concerning the distribution of assets.[43] Second, because a beneficiary has no legal claim to benefits beyond whatever a settlor chooses to provide, the beneficiary's interest may be tied to conditions,[44] including even a prohibition against challenges to the operative agreement.[45]

Finally, it is worth noting that the shape of family business ownership is affected by the *absence* of family law controls over testamentary choices. Unlike many other countries in which children have a legal claim to their parent's wealth,[46] jurisdictions within the United States adhere, with few exceptions, to a principle of testamentary freedom that gives individuals the discretion to distribute their assets in any manner they see fit.[47] While it may be natural to expect that family members will care for each other, and to rely upon family as the institution of first resort for handling illness and infirmity,[48] adult

41 *Id.* at 328 The court properly rejected the defendants' alternative argument that their son could not bring a claim as a minority shareholder because, if his beneficial interest counted as stock ownership for purposes of standing, 98 percent was not a minority position. *Id.* at 326–28. The court instead adopted a functional perspective and allocated fiduciary duties to the parents because they had the power to control the investment. *Id.* at 327–28.

42 *See* Unif. Trust Code § 816(22), 7C U.L.A. 629–30 (2000) (authorizing trustee to "allocate particular assets in proportionate or disproportionate shares"). By contrast, "the law … provides certain core protections to minority shareholders in both public and close corporations, including the prohibition of non-pro-rata distributions." Benjamin Means, *A Voice-Based Framework for Evaluating Claims of Shareholder Oppression in the Close Corporation*, 97 Geo. L.J. 1207, 1239 (2009); *see also* Sinclair Oil Corp. v. Levien, 280 A.2d 717, 721–22 (Del. 1971).

43 *See* Sitkoff, *supra* note 10, at 651 (contending that trust law's flexibility can be explained by the need to reconcile the often "conflicting interests of different classes of beneficiaries"). In a corporation, the law "assumes that all shareholders share the basic aim of profit maximization." *Id.*

44 *See* Adam J. Hirsch, *Freedom of Testation/Freedom of Contract*, 95 Minn. L. Rev. 2180, 2193 (2011) ("A testator may saddle a bequest with conditions.").

45 *Id.* at 2207 (noting that "[s]tates have divided over whether … a 'no-contest' or 'in terrorem' clause is effective").

46 *See* Hirsch, *supra* note 44, at 2233 ("In most countries, bequests to children are compulsory.").

47 *See* Restatement (Third) of Prop.: Wills and Other Donative Transfers § 10.1 cmt. a (2003).

48 *See* Martha Albertson Fineman, *The Vulnerable Subject and the Responsive State*, 60 Emory L.J. 251, 263 (2010) ("The family is the mechanism by which we privatize, and thus hide dependency and its implications.").

children and their parents have no legal claims upon one another, nor do adult children have legal duties between one another. But both probate law and family law protect the spousal relationships through death and dissolution, respectively.[49]

6.2 INHERITANCE CONTRACTS

Instead of implementing a succession plan using trusts or other mechanisms to smoothly transfer control, family members may instead make various, sometimes inconsistent commitments regarding the eventual disposition of business assets. This can create a need to account for informal promises to convey wealth, including family business assets, in exchange for assistance during the testator's lifetime.[50] The details vary, but in each case "the aging person makes the ... promise: 'Take care of me, and someday all this will be yours.'"[51] Notwithstanding the principle of testamentary freedom, as well as the conventional belief that relatives ought to provide services to one another without compensation, courts have generally recognized that inheritances can be the subject of contract.[52]

Thus, private ordering regarding the transfer of family wealth can establish the functional equivalent of a work-to-own employment agreement. For instance, in *Wright v. Trask*, a grandfather promised to leave his ranch and cattle in exchange for his grandson's management of the ranch.[53] As the older man's health declined, he refused to relinquish control of the ranch, and the relationship "became so strained" that the grandfather disinherited his grandson and took away his managerial rights.[54] The grandson sought specific performance of an oral agreement, and the trial court required the grandfather to execute a will leaving the ranch to the grandson and enjoined him from taking any steps to reduce value of the ranch.[55]

49 *See* Chapter 4 at Section 4.3 for a discussion of the intersection between divorce law and family business law.

50 *See generally* HENDRIK HARTOG, SOMEDAY ALL THIS WILL BE YOURS: A HISTORY OF INHERITANCE AND OLD AGE (2012) (exploring the legal and emotional realities of conveying wealth to family members upon old age).

51 Ariela R. Dubler, *All Unhappy Families: Tales of Old Age, Rational Actors, and the Disordered Life*, 126 HARV. L. REV. 2289, 2293–94 (2013).

52 Even when inheritance contracts are not in writing, many jurisdictions allow partial performance to establish clear and convincing evidence. *See* HARTOG, *supra* note 50, at 204.

53 Wright v. Trask, 495 S.E.2d 222, 224 (S.C. Ct. App. 1997).

54 *Id.* at 225.

55 Even though the agreement was oral, the part performance evidenced by prior wills devising the ranch to Wright provided sufficient evidence of the terms. *Id.* at 228 (citing McLauchlin v. Gressette, 79 S.E.2d 149, 158–59 (S.C. 1953) ("'[N]otwithstanding the statute of frauds, the

Other courts have reached similar results. In *Shepherd v. Mazzetti*, the Delaware Supreme Court affirmed a grant of specific performance of a father's oral promise to convey real estate to his son.[56] Likewise, a New York appellate court held that a son's decision to "remain as the manager of the family business ... [and] to forgo other professional opportunities in reliance upon [his mother's] promise constituted sufficient consideration for purposes of imposing a constructive trust."[57] In each case, the bargained-for, economic aspects of the parties' relationship gave rise to an enforceable obligation even though the existence of family connections might otherwise have suggested an alternative explanation for one-sided labor arrangements.

The recognition that inheritance contracts can cement business relationships supports the descriptive claim that family businesses include family bargains. However, in interpreting such bargains, courts seem to treat intimacy as a contaminating factor. For instance, had the court in *Wright v. Trask* concluded that the grandson's services were motivated in substantial part by a sense of family obligation, that finding could have derailed the grandson's legal claim to the family business. Understandably, courts must separate enforceable obligations from gratuitous undertakings, but it does not aid the analysis to insist upon a false category distinction – business or family, not both.

Under existing law, though, lawyers representing family members in inheritance-contracts cases have reason to guide their clients to "repress much ... emotional complexity" in order to fall on the correct side of the category distinction: "It would be the lawyer's job to identify contractual motivations and to make them appear as the dominant and real ones, those that had transformed lives."[58] And yet, in many cases, the attention devoted to the older generation is motivated by love as well as rational calculation.[59]

specific performance of such a contract (to devise real property, interpolated) may be enforced in equity, where there has been part performance of the contract by the party seeking relief.'")). An appellate court affirmed, holding that "Trask and Wright entered into an oral contract to make a will ... [and that] Trask breached the contract by executing a new will, which did not leave the ranch, the cattle, and the equipment to Wright." *Id.* at 229.

56 Shepherd v. Mazzetti, 545 A.2d 621, 622 (Del. 1988).

57 *In re* Urdang, 758 N.Y.S.2d 125, 126–27 (N.Y. App. Div. 2003); *see also* Quadrozzi v. Estate of Quadrozzi, 952 N.Y.S.2d 74, 78 (N.Y. App. Div. 2012) (imposing constructive trust to protect brother's interest in family business).

58 Hartog, *supra* note 50, at 204.

59 *See* Dubler, *supra* note 51, at 2307 (noting that in claims for payment, asserted when a deceased family member failed to convey property as promised, "legal incentives sometimes actually disincentivized any mention of love"). In its zeal for order, "law cannot quite figure out what to do with the role that love should play in people's familial choices and commitments." *Id.* at 2306.

To acknowledge this reality – the overlapping values of business and family – ought not undercut the force of the disinherited plaintiff's grievance.[60] Contractual choices made by family members regarding a family-owned business are embedded in a broader family context of trust and reciprocity.

6.3 OBSTACLES TO SUCCESSION PLANNING

As explained in the previous sections, family business owners can allocate financial and control rights using corporate governance rules and supplemental trust structures. From the standpoint of legal technology, business owners have the capacity to make and implement decisions about how to transition ownership and control. Despite the ample legal resources available, however, very few family businesses survive three generations, and the drop off is steep at each generational handoff.[61]

The tragedy that unfolds in Shakespeare's *King Lear*, a play about the failed handoff of a kingdom from a father to his daughters, provides a classic illustration of why succession plans often fail. Its tropes – an aging king reluctant to relinquish power, squabbling heirs vying for position, a collapse of the distinction between family and business motivations – ring true and can explain the demise of innumerable family businesses. For this reason, a leading treatise suggests that "no one should undertake family business planning without at least three books at hand: a current copy of the state business organization law, a current copy of the Internal Revenue Code, and a copy of *King Lear*."[62]

The main elements of the plot can be described succinctly. In the first Act, Lear makes a surprise announcement. He intends to step aside and give his kingdom to his three daughters: Cordelia, and her elder sisters, Goneril and Regan. Lear has a succession plan "to avoid future strife" in which each daughter takes a roughly equal share. Lear, who is in his eighties, says he is ready to "shake all cares and business from our age, conferring them on younger strengths." However, as a condition of inheritance, Lear requires his

60 *See* HARTOG, *supra* note 50, at 204 ("They were in the lawyer's office and willing to go to court because they believed they had been cheated .... But for promises made, they would have gotten better jobs, learned trades, moved to Montana, not become a drunk, and had happier marriages. They knew ... that taking care of elderly people had been a distraction at best from the lives they were supposed to lead.").

61 *See* George Stalk & Henry Foley, *Avoid the Traps that Can Destroy Family Businesses*, 26 HARV. BUS. REV. 25 (Jan.–Feb. 2012).

62 LARRY E. RIBSTEIN & ROBERT R. KEATINGE, RIBSTEIN AND KEATINGE ON LIMITED LIABILITY COMPANIES § 18:1 n.1 (2018).

daughters to participate in a "love trial."[63] Lear states that his "bounty" will depend on his daughters' declarations of their love for him: "Which of you shall we say doth love us most."[64] Lear's older daughters deliver fulsome praise for their father. Cordelia, however, is unwilling to participate in the charade and remains silent. Lear disinherits her. He also banishes a key advisor, Kent, for protesting Cordelia's treatment. Lear improvises a new plan for succession – Goneril and Regan will now divide the kingdom; Lear will retain the title of king and a retinue of knights as he travels back and forth to be hosted by the two daughters in turn at their expense.

Lear's succession plan breaks down almost immediately. Goneril and Regan take power and refuse to listen to their father's advice and instructions. They are wary of his chaotic impulses and soon strip him of his knights and his dignity. Lear denounces his "unnatural" daughters and refuses to remain in their care to be treated like a wayward child. A struggle for control ensues, matching Cordelia against her sisters.[65] Each has an army at her command.[66] After much bloodshed and betrayal, all three sisters perish.[67] Lear dies of grief. Thus, the strife Lear sought to forestall is inflamed by his mismanagement of succession.

For similar lessons about what not to do, a business owner could turn to *Succession*, an award-winning HBO television show that takes succession of a family media company as its central and titular question. The plot concerns the struggle to determine who will take over the company Waystar Royco when its founder, Logan Roy, either retires or dies. The succession is also literary: Logan Roy is a modern-day King Lear. Just as in Shakespeare's play, *Succession* concerns an aged potentate desperate to hold power and children

[63] Kenji Yoshino, A Thousand Times More Fair: What Shakespeare's Plays Teach Us About Justice 212 (2011).

[64] William Shakespeare, *The Tragedy of King Lear*, act I, sc. 1, l. 56, *in* The Riverside Shakespeare (G. Blakemore Evans et al. eds., 1974).

[65] Meanwhile, in a subplot that amplifies the play's theme of generational conflict and betrayal, the Earl of Gloucester falls victim to the treachery of his illegitimate son, Edmund. The Gloucester subplot also involves sibling rivalry between Edmund and his brother, Edgar, who is the legitimate heir. Professor Boxx points out that while legitimacy is an antiquated consideration for most families, analogous concerns regarding unequal treatment of siblings can arise in "blended" families with children from more than one marriage. *See* Boxx, *supra* note 9, at 755–56 (noting the conflict caused by Rupert Murdoch's decision to give children from a later marriage "diminished voting rights").

[66] Although she was disinherited by Lear, Cordelia married the Prince of France. Shakespeare, *supra* note 64, act I, sc. i, l. 290–303. The French army fights to assert her claim to the British throne.

[67] Goneril murders Regan and then kills herself. Cordelia dies at the orders of Edmund, a villainous character aligned with Goneril and Regan but also playing them against each other.

impatient to seize it from him. Logan Roy has real world parallels, including Rupert Murdoch, but the drama follows an age-old Shakespearean pattern. In a bizarre case of life imitating art imitating life, recent litigation involving Rupert Murdoch's succession plan followed concerns some of his children raised about their prospects after watching episodes of *Succession*.[68]

Lear and his modern counterparts are tragic figures because they cannot let go and, consequently, struggle to conserve and pass down what they have so painstakingly built. If we froze the action in *Succession* just before Logan suffered a stroke halfway through the show's first episode, the ensuing family conflict would be predictable. By that point, we have seen that Logan Roy, who has just turned eighty, is suffering moments of confusion – we first encounter him urinating on a carpet in a walk-in closet, because he cannot find the bathroom.[69] Logan had apparently been persuaded to put a succession plan in place, with his son Kendall slated to take over and press releases already drafted, but then Logan changed his mind, publicly humiliated Kendall, and announced his intention to stay in command.

In a reversal of *King Lear*'s love trial, we learn that Kendall made a key error when he left a tense business negotiation to attend his father's birthday party – Logan took Kendall's performative act of filial devotion as a sign of weakness.[70] Kendall further demonstrated his unfitness in Logan's eyes, when he agreed to sign a change to the family trust that Logan had requested without first seeking independent legal advice.[71] Altering the succession plan on the fly to find a place in the company for his younger son, Roman, Logan fired the chief operating officer, a Kent-like figure named Francis Alfred ("Frank"), one of the few company executives who would have had the gravitas to hold things together in Logan's absence.[72] When

68 *See* Mahler & Rutenberg, *supra* note 21.

69 Jesse Armstrong, Celebration, *in* Succession: Season One – The Complete Scripts 10 (2023) ("An eighty-year-old man, Logan Roy, … pissing towards a laundry basket in a walk-in wardrobe lined with freshly arrived suits and shirts. Dark urine stutters across the deep white pile of the thick carpet …. Logan is momentarily terrified. But then a younger woman, early fifties, is in the doorway."). Logan's wife, Marcia, reassures him: "It's okay. We're in the new place. It's okay, Logan." *Id.* To emphasize the difference between the man and his corporate image, the show cuts to a promotional video: "Logan Roy's face again. But confident. On a screen: a corporate headshot." *Id.* A voice-over: "Waystar Royco is a family. A family that spans four continents, fifty countries, three divisions: Entertainment, News and Resorts. Working together." *Id.*

70 *Id.* at 54.

71 Kendall asked, "Dad – I'm busy, do I need to lawyer all this?" and Logan replied, "It's housekeeping." *Id.* at 29. But, later, Logan says otherwise. *Id.* at 54 ("And you never lawyered the trust change.").

72 *Id.* at 75 ("That's it? To *me*. That's it? After thirty (years) – Jesus Christ, man. Here?").

Logan collapsed soon thereafter, the family business conflict had already been set in motion and was unlikely to end well.

If business owners care about the enterprise they have built and want to reduce the likelihood of its collapse, the most compelling lesson of *King Lear* and *Succession* is to start *early*.[73] Critiques of Lear's supposedly premature abdication of the throne get it backward. Logan Roy's attempt to delay the transition of power indefinitely further illustrates the flaw in this strategy. Whether they hand off their business late in life or die in office, family business owners who stay in control too long jeopardize their life's work. When we first encounter them, Lear and Logan are in their eighties and in declining health. It is long past time for them to have faced the issue of succession. Yet, few family business consultants would be surprised by their failure to do so.

The following sections examine three errors that set the *King Lear* and *Succession* tragedies in motion: (1) the patriarch's conflation of his identity with his kingship; (2) the patriarch's failure to appreciate the different roles his children inhabit as members of his family and as future rulers of the kingdom; and (3) the patriarch's insistence on dictating the terms of succession unilaterally without input from his children or his advisors.[74] If these are tragic flaws in a premodern king, they are flaws shared by Logan Roy and by many contemporary family business owners.

6.3.1 *Identity*

Who is it that can tell me who I am?[75]

For Lear, Logan, and for many family business owners, relinquishing control is difficult because power and identity become intertwined. When Lear announces his intention to hand over his kingdom to his daughters, he is an octogenarian. Yet, he still cannot abide a complete transfer of power. Instead, he specifies that he will retain the title of king and a retinue of knights to attend him. As king, his presence cannot help but cast a shadow over his daughters' rule, leaving open the question of who really is in charge. A perennial problem in family business succession is controlling

[73] *See* Grant Gordon & Nigel Nicholson, Family Wars: Stories and Insights from Famous Family Business Feuds 39 (2010) ("Hoping for peace on your deathbed is rather too late to build a climate of cooperation.").

[74] *See* Benjamin Means, *Solving the* "King Lear *Problem*," 12 Irvine L. Rev. 1241 (2022).

[75] Shakespeare, *supra* note 64, act I, sc. 4, l. 236.

owners who refuse to let go.[76] For this reason, "succession is the ultimate test of a family business."[77]

Consequently, the transfer of power is rarely just a business decision for a controlling owner. Apart from economic considerations, the incumbent's individual identity may be entwined with the status that comes from leadership.[78] Surrendering a business position means leaving behind a major part of what has given an individual's life meaning and allowing "younger strengths" to rise in the workplace and at home.[79] Thus, the patriarch of a family business may wonder whether he will sit at the head of the table for family meals once his children have taken over.[80] Perhaps as a consequence, family business owners often neglect to create or follow a plan for succession.[81]

The problem of identity is at the core of *King Lear*.[82] Lear's situation is tragic because what he wants is impossible to achieve. Lear is the king and must remain so to remain himself. Even though Lear states that he wants to "crawl, unburdened toward death,"[83] he perceives that abdicating the throne is tantamount to a total erasure of self. Yet, by remaining king, if mostly in name, he creates tensions that break the fragile compromise he has sought to achieve and deprive him of peace in his old age.[84] When his older daughters

76 *See* F. Hodge O'Neal & Robert B. Thompson, Oppression of Minority Shareholders and LLC Members § 2.5 (rev. 2d ed. 2005) ("[M]any founders are reluctant to acknowledge their own mortality, or even if they are, are unwilling to deal with possible conflicts between a parental desire to share with all children equally and the reality that one or more children will not be in the family business as it goes forward."); *All Too Human: How Families Can Cause Trouble for Their Firms*, Economist, Apr. 16, 2015 ("Many family patriarchs are larger-than-life figures who are unwilling to make way for their successors.").

77 Kelin E. Gersick et al., Generation to Generation: Life Cycles of the Family Business 193 (1997).

78 *See* Matthias Waldkirch, *Social Identity Theory and the Family Business*, *in* Theoretical Perspectives on Family Businesses 137 (Mattias Nordqvist et al. eds., 2015) (explaining that individual identity is derived in substantial part from "membership in social groups or categories").

79 *See* Blake E. Ashforth, Role Transitions in Organizational Life: An Identity-Based Perspective 13 (2001) (stating that "the more the individual is involved in and identifies with work, the more consequential and potentially taxing the transition process tends to be for the individual").

80 *See* Lee Anne Fennell, *Death, Taxes, and Cognition*, 81 N.C. L. Rev. 567, 584 (2003) ("Maintaining control over assets is consistent with continuing to exercise power and authority in this life; dispersing assets suggests abdication of that power and authority and capitulation to death.").

81 *See* O'Neal & Thompson, *supra* note 76, § 2.5.

82 *See* Ralph Berry, *Lear's System*, 35 Shakespeare Q. 421, 422 (1984) (arguing that "*King Lear* is a tragedy of identity, in the sense that the King has created a system that is his own identity").

83 Shakespeare, *supra* note 64, act I, sc. 1, ls. 42–43.

84 As one commentator puts it, Lear "goes through an abdication without abdicating." Stanley Cavell, Must We Mean What We Say? 255 (1969).

turn their backs on him, Lear experiences not only a betrayal but a loss of identity. Bewildered, he asks, "Who is it that can tell me who I am?"[85] The dual blow is too much for Lear's fragile mind to bear.

Lear's personal identification with the kingship also helps to explain why conflicts with his daughters escalate so rapidly. He perceives their rebukes as earthshaking upheavals of the natural order. By belittling Lear as a doddering old man and asserting their power over him, Goneril and Regan threaten the core of his identity as a king, a father, and a man.

Kendall Roy seeks to assert comparable power over his father and to take charge of Waystar Royco when the opportunity presents itself. At a board meeting for a vote to replace Logan, Kendall declares his love for his father and respect for what Logan has accomplished, but then makes clear that his father is long past his prime, in poor health, and no longer fit to lead. When Kendall concludes his speech with a complaint that his father is gambling the company's money on "a horse that's ready for the glue factory," we are a long way from the blandishments that began the speech.[86] The tension is not just about how the business should be run. The son seeks to take away his father's power. In turn, the father feels compelled to reassert himself at his son's expense.[87] The result departs from *King Lear*, because the older generation prevails, but the dysfunctional dynamic is much the same.

Logan Roy's need to assert his dominance affects his judgment. Regardless of possible merit, Logan views business suggestions from his son as unwelcome challenges to be discarded. He goes so far as to dismantle Vaulter, a company his son had acquired for Waystar Royco at great expense as a signature acquisition toward a new, internet-based business strategy.[88] Given this dynamic, it is unsurprising that Kendall has failed to develop the skills necessary to lead. Apart from the lack of constructive mentoring, it may be that he has been promoted too quickly, or he may simply lack the capacity to serve in

[85] SHAKESPEARE, *supra* note 64, act I, sc. 4, l. 236.

[86] JESSE ARMSTRONG, *Which Side Are You on?*, *in* SUCCESSION: SEASON ONE – THE COMPLETE SCRIPTS 441–42 (2023).

[87] Even when Kendall is running a meeting, Logan's presence undermines him. We observe this dynamic when Logan visits Waystar Royco's offices and joins a meeting already in progress: "*Everyone sits up, adjusting not-too-unsubtly to the new centre of gravity in the room.*" ARMSTRONG, *supra* note 69, at 29.

[88] Logan had previously criticized his son for "paying a billion dollars for a gay little website." ARMSTRONG, *supra* note 69, at 55. Kendall's wounded response – "It is *not* a fucking *website*! It's a portfolio of online brands and digital video content and it's part of a strategy to save us if you'll just let me" – was not persuasive. *Id.* Indeed, the notion that the son could rescue the father was precisely the notion that needed to be stamped out. Of course, such psychodynamics are not conducive to dispassionate business analysis of costs and benefits of various possible courses of action.

executive leadership. In any case, although he chafes at the influence of his father, Kendall lives in his father's shadow.

The father–son conflict that drives interactions between Kendall and Logan is not unusual. In family businesses, "[f]rom a psychological perspective, at the root of the most poisonous conflicts is identity – the idea that one is being diminished or damaged; that one is wounded or threatened in some essential way."[89] Thus, even if a dispute concerns money, "money often represents all kinds of psychological elements, and most powerfully when it stands for how much one is valued or loved."[90] Business succession requires a separation of personal identity and business status; unless family business owners are prepared to cede control, the practicalities of financial and legal arrangements will not matter.

6.3.2 *Role*

Thou Mad'st thy Daughters thy Mothers[91]

Family business owners may fail to distinguish their legitimate expectations as a "king" and as a parent. Role confusion is common and increases the risk of a failed succession. *King Lear* and *Succession* show the importance of roles and role-playing. Although they are not scripted in advance by an omniscient playwright, social roles prescribe behaviors and set expectations that regulate our interactions in the real world.[92] Family members who work together in a business must navigate multiple roles.[93] Parents, for instance, may also be employers. Role confusion can endanger family business succession.

In some situations, family members may leverage their personal connections for business advantage. For example, in *Succession*, Tom Wambsgans is engaged to Shiv, Logan Roy's daughter, and seeks to find a birthday gift that will allow him to ingratiate himself with his father-in-law.[94] To that end, Tom chooses an absurdly expensive watch, and we see Logan's contempt for

89 Gordon & Nicholson, *supra* note 73, at 11.

90 *Id.*

91 Shakespeare, *supra* note 64, act I, sc. 4, ls. 176–77.

92 *See generally* Dramaturgical Analysis of Social Interaction (A. Paul Hare & Herbert H. Blumberg eds., 1988).

93 *See*Ashforth, *supra* note 79, at 24 (stating that social roles are what enable individuals to "categorize themselves and others as a means of ordering the social environment and locating themselves and others within it"). Consequently, if "social roles are incompatible, family business has a built-in conflict." Benjamin Means, *Nonmarket Values in Family Businesses*, 54 Wm. & Mary L. Rev. 1185, 1209 (2013).

94 Armstrong, *supra* note 69, at 21 ("Shiv? Can you – I need to strategize my gift?").

the gesture – recognizing it, correctly, not as a loving gift but as an effort to buy power in the company.[95]

Family and business roles may also be confused. Lear unintentionally collapses the distinction between roles when he demands that his daughters declare their love for him to guide his division of the kingdom.[96] Arguably, Lear's "love trial" makes sense as a merit-based alternative to allocation by birth order.[97] Yet, regardless of Lear's intention, asking his daughters for a display of affection substitutes family intimacy for more appropriate considerations. Even if the purpose of the declarations is ceremonial, the result is to foreground family connections rather than affairs of state.[98]

Relatedly, *King Lear* shows how gender biases can affect family business succession. Lear's succession dilemma arises only because of the absence of a suitable male heir, which forces him to consider how to perpetuate his rule through his daughters and their husbands. Because family roles are often gendered, the expectations imposed on women can limit their opportunities to take on leadership responsibilities.[99] Instead of being evaluated as candidates for succession, women may be valued by their parents mainly as a way of bringing worthy males into the family.[100] As one commentator explains, "Sons-in-law are often expected to join the family business and can be viewed as natural candidates for succession even if they are less capable and competent than daughters."[101]

Gender bias can also endanger succession when the result is an unfair distribution of economic resources.[102] Males in the next generation are often given disproportionate power, which can lead to dissension when they abuse

[95] *Id.* at 67 ("*Tom smiles, Logan walks on, even the box is irritating to him to have to carry.*").

[96] *See* Yoshino, *supra* note 63, at 212 ("Lear is accused of making the category mistake of confusing love and statecraft.").

[97] *See id.*

[98] According to one scholar, "In merging an identity produced by law and one produced by love, Lear abnegates the duties of the sovereign and unseats the affections of the father." Susan Sage Heinzelman, *When Law and Love Are Not Enough*: King Lear *and the Spectacle of Terror*, 28 Quinnipiac L. Rev. 755, 756 (2010). Logan Roy reverses this dynamic and punishes his son Kendall for prioritizing a birthday party over his responsibilities in negotiating a business transaction. Armstrong, *supra* note 69, at 54 ("You left the room. The deal.").

[99] The demonization of Goneril and Regan may be attributed in part "to the sexist expectation that daughters, rarely sons, must care for aging parents." Lesley Kordecki & Karla Koskinen, Re-Visioning Lear's Daughters: Testing Feminist Criticism and Theory 18 (2010).

[100] *See* Calvin Wang, *Daughter Exclusion in Family Business Succession: A Review of the Literature*, 31 J. Fam. Econ. Issues 475, 476 (2010).

[101] *Id.*

[102] *See* Christine Blondel, *The Women of the Family Business*, *in* The Endurance of Family Businesses: A Global Overview 200 (Paloma Fernandez Perez & Andrea Colli eds., 2013).

their control.[103] For example, in one fairly typical case, the parents appointed their sons as directors of the family business and gave them voting stock while leaving their daughters with nonvoting stock.[104] Over time, the sons increased their salaries, stopped paying dividends, and caused the corporation to cover millions of dollars in personal expenses. When the minority shareholders complained and sought redemption of their shares, the majority shareholders implemented a plan to offer approximately 50 percent of the fair market value for the shares. A court found that this pattern of behavior constituted shareholder oppression.[105] Had the parents established a role for their daughters in the business, the abuse of control problem might have been prevented in the first place.[106]

Gender roles are less rigid today than in Shakespeare's time, let alone in the remote England of his *King Lear*, but many family businesses continue to apply traditional, gendered assumptions when allocating opportunities.[107] Part of the problem is that when women wield authority, their presence in the workplace may be perceived in terms of a stereotyped and limited set of family roles.[108] It is sometimes said that women in business roles "must

[103] In one case, two sisters established shareholder oppression after their three brothers, including the company's president, froze them out of a business their parents had founded. Bone v. Coyle Mech. Supply, Inc., No. 5-15-01172, 2017 WL 2403268, *1–2 (Ill. Ct. App. June 6, 2017), *appeal denied*, 93 N.E.3d 1063 (Ill. 2017). In another case, problems arose after a father created family limited partnerships to avoid estate taxes, appointing his two daughters as limited partners and naming another company he owned as the general partner. Boutell v. W.H.B. Co., No. 11-10617, 2012 WL 380238, *2 (E.D. Mich. Feb. 6, 2012). When the father passed away, his son became the president of the general partner and allegedly used his control to deprive his sisters of their fair share of revenue. *Id.* at *3–4. Likewise, a court found breaches of fiduciary duty in a case involving a family business controlled by grandsons of the founder; the plaintiffs were granddaughters of the founder and minority shareholders in the family business. *See* Goret v. H. Schultz & Sons, Inc., No. A-4281-10T1, 2013 WL 4792847, *1 (N.J. Super. Ct. App. Div. Sept. 10, 2013).

[104] *See* White v. Fee, 953 N.Y.S.2d 554, *2 (N.Y. Sup. Ct. 2012).

[105] *See id.* at *15.

[106] *See* Lucia Albino Gilbert & John C. Gilbert, Women Winemakers: Personal Odysseys 235 (2020) ("Women's recognized success in a traditional field can help change stereotypical perceptions of women's abilities and provide opportunities to counter the 'lack of fit' gender-role traditionalism that can influence hiring and promotions.").

[107] *See* Karin Staffansson Pauli, *Gender Theory and the Family Business*, *in* Theoretical Perspectives on Family Businesses 191 (Mattias Nordqvist et al. eds., 2015) (observing that "obstacles to [women's] involvement" include "stereotyped roles, and certain aspects of succession and primogeniture"); Wang, *supra* note 100, at 475 (reporting studies that "females – notably daughters – are almost always overlooked as succession candidates").

[108] *See* Judith G. Greenberg, *Insider Trading and Family Values*, 4 Wm. & Mary J. Women & L. 307, 308 (1998) (contending that "gender is one of the concepts that structures the ways we think about other, seemingly unrelated, issues"). Professor Greenberg notes a contrast between the "male-identified market" and "the women's realm of family." *Id.* at 311.

master a high-wire act that maneuvers around the 'double bind' – a woman executive cannot be too masculine or feminine."[109] Thus, after Lear has relinquished power, his fool scolds him, "Thou Mad'st thy Daughters thy Mothers."[110] The gendered implication is that Lear has become infantilized – an insult that would not have landed with the same force if Lear had vested power in a son.[111]

In *Succession*, Logan Roy's daughter Shiv is repeatedly sidelined because of her gender. In an early power scramble, Kendall brings his brother Roman to his side by dismissing the very idea of allowing Shiv to share control. Kendall dismisses Shiv as a cautious "daddy's girl" who lacks "the nuts to revolutionize."[112] Indeed, the persistence of gender bias in the workplace is one of *Succession*'s most depressing themes. In the final episode, an outside acquirer who has pledged to maintain family continuity to get board approval for the deal decides to appoint Tom Wambsgans as his CEO rather than Shiv Roy, Tom's wife. The acquirer knows that Shiv is pregnant, and he laughingly states a preference for the man who impregnated her rather than "the baby lady" herself.[113] Instead of defending his wife, Tom jumps at the opportunity presented to him.[114]

In family businesses, gender roles may become more salient because of the inevitable overlap of family and business concerns. Lear collapses the distinction between private and public roles entirely, however, when he demands that his daughters declare their love for him to guide his division of the kingdom.[115] Regardless of Lear's intentions, the result is to foreground family connections in what was effectively a business context, the transition of leadership for the kingdom, rather than more appropriate considerations of role suitability.

On the other hand, while family relationships tend to highlight gender roles, parents also typically want the best for all their children and may reject

[109] Marleen A. O'Connor, *Women Executives in Gladiator Corporate Cultures: The Behavioral Dynamics of Gender, Ego, and Power*, 65 MD. L. REV. 465, 468 (2006).

[110] SHAKESPEARE, *supra* note 64, act I, sc. 4, ls. 176–77.

[111] *See* Blondel, *supra* note 102, at 212 ("Daughters accessing leadership roles challenge traditional family relationships.").

[112] JESSE ARMSTRONG, *Shit Show at the Fuck Factory*, *in* SUCCESSION: SEASON ONE – THE COMPLETE SCRIPTS 141 (2023).

[113] JESSE ARMSTRONG, *With Open Eyes*, *in* SUCCESSION: SEASON FOUR – THE COMPLETE SCRIPTS 749 (2023).

[114] *Id.* at 750 ("Well I could do it, I could definitely easily do it.").

[115] *See* YOSHINO, *supra* note 63, at 212 ("Lear is accused of making the category mistake of confusing love and statecraft."). According to Professor Yoshino, Lear's "love trial" could be justified as a merit-based alternative to allocation by birth order. *See id.*

the idea that gender should limit their daughters' opportunities in life. For this reason, family businesses can also create opportunities for women to take on leadership responsibilities that they might not find readily elsewhere.[116] Good intentions, however, are no guarantee of fair treatment in the workplace.[117] When male incumbents fail to prepare wives and daughters for leadership roles, they create a needless risk of future crisis.[118] To limit the effect of gender bias, incumbent owners should seek to include daughters in the business as early as possible – "active involvement in the family business and a close relationship with incumbents (fathers) can be a pathway to leadership and control for some daughters."[119] Again, the lesson for a successful transition is to begin the process as soon as possible.

6.3.3 *Process*

Come not between the dragon and his wrath[120]

Family businesses "link two societal institutions, family and firm, in cooperative ventures for mutual advantage."[121] The joinder is uneasy, however, because each institution is built to serve different values. Families typically allocate their resources to address needs and to reduce vulnerability; businesses prioritize competence and reward merit. Thus, in family businesses, "conflicts unavoidably arise about the appropriate distribution of the advantages gained, and about the principles that should govern the resolution of those conflicts."[122]

[116] As one commentator observes, "[I]n less than the span of a human lifetime, women's roles have changed more than in all of history." Marleen O'Connor-Felman, *American Corporate Governance and Children: Investing in Our Future Human Capital During Turbulent Times*, 77 S. Cal. L. Rev. 1255, 1261 (2004).

[117] Despite social changes, "economic and biological influences lead to the continuation of traditional gender roles." *Id.* at 1273.

[118] *See* Susanna Fellman, *Managing Professionalization in Family Business*, *in* The Endurance of Family Businesses: A Global Overview 276 (Paloma Fernandez Perez & Andrea Colli eds., 2013) (reporting an interview with a female CEO regarding her perception that "her father had never really accepted her as his successor"). The CEO explained the negative consequences when her father's death pushed her into a leadership role for which she had not been prepared: "The day after my father died, I sat in his office with my mother and we knew that we faced a huge challenge. At that point, I had not even been a director. I had to learn a lot and learn it quickly." *Id.* (internal quotation marks omitted).

[119] Wang, *supra* note 100, at 480.

[120] Shakespeare, *supra* note 64, act I, sc. 1, l. 136.

[121] *See* Ludo Van der Heyden et al., *Fair Process: Striving for Justice in Family Business*, 18 Fam. Bus. Rev. 1, 2 (2005); Means, *supra* note 93, at 1189 ("[A] successful family business must find ways to mediate the tension between expectations rooted in family life and expectations inherent to the marketplace.").

[122] *See* Van der Heyden, *supra* note 121.

Family business succession illustrates these concerns.[123] To avoid violating business or family values, families must create a fair set of procedures for making decisions about succession.[124] Without such procedures, succession planning may break down in one of two ways. First, incumbents may be daunted by the sheer complexity of the planning exercise.[125] With more pressing operational challenges to handle, it will be very tempting for incumbent owners to procrastinate. Adding to the temptation to shirk, incumbents may worry about the costs, both financial and emotional, of engaging a difficult topic.[126]

A second risk to succession in the absence of agreed-upon procedures for making decisions is that the older generation will avoid difficult conversations by acting unilaterally. Unfortunately, while incumbents have the prerogative to decide the timing and the allocation of financial and control rights, their raw exercise of power is not enough to convey legitimacy or to command respect.[127] In the face of uncertainty, talented members of the next generation may decide to pursue other opportunities rather than waiting for the family business leaders to make room for them, or they may bristle at having decisions made without their input.

Accordingly, whether incumbents prefer to divide control equally among potential family successors, identify a leader in the next generation, or bring in outside managers, they should strive to create an inclusive process

[123] *See, e.g.*, Kelly LeCouvie & Jennifer Pendergast, Family Business Succession: Your Roadmap to Continuity 3 (2014) ("The impact of family dynamics on business decision-making is often most apparent at the time of a generational transition.").

[124] Although appropriate procedures may vary, it is important to clarify some of the criteria for a fair process. *See* Maxwell L. Stearns, Constitutional Process: A Social Choice Analysis of Supreme Court Decisionmaking 81–82 (2000) ("Unless the term fair is specifically defined, such claims operate as a conversation stopper, but one that fails to identify, let alone resolve, underlying philosophical or methodological disagreements.").

[125] *See* Gregory F. Monday, *A Blueprint for Family Business Succession Planning*, Bus. Law Today (Jan. 16, 2018), https://tinyurl.com/yrkna2wk ("[O]ne reason why so many family businesses do not engage in proper succession planning is because it is difficult and complex. Family business succession planning must take account of countless unknown future circumstances."). Mr. Monday is also the author of a practitioner's guide to family business succession issues. Gregory F. Monday, The Lawyer's Guide to Family Business Succession Planning (2020).

[126] For example, if some family members are not included in a succession plan, "they may just switch off, not just from the business but from the family, losing any sense of emotional bond." Gordon & Nicholson, *supra* note 73, at 168.

[127] *See* E. Allan Lind & Tom R. Tyler, The Social Psychology of Procedural Justice 9 (1988) (reporting "one of the most reliable findings in research on procedural justice: that people react more favorably to procedures that give them considerable freedom in communicating their views and arguments").

that will be perceived as fair even by those who do not get everything they want.[128] To that end, family business owners should engage all stakeholders in dialogue, establish clear criteria for choosing among various alternatives, and, once a decision has been made, articulate the reasons supporting that decision.[129] Succession planning takes time and cannot be thrown together at the last minute.

The time commitment and costs associated with implementing a robust process for succession may seem unappealing to family business owners. If they value the business, however, and wish to see it prosper into the future, succession planning is one of the most important investments they are likely to make. *King Lear* is a stark example of the consequences of neglect. The potential merit of dividing the kingdom – whether in the interests of distributive justice or political strategy – was undermined by the haphazard, arbitrary manner in which Lear imposed his decisions on his children. Lear acted without the benefit of any dialogue with those who would be affected by his decision. He rejected and banished his advisors, issuing threats to those who would intervene: "Come not between the dragon and his wrath."[130]

By disregarding the views of others with a stake in the venture and refusing to take neutral, objective advice, Lear created discord and made future conflict more likely. Indeed, by conditioning his gift on his daughters' statements of love for him, he wounded their pride unnecessarily, stating, in effect, that "to strip him of his power, they [would] have to pay for it by risking a humiliating posture – sitting up and begging, crowing for cheese."[131]

In the same vein, consider Logan Roy's decision, announced before lunch at his birthday party, to casually sweep aside the succession plan he had put in place, and to do so just before Kendall's promotion was due

[128] *See* Van der Heyden et al., *supra* note 121, at 2 ("Conflicts generated by the interface of family, shareholding, and business interests should benefit from an effective application of fair process principles."); GORDON & NICHOLSON, *supra* note 73, at 168 (in a family business, "people can get more upset about what they perceive as an unfair process than the inequality of the division in itself").

[129] *See* Van der Heyden et al., *supra* note 121, at 4–5 (defining key characteristics of fair process).

[130] SHAKESPEARE, *supra* note 64, at act I, sc. 1, l. 136. In the context of family business succession, "some of the most powerful and helpful interventions come from advisers with a background in family therapy who are able to help families develop healthy communications and emotional self-discipline." GORDON & NICHOLSON, *supra* note 73, at 33.

[131] *See* Harry Berger, Jr., *King Lear: The Lear Family Romance*, 23 CENTENNIAL REV. 348, 354 (1979). Although few, if any, family business owners would follow Lear by staging a literal "love trial," it is not uncommon for them to reward "filial loyalty" above all other considerations. See GORDON & NICHOLSON, *supra* note 73, at 117 (describing how Sumner Redstone drove his son out of the family business and awarded power to the daughter who stood by his side during an acrimonious divorce).

to be released publicly. Minutes earlier, Kendall's ex-wife had congratulated him on the promotion.[132] Then, because Logan believed that Waystar Royco belonged to him, and that he could do whatever he wanted with it, he upended Kendall's expected coronation on a whim, announcing that he would instead maintain his position in the firm for the foreseeable future.[133] For Kendall, the swift change in status is bewildering and utterly humiliating. He has not been consulted and has no agency in deciding when or whether he will be entrusted with additional responsibilities. Logan crudely dismisses his son's complaints about the abrupt reversal of months of succession planning: "It's my fucking company!"[134]

When family business succession fails, the older generation's authoritarian approach to decision-making is often to blame. Passing control across generations requires clear communication, which involves listening. Yet, family business owners too often follow Lear's and Logan's example and make decisions unilaterally, presumably because they think "they know best."[135] Worse still, parents may dangle the prospect of future wealth to manipulate their children, treating succession as an exercise of power. Logan engages in this behavior repeatedly. For example, after reversing his plan to put Kendall in charge, Logan reaches out to his daughter, Shiv. He agrees to find a position for her fiancé Tom and asks whether she would consider joining the company.[136]

Lawyers who study these examples should come away with a renewed appreciation for the importance of process. As a matter of distributive justice, there may be no clear answer concerning how the assets of a family business should be passed down to heirs.[137] What matters, then, is not *what* the family decides, but *how* it decides. Lawyers can help to defuse conflict by ensuring that all stakeholders are invited to participate in discussions concerning succession and that key decisions are communicated in a manner that all stakeholders can understand.

[132] Armstrong, *supra* note 69, at 46.

[133] *Id.* at 46–50.

[134] *Id.* at 55.

[135] Gordon & Nicholson, *supra* note 73, at 19 (observing that parents may continue to exercise judgment from "beyond the grave" – specifically, "They can cast a shadow of control in the way they write their wills and construct their family trusts.").

[136] Armstrong, *supra* note 69, at 65.

[137] In some cases, the optimal solution may be to sell the business to outsiders and to distribute cash to family members. *See* Kenneth Kaye, *When the Family Business Is a Sickness*, 9 Fam. Bus. Rev. 347, 347 (1996) ("No one has calculated how many of the [family business succession] 'failures' were actually terrific success stories, creating liquidity that opened new paths of opportunity for the next generation; or, conversely, how many that 'made it' through a transition trapped their successors in misery.").

Outside advisors can help family business owners and other stakeholders to establish a process, but only if those in power are willing to listen. Lear banishes his advisor, Kent. Likewise, in what the *Succession* writers must have intended as a conscious parallel, Logan casually casts aside Frank, the professional advisor who would have been best able to hold the company steady when Logan has a stroke. Kendall, the heir apparent, has not demonstrated the ability to run the business without his father's guidance and is crippled by self-doubt.

In a corporation, the board of directors can ensure that there is an appropriate set of procedures in place for matters such as the employment of family members and succession planning. But, even when a corporation is publicly traded, a controlling owner may have the power to elect a majority of the board and to dominate its decisions. On one occasion, Logan provides a lesson in raw power when he disables the corporation's board of directors from rendering an independent judgment after his son Kendall calls for a vote of no confidence. Logan barges into the meeting, ignores a request that he recuse himself, and bullies his younger son, Roman, into changing his vote.[138] Logan then ignores any further procedural limitations to his exercise of total control over the company, including an asserted power to fire board members (who are elected by shareholders) as he sees fit. The outcome of the board meeting seems to turn not on the law, but on who has the loudest voice and who the company's security guards recognize as wielding power.

In sum, lawyers who advise family businesses must be cognizant of how family dynamics can affect succession planning. A lawyer's technical expertise will be misspent if family dynamics drive succession planning, as when a business owner refuses to surrender control or when parents insist upon bequeathing a business to their children in equal shares regardless of each child's competence or interest. No legal structure can stand if it is built on shifting sands of ego and delusion.

The *King Lear* tragedy is not inevitable. While the world is full of foolish Lears, unworldly Cordelias, and conniving Gonerils and Regans,[139] it also contains supportive families and enlightened business owners who understand that they are running a relay race and need to focus on "passing the baton."[140] The case study that follows describes a father–daughter succession plan that avoids Lear's missteps.

[138] ARMSTRONG, *supra* note 86, at 447.

[139] *See generally* GORDON & NICHOLSON, *supra* note 73; ROGER FRITZ, WARS OF SUCCESSION: THE BLESSINGS, CURSES AND LESSONS THAT FAMILY-OWNED FIRMS OFFER ANYONE IN BUSINESS (1997).

[140] *See, e.g.*, Ben Dooley & Hisako Ueno, *This Japanese Shop Is 1,020 Years Old. It Knows a Bit About Surviving Crises*, N.Y. TIMES, Dec. 2, 2020.

6.4 CASE STUDY: SHARP & SHARP CERTIFIED SEED

Established as a family business in 1947, Sharp & Sharp Certified Seed is a row-crop farm in Allendale, South Carolina. The farm is held as a general partnership and is currently transitioning from Don Sharp, a second-generation owner in his early seventies, to his daughter, Rachael Sharp. Perhaps because she attended law school before joining the family business, Rachael appreciates the importance of a clear process and has insisted on open communication, the involvement of counsel to address tax planning and other considerations in advance, and that the interest of other family members be dealt with beforehand, rather than leaving it to be sorted through later. To his credit, Don has welcomed these suggestions for an orderly process.

Historical Context. Rachael's paternal great, great-grandmother established a farm at the current location, and it was female owned for another two generations. Rachael's great-grandmother died young, when Rachael's grandmother was only six years old. Rachael's great-grandfather had a life estate but was not permitted to diminish the value of the estate. He was not dedicated to farming, however, and later decided to cut timber on the property to make money. Rachael's grandmother sued for injunctive relief and prevailed.

Rachael's grandmother continued to run the farm until she married. Her husband served in the military during World War II, and the family moved to Texas, allowing the farm to go fallow. After the war, Rachael's grandfather earned a degree at Clemson University, and the family returned to the farm. He had no experience farming but had majored in agriculture at Clemson and was successful as a farmer.

Rachael's grandfather started Sharp & Sharp Certified Seed. The second Sharp partner was his son, Don, who joined in the farming work when he was old enough to do so. Rachael's grandmother also worked the farm but was not considered to be a co-owner, notwithstanding the fact that she had brought the property with her into the marriage. Although the farm was a matriarchy in its first generations, the power structure had become patriarchal. Despite her lack of formal status as a paid employee, Rachael's grandmother handled payroll, made hamburgers and sweet tea for employees every day (taking care to pour unsweet tea with a packet of Sweet'N Low taped to the glass for a diabetic employee), and otherwise helped run the farm.[141] The farm grew soybeans, corn, cotton, peanuts, and wheat.

[141] *See* SARAH WHATMORE, FARMING WOMEN: GENDER, WORK, AND FAMILY ENTERPRISE 1–4 (1991) (discussing women's behind-the-scenes roles in farming).

The Second Generation. Don has lived his entire life on the farm, except for when, like his father before him, he attended Clemson. Don has a sister who does not have an interest in farming. Rachael's grandfather died in 2001, and her grandmother passed away in 2006. The farm was left equally to Don and his sister.[142] In order to continue the farm, Don had to buy her out. However, because the value of the farm is tied up in the property and not in cash flow, there was not enough money available to complete a buyout.

Creating a predicament reminiscent of *King Lear*, the parents had established an estate plan without consulting their children. If they had addressed the dilemma ahead of time, the cash flow issues might have been handled in different ways – perhaps with a life insurance policy. Also, the parents could have spoken with their children about the value of the farm as a part of the family's heritage and their expectations for how it might be preserved. Instead, the siblings were left to hash through the ownership issues after their parents died. It strained the sibling relationship, but they did achieve a compromise that allowed Rachael's father to retain the property.[143] Even when a lack of planning creates a risk of conflict, bloodshed (real or metaphorical) is not the only possibility.

Consequently, Rachael's aunt still owns a significant percentage of the farm's property – about 500 acres – and receives rental payments each year. Rachael's aunt does not have an unrestricted ownership interest in the land. Importantly, Don has a right of first refusal to buy the remaining property, should his sister negotiate a sale outside the family. Also, because the farm's irrigation systems are expensive fixtures, Rachael's aunt's rights are subject to permanent easements to ensure that the farm's operations are not threatened by her ownership interest. Although the family has made it work, the lack of careful succession planning saddled the farm with debt and uncertainty and did not maximize value for the passive owner.

The failure to separate the interests of next-generation family members outside the business is not uncommon in businesses with illiquid assets. Sometimes, families prefer to keep all members of the family involved as owners, but this approach can create predictable conflicts between those who are active in managing the business and those who are only interested in receiving distributions of profits. Alternatively, to provide equivalent wealth to children who will not have an active role in the business, parents might be better advised to harvest cash from the business that can be transitioned

[142] *See* General Warranty Deed on file with author.

[143] *Id.* (reporting "a private family settlement agreement … to alter the shares they are entitled to … as part of that global settlement and division of the real property of this Estate and Trust").

separately, or to acquire life insurance policies that can fund a one-time cash payment to children who are not selected to take over the business. Also, although equal treatment is a common goal for family inheritances, parents might prioritize the needs of the business venture and divide their assets unequally. Regardless of the approach the older generation takes, a lack of communication can create resentment and uncertainty. Rachael noted that the whole issue of the farm split between her father and her aunt remains a "taboo topic." In her view, southern farms are vulnerable because "nobody wants to bring up anything uncomfortable." Rachael speculates that this hesitancy may be a "farm thing" or a "southern thing" but problems cannot be solved by ignoring them.

The Third Generation. At present, as a practical matter, Sharp & Sharp Certified Seed is controlled by Don. Unlike King Lear, Don has squarely faced the question of succession, electing not to divide his kingdom but to bequeath it to the heir most capable of preserving it. The family's original expectation was that Rachael's brother would one day take over the farm. He grew up working the farm, driving a tractor, and learning the business. Unfortunately, a serious opioid problem forced the family to reevaluate that plan, and Rachael agreed to step in. The farm is a legacy that has been handed down across generations, and Rachael does not want to be the one who lets it drop.

Rather than dictating the terms of succession unilaterally, as Lear might have done, Don has agreed to a process that gives his daughter a voice in how the transition will be effectuated. Rachael believes that her family's plan for the farm is unusual in that she and her father have learned to have difficult conversations with each other, separating their relationship as father and daughter from their working relationship. For the past five years, Rachael has been a full-time employee. She handles the books and finances, orders chemicals, ships seeds, and generally takes care of logistics. Don has emphasized that there can be no appearance of favoritism – she needs to be at work on time and to stay until the other employees have left. Each year, they take a one-week vacation together and that gives them the opportunity to relate to one another as father and daughter. (It is also the only week each year when her father leaves the farm.)

In terms of legal structure, the farm is currently a general partnership, and Don has retained counsel to advise him regarding the transition of business ownership as well as related estate planning issues. Don holds some property in trust, and he has slowly transferred property and business equity to Rachael and to her mother. Currently, Rachael has 30 percent, Don has 50 percent, and Rachael's mother holds the remaining 20 percent. Pursuant to a Farm Services Agency program that provides financial incentives for succession planning, Don will transfer 5 percent each year until Rachael has 50 percent. The farm's liabilities are addressed via an insurance policy, but it is likely that the business structure will change and that the general partnership will be replaced with one or more formal business entities.[144]

It has not always been easy. Rachael's business relationship with her father has taken time to build. She describes it as "a work in progress."[145] Rachael treads lightly when she can because there are several different relationships that must be negotiated – father–daughter; employer–employee; and co-owner. In the beginning, it was "rough." Her father is, in her words, "stubborn" and can be "hardheaded as all get out." Like many business owners, Don was accustomed to making the decisions unilaterally and struggled to give up control. Gradually, though, Rachael has been able to influence farm operations. She has learned that sometimes she needs to "let it soak in a little bit." For example, one year she ran the numbers and persuaded Don not to rent additional acres because the risks far outweighed the possible benefits. This ran counter to his general view that bigger is better when it comes to farming. He did not admit that he agreed with her, but when the time came to rent the land, Rachael discovered that he had let it go. Rachael's analysis was correct, saving the farm a significant sum of money, and that has given her additional credibility with Don. On other issues, such as the use of technology, father and daughter continue to disagree.

Even if he shares Lear's stubborn streak, however, Don has never insulated himself from criticism. To the contrary, he has enlisted professional advisors (rather than banishing them), and he has created a transition process that gives Rachael the opportunity to learn the business before he entrusts her with it entirely. The Sharp family's approach to business succession for their 1,000-acre farm thus presents an instructive contrast to *King Lear*, and, in factually similar circumstances, the farming family that is the subject of Jane Smiley's *Lear*-patterned novel, *A Thousand Acres*. The novel describes the battle for control of a family farm from the perspective of the eldest daughter Ginny.[146] Notably, when one of the daughters, who is a lawyer, has the temerity to ask about her father's succession plans, she is cut out of her inheritance. Rachael Sharp, too, has a legal education, but her contributions have been appreciated by her father and not perceived as a sign of disrespect.

144 *See generally* Dwight Drake, Business Planning: Closely Held Enterprises 314 (5th ed. 2018) (discussing how companies can divide a business into a holding company with multiple subsidiary operating companies).

145 Interview with Rachael Sharp (Sept. 14, 2022).

146 *See* Jane Smiley, A Thousand Acres (2001).

It is difficult being the only woman farming "within a thirty-mile radius," and there is stress that comes with the job, but Rachael sleeps well at night because she is comfortable with what she does. Although she recognizes that handling her aunt's interest in the property will be an ongoing challenge, and that her brother's potential expectations regarding the farm may also be a source of tension, Rachael is optimistic about her ability to manage the farm and to preserve it for the future.[147] In sum, while the business succession has not yet been completed, and it is always possible that the family's plans will change, the prospects for a third generation of Sharp & Sharp Certified Seed are bright.

147 In a recent conversation with me, Rachael noted that it would have been even better to "have started twenty years ago."

PART III

LEGAL FRAMEWORKS

The chapters in this section further explore the intersection of legal principles and family business dynamics. Chapter 7 argues that the statutory default rules for existing forms of business association must be customized to fit the needs of family businesses. Because it is often unrealistic to expect bespoke bargains among family members, the chapter further proposes the creation of an "F Corp" entity form for family businesses that would create an integrated set of default rules to better accommodate typical family dynamics.

Chapter 8 focuses on dispute resolution, explaining how the misalignment of family and business concerns can lead to claims of shareholder oppression and protracted and expensive litigation. For example, because of the relative informality of many family businesses, it may not even be clear who has an ownership stake. The chapter emphasizes the need for a contractual framework that balances the preservation of family relationships with the resolution of business disputes, offering practical solutions for courts, lawyers, and business advisors.

Together, the two chapters in this section argue for the creation of an integrated legal framework for family businesses flexible enough to accommodate their complexities while robust enough to protect all stakeholders, including minority shareholders, employees, and the broader community.

7

Improving Corporate Governance

Family businesses have distinctive characteristics that the law should account for to better serve the needs and the values of family business participants. At a minimum, reconciling family and business values requires a more nuanced approach to contract law. This was the argument advanced in Chapter 3. Courts that perceive the interplay of business and family relationships will do a better job of interpreting legal obligations consistent with the parties' own expectations. However, family business participants are not ordinarily inclined to bargain carefully before investing. Consequently, when a dispute arises as to some aspect of their business, it is commonplace that the parties will not have addressed the topic of concern ahead of time.

The default settings provided by statute matter a great deal, because they will often be left untouched. Yet, no existing form of business association has been drafted for use by family business owners. Accordingly, to accommodate family dynamics, lawmakers and advisory groups, such as the American Law Institute and the Uniform Law Commission, should consider drafting a new "F Corp" form of business association tailored to the needs of family businesses. The F Corp could facilitate succession planning through, for example, an independent board committee with authority to oversee the succession process, a mandatory retirement age for senior executives to ensure a timely turnover of managerial responsibilities, and a required election concerning whether the business will be run by family members or nonfamily professional managers. Lawmakers should also consider creating financial incentives for lifetime transfers of ownership and control.

Even without legislative reform, courts can use existing law to bolster family business governance. To that end, courts should clarify the fiduciary duties owed by boards of directors in the context of succession planning. In particular, courts should hold that the fiduciary obligation of care requires a board of directors to implement a succession plan and review it on a periodic basis.[1] When there are challenges to the capacity of incumbents, courts should establish an evaluative standard sufficient to ensure that those in control of a family business are capable of acting with ordinary prudence when making decisions concerning succession. That is, courts should invoke the fiduciary duty of care, both to require boards to initiate succession planning, and as a standard for evaluating the capacity of incumbents. Notably, the proposed standard would be higher than the level of cognitive functioning currently required for other types of testamentary capacity. Under current law, courts have stated that "[e]ven the weak, aged, powerless, ignorant, and uninformed have the right to create a testamentary document."[2]

Family business governance can also be shaped by lenders, customers, suppliers, distributors, and key nonfamily employees. The stability of a family business is of legitimate concern to those who depend on it. To the extent counsel for these counterparties include "business continuity" on their due diligence checklists, they can mitigate risk for their clients by requiring a clear succession plan as a condition for business dealings.[3] Taken together, a mix of private ordering and public incentives offers the best prospect of improving the governance of family businesses, making successful transfers across generations more likely.

7.1 LEGISLATIVE INITIATIVES

The law governing business associations is principally state law.[4] States offer partnership, limited partnership, corporate, and limited liability company (LLC) choices, among others, each with a different set of default and mandatory governance rules.[5] No state, however, offers a form of business

[1] In smaller businesses that lack a formal board structure, an analogous fiduciary obligation could be imposed on the control group.

[2] *See, e.g.*, Govan v. Brown, 228 A.3d 142, 150 (D.C. Ct. App. 2020).

[3] *See* Donald V. Fites, *Make Your Dealers Your Partners*, HARV. BUS. REV., Mar.–Apr. 1996, at 178–79 (reporting that Caterpillar, a major manufacturer of construction and mining equipment, prefers to work with family-owned dealers and describing several steps it takes to ensure that those family businesses will be able to transfer control across generations without disruption).

[4] *See* STEPHEN M. BAINBRIDGE, CORPORATION LAW AND ECONOMICS 14 (2002) (explaining that "[s]electing a state of incorporation has important consequences, because of the so-called 'internal affairs doctrine' – a conflicts of law rule holding that corporate governance matters are controlled by the law of the state of incorporation").

[5] For example, corporate law imposes mandatory fiduciary duties that may be waived in an LLC. *See* AM Gen. Holdings LLC v. The Renco Grp., Inc., 2016 WL 4440476, at *15 (Del. Ch. Aug. 22, 2016) (stating that "the LLC Act enables contracting parties to alter and even eliminate equitable fiduciary duties").

association designed specifically for use by family businesses. Nor, with limited exceptions, have legislators at the federal, state, or local level created financial incentives for family businesses to engage in succession planning. Given the economic importance of family businesses, and the social cost of avoidable business failures, lawmakers should consider the utility of both types of intervention.

7.1.1 *The F Corp*

The best way to avoid crippling dissension in a family business (or any other venture) is to anticipate potential problems and plan around them. By picking the most suitable jurisdiction and business entity form, investors can take advantage of default rules that structure their business relationships in at least rough accord with their intentions.[6] However, no available form of business entity can resolve in advance the various potential conflicts that loom when family interests substantially overlap with business ownership and management interests.

For many family businesses, the flexibility of the LLC makes it the best choice among existing options. Before the advent of the LLC, investors once had to choose either desirable flow-through taxation rules or limited liability and could not achieve both without following cumbersome procedures.[7] The great advantage of the LLC is that investors have limited liability and can simply elect flow-through or entity taxation while also tailoring governance rules in an operating agreement.[8] Many LLC statutes have standard default options that provide either a partnership or corporation governance structure.

[6] *See* JONATHAN R. MACEY, CORPORATE GOVERNANCE: PROMISES KEPT, PROMISES BROKEN 23 (2008) (noting that "by incorporating their businesses in a jurisdiction that contains statutory provisions that are to their liking people organizing new business (or reorganizing existing businesses) can select or 'opt into' the set of 'off-the-rack' legal rules that best fit their needs .... [E]ven within a single jurisdiction, people organizing a business can select among a variety of different forms of business organization, such as the traditional corporate form, as well as the limited partnership, the limited liability company, and the limited liability partnership").

[7] *See* Susan Pace Hamill, *The Story of LLCs: Combining the Best Features of a Flawed Business Tax Structure, in* BUSINESS TAX STORIES: AN IN-DEPTH LOOK AT TEN LEADING DEVELOPMENTS IN CORPORATE AND PARTNERSHIP TAXATION (Steven A. Bank & Kirk J. Stark eds., 2005). For instance, a corporation could choose flow-through taxation by selecting "S" status only if it met a number of rigid requirements concerning number of shareholders, principal place of business, and the like. Alternatively, in more recent years, a business venture might use the limited partnership form to shield the investors from liability while preserving flow-through taxation and establish a corporation to serve as the general partner and to hold the liability. The same individuals would serve as the directors and officers of the corporation and as the limited partners.

[8] For analysis of the LLC and a discussion of its evolution, *see id.*

Yet, the LLC form does not solve the problem of minority owner oppression because abuse of control is an inherent structural feature of closely held businesses with limited exit rights and majority rule as the basic gap-filling mechanism.[9] General default rules cannot hope to cover more than a fraction of the possible disputes that could occur over the course of a long-term business relationship.[10] Therefore, minority investors must either depend on specific bargaining or judicial intervention to enforce standards of conduct among shareholders.

Given the variety of family business structures, it is unrealistic to expect that an off-the-rack business entity would meet each business's idiosyncratic needs. But that is true of any business in any business entity form. If a family business entity choice could more closely match the interests of participants, it could narrow the range of issues to be adjusted via contract. Moreover, a family business entity could create a template that identifies issues that participants should consider, regardless of how they resolve those issues. Business entities designed for use by social enterprises provide a helpful model for this type of governance innovation.

In the past decade, interest in forms of business association designed to facilitate social enterprise has skyrocketed.[11] The most popular social enterprise statutory form in the United States, the benefit corporation or "B Corp," has now been adopted by thirty-seven states and is on the legislative agenda in another four states.[12] The B Corp explicitly authorizes managers to combine

[9] *See* Robert B. Thompson, *The Shareholder's Cause of Action for Oppression*, 48 Bus. Law. 699, 699 (1993) ("The statutory norms of centralized control and majority rule, when combined with the lack of a public market for shares in a close corporation, leave a minority shareholder vulnerable in a way that is distinct from the risk faced by investors in public corporations.").

[10] *See* Macey, *supra* note 6, at 29 (stating that, "by definition, shareholders and other parties to corporate governance disputes that wind up in litigation have not actually specified a preferred outcome *ex ante*"). Professor Macey observes that, as a consequence, "a court's hypothesis that a particular result is the one that the shareholders would have preferred cannot be refuted." *Id.*

[11] *See* Emily Winston, *Benefit Corporations and the Separation of Benefit and Control*, 39 Cardozo L. Rev. 1783, 1796–97 (2018) (stating that the "social enterprise movement … was likely accelerated by the widespread negative social effects of the 2008 financial crisis and subsequent Great Recession"). For an overview, *see generally* The Cambridge Handbook of Social Enterprise Law (Benjamin Means & Joseph W. Yockey eds., 2019).

[12] *See State by State Legislative Status*, Benefit Corp. Info. Ctr, https://tinyurl.com/2vf5de2p (last visited Mar. 13, 2024). There are actually two closely related concepts at issue: The nonprofit B Lab entity that drafted the model benefit corporation legislation also promotes a "B Corp" certification for businesses that "meet the highest standards of verified social and environmental performance, public transparency, and legal accountability to balance profit and purpose." *What's Behind the B?*, B Lab, https://usca.bcorporation.net/about-b-corps (last

the pursuit of profit with the achievement of other social objectives.[13] An analogous "F Corp" entity could establish a structure for the dual family and business purposes typical of a family firm. In particular, drafters of F Corp model legislation should consider including the following best practices for succession planning.

Independent Board Committee. The F Corp statute should require the creation of an independent committee with authority to establish criteria for hiring and evaluating family members within the organization. The committee should also have primary responsibility for vetting candidates for leadership succession and should be required to have a majority of independent members.[14] Even if its rulings were advisory, an independent committee would play an important mediating role and could help family constituents sidestep the role conflicts that can endanger family business succession.

Some family businesses have already established committees along these lines. For example, *The New York Times*'s Ochs-Sulzberger family used an independent committee to evaluate candidates for the position of publisher.[15] The position had been family held since 1896, but that was no guarantee that a family member would be deemed ready for the responsibility. Likewise, the Brown-Forman Corporation, which makes spirits including Jack Daniel's and Woodford Reserve, relies upon an independent "Nominating Committee" to identify candidates for the board of directors and "lead the work of the Board in succession planning for the Chief Executive Officer."[16] To ensure its independence, the Nominating Committee must "consist of at least three directors, at least one of whom is a member of the controlling shareholder family group and a majority of whom are 'independent' as that term is defined by the listing standards of the New York Stock Exchange."[17]

visited Mar. 13, 2024). I use the B Corp label inclusively to refer to benefit corporations and to third-party certifications.

13 *See* Winston, *supra* note 11, at 1786.

14 One scholar has defended the role of independent directors in family businesses, noting that they can provide "a reality-check function … when questions of management succession are on the table." *See* Deborah A. DeMott, *Guests at the Table?: Independent Directors in Family-Influenced Public Companies*, 33 J. CORP. L. 819, 853 (2008).

15 *See* Sydney Ember, *A.G. Sulzberger, 37, to Take Over as New York Times Publisher*, N.Y. TIMES, Dec. 14, 2017.

16 *See Corporate Governance and Nominating Committee Charter*, BROWN-FORMAN CORP., 1, https://tinyurl.com/mua8284a (last visited Mar. 6, 2025) (describing duties of Corporate Governance and Nominating Committee ("the Nominating Committee")). Brown-Forman was founded in 1870, and is a family-controlled, publicly traded corporation. *See Discover Our Roots*, BROWN-FORMAN CORP., www.brown-forman.com/history-timeline (last visited Mar. 6, 2025).

17 *Id.*

The Nominating Committee provides a neutral venue for addressing potential conflicts between business and family values.[18]

Retirement Age. The F Corp framework should formalize another governance best practice by mandating that the board establish a retirement-age policy for board members and senior officers. As Justice O'Connor observed in a decision upholding a mandatory retirement age for state court judges, "It is an unfortunate fact of life that physical and mental capacity sometimes diminish with age."[19] The F Corp statute might also provide for periodic cognitive screening beginning at age fifty and increasing in frequency over time. Regular cognitive screening could be in lieu of a mandatory retirement age or a supplemental measure.

Brown-Forman's corporate governance guidelines are instructive in this regard. The guidelines state that "[n]o director may stand for re-election to the Board at the Annual Meeting of Stockholders immediately following his or her 72nd birthday."[20] The company allows limited exceptions to that policy, but only upon recommendation of the Committee and "a special vote by the Board, with two-thirds of directors approving, without the vote or participation of the affected director."[21] Brown-Forman's written policy facilitates succession planning because it makes clear that the retirement of an incumbent is not a judgment regarding that person's capacity to continue in the role. Instead, by shifting the focus from individual competence to business policy, a preset retirement age recognizes that the timely transition of ownership and control is beneficial for a family business.[22]

Family Managed Versus Professionally Managed. Drafters of F Corp legislation might also borrow from LLC statutes, which distinguish between

[18] *Id.* Although disputes must be resolved on their own merits, the Committee's charter makes clear that family values should not be ignored: "[T]he Committee shall pay due attention to the corporate governance implications of the Brown family's control of a majority of the Company's outstanding voting stock, including by staying apprised of the family's own governance initiatives and by appropriately balancing the governance needs of a public company with those of a family controlled company." *Id.*

[19] Gregory v. Ashcroft, 501 U.S. 452, 472 (1991). One commentator argues that because cognitive decline is neither inevitable nor uniform, it would be better to "empower" individual judges by providing them with information about their cognitive functioning. *See* Francis X. Shen, *Aging Judges*, 81 OHIO ST. L.J. 235, 238 (2020).

[20] *Leadership & Governance*, BROWN-FORMAN CORP., www.brown-forman.com/leadership-and-governance (last visited Mar. 6, 2025).

[21] *Id.* In exceptional cases, the board might recognize the continuing contributions of a director, especially since "there is no published neuroscientific research suggesting that a particular age … should serve as the bright line cutoff for cognitive decline." Shen, *supra* note 19, at 281.

[22] A retirement policy also recognizes the reality that, for most people, cognitive decline is a natural part of aging. *See, e.g.*, Jonas Persson et al., *Structure–Function Correlates of Cognitive Decline in Aging*, 16 CEREBRAL CORTEX 907 (2005).

manager-managed and member-managed organizational structures.[23] In that regard, an F Corp could require family businesses to designate whether they wish to adopt a "family control" or "family ownership" structure. A family business would select "family control" so long as it intends for family members to occupy the CEO and other senior officer positions.[24] By contrast, the choice of "family ownership" would indicate that family involvement is limited to board oversight and that independent managers will hold the senior management positions and exercise operational control.[25] Although the choice would be alterable, perhaps subject to a supermajority vote, clarifying the basic parameters of succession planning would help reduce the grounds for conflict.

These are just a few examples of how an F Corp choice of entity could offer governance principles designed to meet the needs of typical family businesses.[26] Although well-run family businesses like Brown-Forman Corp. may not need assistance, off-the-shelf family business best practices could provide guidance for the vast majority of family businesses that lack the time, resources, or inclination to develop tailored governance procedures. Nor is the prospect of an F Corp entity unrealistic. The widespread adoption

[23] *See* Douglas K. Moll, *Minority Oppression & the Limited Liability Company: Learning (or Not) from Close Corporation History*, 40 WAKE FOREST L. REV. 883, 917–18 (2005) ("LLC statutes typically provide for partnership-like management by members … or for corporate-like management by managers.").

[24] If family owners have the skill set and interest to handle operations directly, the "elimination of the separation between owners and management" allows for more efficient operations. *See* Johan Lambrecht & Jozef Lievens, *Pruning the Family Tree: An Unexplored Path to Family Business Continuity and Family Harmony*, 21 FAM. BUS. REV. 295, 298 (2008). For family businesses of this type, it is often best to mandate buyouts of passive family owners to avoid conflict about dividends and salary. *See id.*

[25] The Brown-Forman Corp. falls into this category, although there is no formal written policy to that effect. After several generations of direct family control, the family made the strategic choice to delegate operational decisions to professional managers and to focus on larger questions of strategy and vision. Interview with Matthew Hamel, Brown-Forman Corp. General Counsel (Nov. 16, 2020) (notes on file with author).

[26] Other topics of interest might include disclosure requirements regarding the prioritization of family and business interests, the extent to which the family would be authorized to maintain voting control without holding a majority of the firm's equity, the establishment of buy-sell agreements or other exit rights for nonparticipating family members, whether to create a family advisory board separate from the board of directors, and whether to authorize greater latitude for ownership and control exercised through trusts and foundations. Some issues might be resolved through a mandatory family business structure; others might be better accommodated by presenting a template of choices for family owners to review on a periodic basis. Also, some governance features might be bundled together, so that, for example, electing a family ownership model would come with one type of buy-sell arrangement and a separate advisory board to represent the interests of a greater number of family members.

of B Corp statutes in the last decade demonstrates that, if backed by determined advocates, there is a pathway for state-by-state adoption of new forms of business association.

Objections. In addition to its value as precedent, the recent history of the B Corp provides a helpful preview of objections that are likely to be lodged against the F Corp. Those objections largely fall into two categories: (1) that the new entity form departs from other forms of business association in ways that are normatively undesirable; and (2) that the new entity form is unnecessary, because its structure can be achieved by modifying existing entity forms through tailored organizational documents and related contracts.

Regarding the asserted undesirability of the B Corp and other forms of social enterprise, commentators have argued that allowing managers to sacrifice profits to pursue an unrelated social purpose exacerbates agency costs.[27] When questioned about poor economic performance, managers can gesture toward nonfinancial goals; when asked why the business failed to dedicate more resources toward a social mission, managers can remind critics that, as a business venture, the social enterprise is also obligated to earn a reasonable return on investment.[28] In short, those who serve two masters serve none.[29] On similar grounds, critics might object to an F Corp structure that allowed managers to operate the business to serve the interests of a controlling family at the expense of profitability.

In response, advocates of social enterprise have observed that corporate managers already enjoy substantial discretion to pursue a variety of objectives over varying time horizons and that managers need not seek to maximize short-term profits.[30] Indeed, the business judgment rule permits managers

[27] *See* Charles M. Yablon, *Mixed-Motive Investments and Agency Costs*, *in* The Cambridge Handbook of Social Enterprise Law 384 (Benjamin Means & Joseph W. Yockey eds., 2019).

[28] Managers act on behalf of owners and, like other agents, have incentives that may not be fully aligned with the goals of the owners. *See generally* Michael C. Jensen & William H. Meckling, *Theory of the Firm: Managerial Behavior, Agency Costs and Ownership Structure*, 3 J. Fin. Econ. 305 (1976); Eugene F. Fama, *Agency Problems and the Theory of the Firm*, 88 J. Pol. Econ. 288 (1980).

[29] *See* Stephen Bainbridge, *In Defense of the Shareholder Wealth Maximization Norm*, 50 Wash. & Lee L. Rev. 1423, 1427–28 (1993) ("In economic life, as in religious life, no one can serve two masters at the same time. Directors thus cannot be loyal to both shareholders and nonshareholder constituencies.").

[30] *See* Paramount Commc'ns Inc. v. QVC Network Inc., 637 A.2d 34, 42 (Del. 1994) ("Under normal circumstances, neither the courts nor the stockholders should interfere with the managerial decisions of the directors."); Eric W. Orts, Business Persons: A Legal Theory of the Firm 41 (2013) ("In the United States, the 'business judgment rule' bestows significant discretion to corporate managers and directors to exercise independent decision-making authority on a wide range of decisions.").

to assert, without offering hard evidence to support their claims, that community investment, environmental responsibility, and other forms of stewardship are the best way to preserve long-term business value.[31] For this reason, while organization as a B Corp may signal to investors the heightened importance of social mission, managers already have the practical ability to pursue such objectives if they choose to do so.[32] The same could be said of F Corps. Whether or not family stewardship produces greater economic value, there are limited avenues for external attack under existing business association statutes. Social enterprise and family stewardship alike are shielded from scrutiny by the business judgment rule.

Taking nearly the opposite tack, a second major line of objection to B Corps is not that they are dangerous, but that they are superfluous.[33] With a modicum of creativity, almost any form of business association can be adapted to suit the needs of its owners. The majority of new businesses are organized as LLCs, in part because LLC statutes defer most questions to the parties' operating agreement. Delaware's LLC Act declares, for example, that it is state policy to give "the maximum effect to the principle of freedom of contract."[34] Using this freedom, entrepreneurs can create a dual-purpose entity to pursue environmental or other social goals. Likewise, a family could allocate economic and voting rights in any fashion it chose.[35] To the extent specialized provisions governing

[31] *See, e.g.*, Shlensky v. Wright, 237 N.E.2d 776, 781 (Ill. 1968) (rejecting shareholder suit based on management's refusal to install lights at Wrigley Field in order to schedule night baseball games). The court speculated that "the long run interest of the corporation in its property value at Wrigley Field might demand all efforts to keep the neighborhood from deteriorating." *Id.* at 780. Ultimately, the court concluded that the merits of the decision were not subject to review as long as there were no allegations of "fraud, illegality or conflict of interest in [the] making of that decision." *Id.*

[32] *See* Joseph W. Yockey, *Using Form to Counter Corruption: The Promise of the Public Benefit Corporation*, 49 U.C. DAVIS L. REV. 623, 639 (2015) ("The business judgment rule provides ample flexibility to corporate managers to make any socially driven decision they desire. All they must do is act in due care, in good faith, and stay free of conflicts of interest."). Professor Yockey argued that a public benefit corporation could help spur social enterprise, not by creating new legal possibilities, but by "disrupting norms and expectations." *Id.* at 640.

[33] *See* Peter Molk, *Do We Need Specialized Business Forms for Social Enterprise*, *in* THE CAMBRIDGE HANDBOOK OF SOCIAL ENTERPRISE LAW 242 (Benjamin Means & Joseph W. Yockey eds., 2019) (arguing that the LLC combined with external certifications provides sufficient flexibility for social enterprise).

[34] DEL. CODE ANN. tit. 6 § 18–1101(b) (2013).

[35] Alternatively, a family could use a trust to hold equity and direct the trustee to allocate business assets according to whatever rules the family saw fit. *See generally* Karen E. Boxx, *Too Many Tiaras: Conflicting Fiduciary Duties in the Family-Owned Business Context*, 49 HOUS. L. REV. 233 (2012).

social enterprises or family businesses are not already commonplace, therefore, it may be evidence that there is not a market demand for them.[36]

Although accurate as far as it goes, the objection overlooks the significance of transaction costs.[37] Even though a social-enterprise mission or a distinctive family business structure could be built using existing business entity forms, the modification of legal forms requires the involvement of lawyers and the attention of entrepreneurs who might prefer to simply adopt a useful off-the-shelf governance form. Commentators have observed that social-enterprise statutes make a difference, because "[s]ocial entrepreneurs are likely not going to want to reinvent the 'legal' wheel."[38] Regardless of what is theoretically possible under existing law, "it is far more efficient for a deliberate, off-the-shelf hybrid alternative to be made available than to expect every social enterprise to design its own one-off supporting infrastructure."[39] For substantially the same reasons, an F Corp that provides a workable model for family business owners could save considerable time and effort.

Another potential objection to a special, family business statute might draw from the history of LLCs. Although many LLC statutes once had provisions that enabled easy, partnership-like exit, the default rules were later changed to mirror corporate law rules that do not guarantee liquidity.[40] This was done to accommodate tax planning in family businesses.[41] In order to qualify for a lack-of-marketability deduction in shares transferred through inheritance, the holder cannot also have the right to exchange them for fair value.[42] An automatic exit right provided by statute, in any case, would have other undesirable features, including exposing the business to risk of minority opportunism.[43] Also, strong exit rights could be destabilizing and creditors might worry about the possibility of "a relatively trivial falling out among the equity investors …

[36] In this regard, it may be notable that while many states have passed B Corp legislation, very few businesses have availed themselves of it.

[37] *See* Ofer Eldar, *Designing Business Forms to Pursue Social Goals*, 106 VA. L. REV. 937, 952 (2020) ("A legal form would be unnecessary if it was costless for firms and subsidy providers to use standard private ordering mechanisms, such as contracts.").

[38] *See* Carol Liao, *Early Lessons in Social Enterprise Law*, *in* THE CAMBRIDGE HANDBOOK OF SOCIAL ENTERPRISE 120 (Benjamin Means & Joseph W. Yockey eds., 2019).

[39] *See id.* at 121.

[40] *See* LARRY E. RIBSTEIN, THE RISE OF THE UNCORPORATION 179–80 (2010).

[41] *See id.*

[42] *See id.*

[43] For instance, minority investors could threaten to exercise the exit right at a time when the business lacked cash and extract a greater percentage of the value of the business in exchange for not exiting. For further discussion of the problems associated with automatic exit rights, see Benjamin Means, *A Voice-Based Framework for Evaluating Claims of Minority Shareholder Oppression in the Close Corporation*, 97 GEO. L.J. 1207, 1252 (2009).

thus raising the cost of capital."[44] In sum, though imperfect, current corporate and LLC forms may offer the best mix of governance, tax, and liability rules.

Finally, even if one had concerns about the normative desirability of family businesses *and* believed that existing forms of business association could be tailored to suit the purposes of family owners, a dedicated family business statute could be useful as a way of surfacing normative concerns and developing best practices for governance.[45] As one scholar argues in the B Corp context:

> [T]he value of the benefit corporation form comes from its ability to create an important new institutional structure to govern the evolving social enterprise space. For example, the form provides a focal point that ought to make it easier for like-minded actors to cooperate and collaborate on issues ranging from corporate governance practices to capital formation. It is a highly visible archetype that provides common ground and a clear framework for firms and stakeholders to coordinate their activities.[46]

In much the same fashion, an F Corp model could facilitate a constructive dialogue concerning the value of various approaches to family business ownership and control. Over time, the F Corp could be revised accordingly.

As a first step, a draft of model F Corp legislation would need to be created by an enterprising state, the Uniform Law Commission, the American Law Institute, or by a private advocacy group like B Lab, which has promoted the B Corp model. For family businesses, there are a number of national organizations, such as the Family Firm Institute,[47] the Cambridge Family Enterprise Group,[48] and the John L. Ward Center for Family Enterprises at the Kellogg School of Management[49] that might be interested in sponsoring

44 BAINBRIDGE, *supra* note 4, at 831; MACEY, *supra* note 6, at 24 ("[B]uy-sell arrangements are very costly for companies. In particular, creditors understandably view such arrangements as a significant source of risk, since the exercise of a buy-sell agreement by a shareholder reduces the 'equity cushion' available to creditors whose loans have not been repaid when the shareholder's stock is purchased by the company.").

45 Unlike statutory provisions, individually tailored LLC agreements are not standardized and can create considerable confusion. *See generally* Leo Strine & J. Travis Laster, *The Siren Song of Unlimited Contractual Freedom*, *in* RESEARCH HANDBOOK ON PARTNERSHIPS, LLCS AND ALTERNATIVE FORMS OF BUSINESS ORGANIZATIONS (Robert W. Hillman & Mark J. Loewenstein eds., 2015).

46 Joseph Yockey, *Does Social Enterprise Law Matter?* 66 ALA. L. REV. 767, 770 (2015).

47 Information about the Family Firm Institute can be found on its website. *See* FFI FAM. FIRM INST., www.ffi.org/ (last visited Mar. 6, 2025).

48 *See Successful Families. Enduring Enterprises*, CAMBRIDGE FAMILY ENTERPRISE GROUP, https://cfeg.com/ (last visited Mar. 6, 2025).

49 *See The John L. Ward Center for Family Enterprises*, NW. KELLOGG, https://tinyurl.com/3xvrae2k (last visited Mar. 6, 2025).

the effort. Even if a family business entity were authorized by statute in only a small handful of jurisdictions, family businesses located elsewhere could choose to organize themselves under the law of one of those jurisdictions.[50]

7.1.2 *Financial Incentives*

Apart from the practical and emotional difficulties associated with identifying business leaders for the next generation, family business succession also poses a financial challenge.[51] Family businesses often lack the accumulated assets necessary to buy out incumbent owners who are ready to retire, and banks may be reluctant to provide credit to younger, unproven managers.[52] To reduce the financial burden, thereby incentivizing lifetime transfers of ownership and control, lawmakers could offer low-cost loans, tax subsidies, bidding preferences for government contract work, and free counseling.[53]

Regardless of the form of support, legislative intervention would necessarily involve an allocation of societal resources to family businesses. For example, below-market loans would not only return a lower-than-market profit but would also, in the aggregate, expose the government to losses in the form

[50] Businesses are not limited to the entity choices in their home jurisdiction. Notably, the state of Delaware benefits from out-of-jurisdiction incorporation choices for publicly traded corporations: "The website for Delaware's Division of Corporations recites that '[m]ore than half a million business entities have their legal home in Delaware including more than 50 percent of all U.S. publicly traded companies and 60 percent of the Fortune 500.'" Lawrence A. Hammermesh, *The Policy Foundation of Delaware Corporate Law*, 106 COLUM. L. REV. 1749, 1749–50 n.1 (2006) (citation omitted). Delaware or another state might seek to claim similar status for F Corps. Once the F Corp form became available, it would be important to line up a strong cohort of early adopters to demonstrate its viability. *See* Liao, *supra* note 38, at 116 (noting that "[t]he B Corporation movement … began with eighty founding companies").

[51] *See* Glenn R. Ayres, *Rough Corporate Justice*, 11 FAM. BUS. REV. 91 (1998) (noting that, while leadership succession in a public corporation is "normally not a major cost-allocation issue," the situation is different for most family businesses, because succession is "not only a highly charged emotional transition, but it also may put the capital integrity of the firm at risk").

[52] Even if parents are willing to take less than fair market value, they still need enough to fund a comfortable retirement. *Id.* at 93.

[53] For an assessment of different forms of government intervention in markets, including cash grants, tax credits, and the deferral or exclusion of gains from taxable income, see Samuel Estreicher & Clinton G. Wallace, *Equitable Health Savings Accounts: Bridging the Left-Right Divide*, 56 HARV. J. LEGIS. 396, 412–13 (2018). If the government chose to employ a tax-subsidy strategy, it would need to take into account existing tax-driven timing considerations. *See* Dwight Drake, *Transitioning the Family Business*, 83 WASH. L. REV. 123, 132 (2008) (noting that, from a tax standpoint, succession planning "is helped by focusing on three time-frames: the period both parents are living, the period following the death of the first parent, and the period following the death of the surviving parent").

of unrepaid principal. Also, unless developed in partnership with banks and other private lending institutions, a government loan program would come with a significant administrative apparatus, adding to its overall cost.

Accordingly, before offering low-cost loans, enacting a tax subsidy, or otherwise committing public resources to facilitate family business succession, lawmakers should evaluate the costs and benefits to assure themselves that the policy would be worthwhile. As one commentator explained, in the context of tax subsidies for social enterprise, proponents of any such program should be able to address four concerns:

> First, what aspects … should be considered for incentivization? Second, is it in fact desirable as a policy matter to incentivize one or more of those aspects? Third, could tax law in theory incentivize a desired aspect; that is, are the tools that tax law deploys suitable for accomplishing this goal? Fourth, would tax law sufficiently incentivize the desired aspect to justify the cost of doing so in terms not only of lost revenue to the government but also of increased complexity and other unintended consequences (including the feasibility of measuring how well the incentive actually works and the costs it imposes)?[54]

Public support for family businesses ought to reflect a normative judgment that family businesses are socially valuable. It is one thing to observe that delayed transfers of power can endanger the viability of a family business; it is another to conclude that the state should put its thumb on the scale by creating a financial incentive for lifetime transfers.

Indeed, it might be objected that the effort to preserve family ownership reflects a romanticized view of a particular form of economic activity. Perhaps, we can value the contributions of family businesses in general without intervening in the marketplace to ensure the survival of any particular family business.[55] At a minimum, though, I presume that there are costs associated with the avoidable failure of a family business. Those costs, borne by the family but also by a wider circle of stakeholders, include the

[54] *See* Lloyd Hitoshi Mayer, *Creating a Tax Space for Social Enterprise*, *in* The Cambridge Handbook of Social Enterprise Law 165 (Benjamin Means & Joseph W. Yockey eds., 2019).

[55] In this regard, for example, lawmakers might pay more attention to antitrust-adjacent problems caused by economic concentration in industries. *See* Farah Stockman, Opinion, *A Good Reason for Rural Rage: The Crushing Power of Corporate Meat*, N.Y. Times, Sept. 30, 2024 ("It's no secret that rural Americans are angry with the Washington elite. Less discussed are some of the sensible reasons for it. For far too long, family farms have been crushed under the monopolistic power of Big Ag. And for decades, politicians from both parties either turned a blind eye to the oligopolies that rule over rural America – or climbed right into bed with them.").

inefficiency of destroying a profitable business, the collateral expenses of litigation, and, sometimes most consequential, the toll taken on marriages, sibling bonds, and parent–child relationships. Accordingly, without attempting to determine the optimal level or mode of intervention, it seems safe to conclude that some level of public support of family business transitions would increase overall social welfare.[56]

Moreover, the normative question need not have a single answer. In sectors of the economy resembling family farming, lawmakers may wish to prioritize the ideal of small-scale ownership, whether by the incumbent family or by others interested in entering the business.[57] Lawmakers might also take into account the promotion of business ownership by underrepresented or vulnerable populations. For example, the Conservation Reserve Program-Transition Incentive Program applies to land that has already been designated as farm eligible and facilitates the transfer "from a retired or retiring owner or operator to a beginning, veteran, or underserved farmer or rancher."[58] Other government programs provide benefits to businesses that are owned by women or those from minority groups.[59]

Whether applied broadly, only in particular economic sectors, or only to family businesses of a particular type or scale, the operational parameters of a financial incentives program would need to be clarified. For example, lawmakers would need to decide whether their goal is to encourage transfers within the family, or to remain neutral between succession plans that

56 The dominant view of regulation is that the goal should be to maximize welfare, leaving distributional concerns to the income tax. *See* Louis Kaplow & Steven Shavell, *Fairness Versus Welfare*, 114 HARV. L. REV. 961, 993–94 (2001). For a dissenting argument that distributional concerns should count when evaluating policy, *see generally* Richard L. Revesz, *Regulation and Distribution*, 93 N.Y.U. L. REV. 1489 (2018). Even if distributional concerns were considered explicitly, it is not clear how they might affect the analysis. *See generally* Benjamin Means, *Wealth Inequality and Family Businesses*, 65 EMORY L.J. 937 (2016) (arguing that family businesses provide a pathway to the middle class for many families but can also entrench disparities in wealth across generations).

57 *See, e.g.*, Edward W. De Barbieri, *Supporting Small Businesses in Place*, 48 FORDHAM URB. L.J. 1107 (2021).

58 *See Investing in the Next Generation of Agricultural Scientists*, SARE: SUSTAINABLE AGRIC. RSCH. & EDUC. (2016), https://tinyurl.com/46nz5eu6; *USDA Announces up to $550 Million in American Rescue Plan Funding for Projects Benefiting Underserved Producers and Minority Serving Institutions that Create Career Development Opportunities for Next Generation Leaders*, USDA: U.S. DEP'T OF AGRIC. (Aug. 24, 2022), https://tinyurl.com/vknby6ja.

59 *See, e.g.*, *Women-Owned Businesses*, U.S. SMALL BUS. ADMIN. (Feb. 5, 2025), www.sba.gov/business-guide/grow-your-business/women-owned-businesses (providing an overview of resources for women entrepreneurs including loan programs and assistance in competing for federal contracts).

preserve family ownership and those involving a sale outside the family. Also, in the latter case, lawmakers might further distinguish between sales to outsiders that also could be classified as a family business and sales to nonfamily business investors. Although imperfect in its execution, the government's provision of short-term funding to help small businesses survive the COVID-19 crisis offers a model for how a legislative initiative might bolster family business succession by incentivizing planning and helping bridge the gap between a succession plan and available assets.[60]

Finally, whether or not lawmakers choose to authorize loans, tax subsidies, or other types of financial aid, government agencies can also help by providing information concerning succession planning. In the context of family farms, for example, the United States Department of Agriculture (USDA) has amassed written guidelines, videos, and offers access to in-person consultation through USDA Farm Service Agency county offices. Materials available via the USDA website include, *Farm Succession and Transfer: Strategies for the Junior Generation*; *Workshop Addresses Steps to Transfer the Family Farm*; *When to Start Planning Your Legacy*; *Fair vs. Equal Exercise*; and *Farm Succession Dos and Don'ts.*[61] Although not a substitute for advice of counsel, compilations of general advice can encourage family businesses to begin the succession planning process and inform them about the nature of the task.

There are also nonprofit and university-based organizations that can help business owners. For example, as the director of a family and small business program, I have addressed rotary clubs to raise awareness concerning sources of family business conflict, given webinars on business entity choices for small businesses, hosted continuing legal education sessions on cybersecurity and estate planning, and led succession planning workshops.[62] When business owners contact the program, we can also make referrals for legal, financial, and business advice. We work in partnership with groups like SCORE, the South Carolina Small Business Development Center, the South Carolina Council on Competitiveness, Independent Banks of South Carolina, and the Kim S. Miller Family Enterprise Institute of South Carolina.

[60] For an assessment of the program's successes and shortcomings, see Patrick D. N. Perkins, *Crisis Legislation: Analyzing the Noble Quest of the Paycheck Protection Program to Save Small Businesses*, 101 NEB. L. REV. 945, 969–71 (2023).

[61] *See Farm Transition Planning Toolbox*, U.S. DEP'T AGRIC. (Feb. 12, 2025), https://farmanswers.org/Toolbox/farm_transition_planning_toolbox.

[62] More detailed information about the Family and Small Business Program at the University of South Carolina Joseph F. Rice School of Law is available on our website, go.sc.edu/fsb.

7.2 JUDICIAL INTERVENTION

Unlike lawmakers, courts resolve individual disputes and are not well positioned institutionally to make broader judgments concerning social policy.[63] Nevertheless, the law has a prospective effect, and judicial decisions shape behavior. To illustrate the judicial role, this section focuses on board-of-director fiduciary duties and challenges to the capacity of incumbent family owners, two topics that are relevant to family business governance and comfortably within the purview of judicial review. Notably, both topics overlap with the proposed F Corp statutory provisions described earlier: an independent committee would help the board satisfy its fiduciary duties; a mandatory retirement policy would reduce concerns regarding the capacity of aging incumbents.

7.2.1 *Fiduciary Duty*

A corporation's board of directors owes fiduciary duties to the corporation and its shareholders.[64] Even in corporations with public shareholders, these duties leave wide discretion to run a family business consistent with the controlling family's values. Unlike regulations that might, for example, limit insider control by imposing sunset provisions[65] or by preventing companies with unequal classes of stock from listing on stock exchanges or indices,[66] the availability of judicial monitoring to police alleged breaches of fiduciary duty should not impede family ownership. Unless noncontrolling shareholders can specifically allege breaches of the duty of care or loyalty, the board has "virtually unconstrained freedom to exercise business judgment."[67] As discussed in Sections 7.2.1.1 and 7.2.1.2, however, while fiduciary duties leave ample room for discretionary

63 *See* Felix Frankfurter, *A Note on Advisory Opinions*, 37 HARV. L. REV. 1002, 1002–04 (1924) (stating that courts are limited to the facts before them and may not have adequate factual context to make broader policy determinations).

64 *See* Stanziale v. Nachtomi, 416 F.3d 229, 238 n.12 (3d Cir. 2005); Malone v. Brincat, 722 A.2d 5, 10 (Del. 1998). Fiduciary duties can also attach to controlling shareholders. *See* Ivanhoe Partners v. Newmont Mining Corp. 535 A.2d 1334, 1344 (Del. 1987) (holding that "a shareholder owes a fiduciary duty only if it owns a majority interest in or exercises control over the business affairs of the corporation"); D. Gordon Smith, *Firms and Fiduciaries, in* CONTRACT, STATUS, AND FIDUCIARY LAW 294 (Paul B. Miller & Andrew S. Gold eds., 2016) (arguing that fiduciary duties are linked to control over critical resources).

65 *See* Lucian A. Bebchuk & Kobi Kastiel, *The Untenable Case for Perpetual Dual-Class Stock*, 103 VA. L. REV. 585 (2017).

66 *See* Press Release, Elizabeth Warren, U.S. Senator for Massachusetts, *Senator Elizabeth Warren Urges NYSE, NASDAQ to Propose Rules Requiring "One Share, One Vote" Structures* (June 5, 2013), https://tinyurl.com/zjd7j82e.

67 BAINBRIDGE, *supra* note 4, at 251.

choices that can serve the interests of multiple corporate constituencies, they require a well-informed decision-making process and prevent controlling owners from expropriating the value of a business for their own benefit. Given proper scope, they should function as a backstop to support good governance.[68]

7.2.1.1 The Duty of Care

As set forth in the 1984 Model Business Corporation Act, the duty of care provides that "[a] director shall discharge his duties ... with the care an ordinarily prudent person in a like position would exercise under similar circumstances."[69] To satisfy the standard, board members "need not achieve perfection."[70] Accordingly, while the fiduciary duty of care cannot be leveraged to require directors to follow "ideal corporate governance practices,"[71] it sets a minimum standard of competence.

The board's fiduciary duties are not excused when there is a controlling owner, even if the controlling owner is the chair of the board. For example, in *ATR-Kim Eng Financial Corp. v. Araneta*, a family business incorporated a holding company in Delaware, but the holding company had "no reporting system ... in place" and its nonfamily directors "entirely deferred" to the controlling owner.[72] Mr. Araneta, the controlling owner, "caused the corporation to transfer its key assets – its ownership of several businesses worth over $35 million ... to members of his family in violation of his fiduciary duties."[73] Although the other board members did not benefit personally, they violated their own fiduciary duties to the corporation because they "did nothing to make themselves aware of [the controlling owner's] blatant misconduct or to stop it."[74]

68 Professor Carrie Stanton argues that fiduciary duties are crucial as a mechanism to address matters beyond the scope of typical private ordering in a family business. *See* Carrie Stanton, *Scrutinizing Succession*, 2025 Wis. Law. Rev. 741, 755 ("Fiduciary duties' comprehensive overlay across nearly every aspect of corporate governance allows situation- and company-specific application for different companies in different circumstances.").

69 Rev. Model Bus. Corp. Act § 8.30(a) (1984).

70 Cooke v. Oolie, No. CIV. A. 11134, 2000 WL 710199, at *17 (Del. Ch. May 24, 2000); Michael P. Dooley & E. Norman Veasey, *The Role of the Board in Derivative Litigation: Delaware Law and the Current ALI Proposals Compared*, 44 Bus. Law. 503, 521 (1989) (observing that "the duty of care is more aspirational than consequential").

71 Brehm v. Eisner, 746 A.2d 244, 256 (Del. 2000).

72 ATR-Kim Eng Financial Corp. v. Araneta, No. CIV.A. 489-N, 2006 WL 3783520, at *20 (Del. Ch. Dec. 21, 2006), *aff'd*, 930 A.2d 928 (Del. June 14, 2007).

73 *Id.* at *1.

74 *Id.* at *20. The court concluded that because the board members "acted as ... stooges for Araneta, seeking to please him and only him, and having no regard for their obligations to act loyally towards the corporation and all of its stockholders," they were "jointly liable for Araneta's fiduciary violations." *Id.* at *1 and *21.

Likewise, Sumner Redstone's control of CBS and Viacom should not have prevented board members from insisting upon a well-documented succession plan.[75] (A dual-class stock scheme adopted in 1990 allowed Sumner Redstone to retain complete control of Viacom, even a quarter century later when serious questions regarding his mental competence arose.)[76] Had board members intervened, CBS and Viacom might have avoided years of costly litigation. Instead, as a consequence of Sumner Redstone's refusal to acknowledge his own mortality, the businesses suffered turmoil as Redstone's daughter, Shari Redstone, struggled to assume command over the objections of senior management.[77] Sumner Redstone owned CBS and Viacom indirectly through a family-owned holding company, National Amusements, as well as a series of trust instruments, but the boards of CBS and Viacom owed their fiduciary duties to their respective corporations and all shareholders. As board members, they could not fulfill their duty to provide oversight of each corporation's activities without satisfying themselves concerning the existence and suitability of a succession plan.[78] Mr. Redstone's public statements concerning his disregard of succession planning were a "red flag" the directors ignored.[79]

75 In connection with the acquisition of Paramount in the late 1990s, Redstone did disclose a succession plan, which involved Viacom's CEO Philippe Dauman assuming control, but the succession plan was not binding: "'Sumner had no intention of naming a successor. As long as he had control, he could have named the Man in the Moon and then taken it back.'" KEACH HAGEY, THE KING OF CONTENT: SUMNER REDSTONE'S BATTLE FOR VIACOM, CBS, AND EVERLASTING CONTROL OF HIS MEDIA EMPIRE 151 (2018) (quoting an unnamed "family associate").

76 "Sumner Redstone indirectly controls Viacom through National Amusements, Inc. …, while holding only 8 percent of Viacom's equity capital." Bebchuk & Kastiel, *supra* note 65, at 587 (quoting Viacom Inc., Proxy Statement (Form DEF 14A) 22 (Dec. 16, 2016), https://tinyurl.com/5a55mnnp).

77 *See generally* Matthew Garrahan & Shannon Bond, *Succession Battle Engulfs Sumner Redstone's Media Empire*, FIN. TIMES, Feb. 4, 2016.

78 In 2015, a lawsuit challenging Sumner Redstone's capacity in the context of a private dispute exposed the possibility that the boards of Viacom and CBS had been pretending that he was still in charge while knowing that he was not capable of making decisions. As one commentator put it, if the allegations were true, "then a great fraud had been perpetrated upon the shareholders of Viacom and CBS, who had been paying tens of millions of dollars to an 'executive chairman' who could not manage to stay awake until the end of a televised baseball game and sobbed through the opening credits of *Deadpool*." HAGEY, *supra* note 75, at 266–67.

79 Ordinarily, boards satisfy the duty of care by "gaining assurances from management and advisers that systems believed appropriate have been established coupled with ongoing monitoring of systems in place, such as those concerned with compliance or internal controls." Rev. Model Bus. Corp. Act § 8.30 (1984) Official Comment at 8–195. Directors are "entitled to rely on the honesty and integrity of their subordinates" but not when they are on notice of a potential problem. *See* Graham v. Allis-Chalmers Mfg., 188 A.2d 125, 130 (Del. 1963).

Given the importance of succession planning and the disastrous consequences of neglecting it, courts should hold that a board of directors falls short of its fiduciary obligation if it fails to require succession planning. Ideally, and consistent with the F Corp concept, the board would create an independent committee to evaluate the issue. As exemplified by Sumner Redstone's obstinance, the absence of succession planning exposes a family business to the risk of a leadership vacuum and destabilizing conflict among members of the next generation. Therefore, upon proper petition, courts should not hesitate to enter injunctive relief to order a corporation's board to put into place a succession plan.[80] Courts may not be well positioned to judge the merits of a particular succession plan, but they can evaluate the adequacy of the underlying process.

Modern corporate governance should prevent the entrenchment of Lear-like leaders. The only person capable of avoiding tragedy in *King Lear* was Lear; there was no independent legal mechanism to force Lear to confront his mortality or to review the merits of his succession plan, once he decided to put one in place. The fiduciary structure of corporate law, however, vests authority and responsibility in the board of directors, even when there is a controlling owner. Moreover, "to the extent controlling owners hold board positions or senior managerial roles, the controlling owners owe the same fiduciary duties as any other board member or manager when acting in that capacity."[81] By holding that the duty of care requires the board of directors to plan for succession, courts can motivate board members to act, thereby ensuring that succession planning will not be ignored or made subject to the whims of a controlling owner.

Although some commentators might object that the duty of care is toothless in controlled companies because boards lack independence, the presence of fiduciary obligations can still shape behavior. As an initial matter, it cannot be presumed that directors will violate their fiduciary obligations in order to seek reappointment in the future or out of misplaced loyalty to those who appoint them.[82] Equally important, if the board lacks

80 Plaintiffs might also seek monetary damages in the wake of a failed business succession. Causation issues aside, however, "[c]ases holding directors liable for a breach of the duty of attention or care, uncomplicated by self-dealing or conflict of interest are rare." Cinerama, Inc. v. Technicolor, Inc., 663 A.2d 1134, 1147 (Del. Ch. 1994).

81 *Id.* at 925 (citing Zahn v. Transamerica Corp., 162 F.2d 36, 45 (3d Cir. 1947)).

82 For example, in a bitter takeover battle between Air Products and Chemicals, Inc. ("Air Products") and Airgas, Inc. ("Airgas"), nominees to the Airgas board appointed by Air Products ultimately endorsed the defensive measures put in place by the Airgas management team. *See* Air Prods. & Chems., Inc. v. Airgas, Inc., 16 A.3d 48 (Del. Ch. 2011).

independence because of a controlling shareholder, then the fiduciary duties can be enforced against the shareholder.[83]

Consistent with the F Corp proposal set forth earlier, it may be that courts should apply closer scrutiny to ensure that the duty of care has been met in cases involving insider control. If judicial relief were seen by all parties as a realistic option, controlled companies would have reason to adopt succession plans. When necessary, shareholders could use the prospect of litigation to force corporations to engage in meaningful succession planning or to adjust outdated plans that might already exist.

To be clear, the duty of care does not preclude family business succession or other similar exercises of insider prerogative; it simply requires an appropriate process before decisions are made. Consider in this regard the way *The New York Times* selected its most recent publisher. Even though there was a strong presumption in favor of the Ochs-Sulzberger family, the succession decision was delegated to an independent committee. The newspaper is publicly held and proceeded in apparent recognition of the fact that there were nonfamily equity investors with financial interests at stake. Moreover, *The New York Times* has long served nationally and perhaps internationally as the paper of record. As the controlling family surely understood, an improperly handled transition could damage the paper's ability to fulfill this vital role to the detriment of its shareholders, the journalists who work for it, and the general public who rely on its integrity.[84] Indeed, abiding by the duty of care is part of what it means to be a steward. The applicable fiduciary standard reflects and reinforces benign explanations for insider control.

7.2.1.2 The Duty of Loyalty

The duty of loyalty offers further protection against abuses of control. As a general matter, managerial decisions are protected from substantive judicial review by what is known as the "business judgment rule."[85] However, courts apply heightened scrutiny to challenged transactions if plaintiffs can properly

[83] *See* BAINBRIDGE, *supra* note 4, at 336.

[84] Similar concerns were raised when the Bancroft family sold its stake in *The Wall Street Journal* to Rupert Murdoch. Although Murdoch's own businesses are family controlled, and so it could be said that *The Wall Street Journal* remains in family hands, it is now harnessed to a media empire in which journalism plays only a part alongside entertainment properties and apparent political ambitions. *See* Richard Perez-Pena & Andrew Ross Sorkin, *Dow Jones Deal Gives Murdoch a Coveted Prize*, N.Y. TIMES, Aug. 1, 2007.

[85] *See* ORTS, *supra* note 30, at 41 ("In the United States, the 'business judgment rule' bestows significant discretion to corporate managers and directors to exercise independent decision-making authority on a wide range of decisions under ordinary circumstances.").

allege that controlling shareholders or directors have a conflict of interest that calls their loyalty into question.[86] Such conflicts include "transactions with close relatives of managers or with companies owned by their families."[87] For example, in one famous case, the corporation hired the spouse of a board member to sing as part of the corporation's new advertising campaign.[88] Shareholders challenged the use of corporate funds as an improper transfer in violation of the duty of loyalty. The court approved the hiring decision, but only after closely scrutinizing it to ensure that the substantive terms were entirely fair to the corporation.[89]

Supplementing the duty of care, the duty of loyalty provides another mechanism for regulating controlling shareholders in conflict-of-interest transactions. Thus, regardless of the voting power of a controlling owner, business succession should not receive automatic business judgment rule deference when controlling owners rely upon kinship preferences. Although family succession may survive enhanced scrutiny, the perpetuation of family ownership must be justified if there are objecting minority owners. To avoid the prospect of judicial scrutiny after the fact, controlling owners may choose to disclose the existence of the conflict and seek ratification by independent board members or shareholders. Indeed, the use of an independent committee to make hiring and promotion decisions for family members would send an important signal of compliance with the duty of loyalty.

The safeguard provided by the duty of loyalty is important because there is always the risk that controlling owners will take advantage of their position to achieve private benefits of control.[90] In the context of family ownership, family members who are employed by a family business sometimes earn salaries greater than they could expect elsewhere, dividends can be issued to meet the needs of family members, and business ownership may come with meaningful nonpecuniary benefits for the controlling family. Accordingly, "[t]o the extent that the controlling shareholder or her heirs wish to go on

86 *See* Kahn v. Lynch Commc'ns Sys., Inc., 638 A.2d 1110, 1115 (Del. 1994).

87 Reinier Kraakman et al., The Anatomy of Corporate Law: A Comparative and Functional Approach 153 (2d ed. 2009).

88 Bayer v. Beran, 49 N.Y.S.2d 2 (N.Y. Sup. Ct. 1944).

89 *See id.*

90 To be clear, the existence of self-interested motivation does not mean that family owners will adopt entrepreneurial strategies that fail to produce value for other investors. Nor should successful stewardship require family owners to act with total selflessness. Notwithstanding the potential for misalignment, some scholars conclude that "family ownership, instead of exacerbating the agency costs with minority-equity claimants, appears to reduce conflicts of interest." Ronald C. Anderson & David M. Reeb, *Founding-Family Ownership, Corporate Diversification, and Firm Leverage*, 46 J. L. & Econ. 653, 656 (2003).

directly managing the company, there may be a powerful inclination to overinvest in the company's existing businesses – those with which the family manager is more comfortable – even though other opportunities that require different managerial skills may offer higher returns."[91] The duty of loyalty comes into play when a controlling owner's choices benefit insiders at the expense of other constituencies.

However, the duty of loyalty should constrain managerial discretion principally when those in control stand on both sides of a transaction. Taken too far, the duty of loyalty could be used to blanch family stewardship of its ameliorative powers and to enshrine profit-maximization at the expense of other corporate objectives. Applied in this fashion, the duty of loyalty would undermine the business judgment rule and prevent controlling owners from exercising their discretion to define business objectives and to formulate a strategy to achieve them.[92]

7.2.2 *Incapacity*

There is another risk of delayed succession planning: Changes in an incumbent's cognitive ability and emotional temperament can jeopardize the transfer of power.[93] This, too, is a lesson of *King Lear*. Having held onto his kingdom until he was in his eighties and in poor health, Lear badly mismanaged the transition to his daughters. In a fit of pique, he disinherited the daughter he most admired, because she failed to participate in a demeaning pageant of public flattery. He banished his closest advisor for questioning his judgment. Lear's behavior betrayed the "infirmity of his age."[94]

And, yet, a challenge to a present-day Lear's testamentary capacity would almost certainly be rejected.[95] Testators are entitled to a presumption of

[91] Ronald J. Gilson, *Controlling Shareholders and Corporate Governance: Complicating the Comparative Taxonomy*, 119 Harv. L. Rev. 1641, 1667 (2006).

[92] *Cf.* Einer Elhauge, *Sacrificing Corporate Profits in the Public Interest*, 80 N.Y.U. L. Rev. 733, 772–76 (2005) ("[S]ome discretion to sacrifice profits is an inevitable byproduct of the business judgment rule.").

[93] *See* Timothy A. Salthouse, *When Does Age-Related Cognitive Decline Begin?*, 30 Neurobiology Aging 507, 508 (2009) (stating that cognitive decline typically commences before the age of sixty and becomes more pronounced after seventy).

[94] William Shakespeare, *The Tragedy of King Lear*, act 1, sc. 1, l. 339, *in* The Riverside Shakespeare (G. Blakemore Evans et al. eds., 1974).

[95] *See, e.g.*, *In re* Will of Goldberg, 582 N.Y.S.2d 617, 620 (N.Y. Sur. Ct. 1992) ("It is hornbook law that less mental capacity is required to execute a will than any other legal instrument."); Weeks v. Drawdy, 495 S.E.2d 454, 461 (S.C. Ct. App. 1997) ("The degree of capacity necessary for the execution of a will is less than that needed for the execution of a contract."); *In re* Will

capacity, and the standard for evaluating capacity requires only that testators know what assets they hold, that they recall the people who are "the natural objects of their bounty," and that they understand the nature of their testamentary act.[96] Cases finding incapacity tend to involve dementia or severe mental illness.[97] At the time he made his disposition, Lear understood that he was king, recognized his daughters, and was fully aware that he was dividing his kingdom among them according to a plan he had drawn for the purpose.[98]

If adopted, a mandatory retirement policy would reduce the likelihood of serious capacity issues in family businesses. When issues concerning capacity do arise, however, courts should apply a more exacting test than the usual standard for testamentary capacity. In a family business, the disposition of assets is, among other things, a business decision, and the legal deference to a testator's disposition of property should not exceed the deference accorded to other business decisions.[99] Failure to engage in succession planning is not protected by the business judgment rule.[100] Further, while courts are reluctant to second-guess the choices of those charged with running a business, the business judgment rule is subject to fiduciary constraints of care and loyalty.[101] An incumbent who has suffered serious cognitive decline cannot be relied upon to act with the reasonable prudence required by the duty of care.

of Rasnick, 186 A.2d 527, 534 (N.J. Super. Ct. Prob. Div. 1962) ("As a general principle, the law requires only a very low degree of mental capacity for one executing a will.").

96 *See, e.g.*, Matter of Estate of Killen, 937 P.2d 1368, 1371 (Ariz. Ct. App., 1996).

97 *See, e.g.*, Riddell v. Edwards, 32 P.3d 4, 9–10 (Alaska 2001) (upholding finding of incapacity based on diagnosis of dementia or Alzheimer's disease and trial court's assessment "that '[a]t numerous points in her conversation with the court, [testator] was utterly confused about the status of people in her life and about her own capabilities'").

98 Lear probably lacked capacity by the end of the play (heath, lightning), but capacity is judged at the time of the testamentary act, so Lear's eventual madness would not be relevant to the inquiry.

99 For a broader analysis of the relationship of family and business law in family businesses, see Benjamin Means, *The Contractual Foundation of Family-Business Law*, 75 Ohio St. L.J. 675, 689 (2014) (arguing that "family law's influence runs through the essential questions of business organization law: who the members are, what obligations they owe to one another, and how the assets of the firm will be controlled and distributed").

100 *See* Stephen A. Radin, The Business Judgment Rule: Fiduciary Duties of Corporate Directors 88 (6th ed. 2009) ("'Technically speaking, [the business judgment rule] has no role where directors have either abdicated their functions, or absent a conscious decision, failed to act.'") (quoting Aronson v. Lewis, 473 A.2d 805, 813 (Del. 1984)).

101 *See id.* at 53 ("Numerous Delaware decisions hold that the presumption of the business judgment rule 'can be rebutted if the plaintiff shows that the directors breached their fiduciary duty of care or of loyalty or acted in bad faith'") (quoting *In re* Walt Disney Co. Deriv. Litig., 906 A.2d 27, 52 (Del. 2006)).

To operationalize the recommended standard, courts could order medical evaluations based on well-pled allegations of incapacity.[102] Where necessary, courts could then invoke the remedy for incapacity under existing law, which authorizes the appointment of a conservator when an individual has lost the ability to manage their assets.[103] Applying an evaluative standard tied to ordinary business judgment rule considerations would leave incumbent family business owners with broad, but not entirely unchecked, authority. Moreover, judicial intervention could still be limited if the incumbent had created a private mechanism to address the problem of capacity, perhaps through the terms of a revocable trust.[104]

One commentator has defended the minimal threshold for testamentary capacity by arguing that the "inquiry is not at all concerned with the testator's ability to manage her property adequately during her lifetime."[105] Even assuming that distinction is valid in nonfamily business contexts, managerial and testamentary decisions are not "completely different" when what is at stake is the future of a family business.[106] To the contrary, succession planning is a crucial component of managing a family business. Accordingly, it would be a mistake to defer to the testamentary decisions of an incumbent who would not otherwise be deemed fit to manage their affairs.

Sumner Redstone's later years illustrate the importance of evaluating the capacity of family business owners. During his prime, he built a business empire. In his later years, however, Redstone lost the power of speech and was reduced to only a few words, reportedly using an iPad to indicate "yes," "no," and "f*** you."[107] Yet, he remained in his position as CEO and board chair of National Amusements, Inc., the holding company that held a controlling

[102] *See* Denise C. Park & Patricia Reuter-Lorenz, *The Adaptive Brain: Aging and Neurocognitive Scaffolding*, 60 Ann. Rev. Psychol. 173, 174 (2009) (describing advances in clinical evaluations including "neuroimaging tools"); Timothy A. Salthouse, *Neuroanatomical Substrates of Age-Related Cognitive Decline*, 137 Psychol. Bull. 753, 759 (2011) (same).

[103] Ralph C. Brashier, *Conservatorships, Capacity, and Crystal Balls*, 87 Temp. L. Rev. 1, 7 (2014) ("Painting with the broadest of brushes, one might state that the essential question a conservatorship court must answer is whether the respondent so lacks the *ability to manage* his assets that the state must intervene by appointing a conservator to assist him.") (emphasis in original).

[104] *See* David J. Feder & Robert H. Sitkoff, *Revocable Trusts and Incapacity Planning: More than Just a Will Substitute*, 24 Elder L.J. 1, 3 (2016) (stating that revocable trusts "are also commonly used for *incapacity planning* as a substitute for a court-appointed conservator (or guardian)") (emphasis in original).

[105] *Id.* at 10.

[106] *Id.*

[107] Keach Hagey, *Sumner Redstone Wouldn't Have Last Word on a CBS-Viacom Merger*, Wall St. J., Apr. 3, 2018 ("Questions have surfaced in recent years about Mr. Redstone's mental standing. To help him communicate, some people who recently have met with him say that

stake in Viacom and CBS. Reports concerning the extent to which he was capable of making decisions were, at best, uncertain. In one lawsuit, opposing counsel addressed a geriatric psychiatrist's report that Sumner Redstone met the standard for legal capacity by observing that the report "did not answer whether Sumner Redstone 'had sufficient capacity to make complex decisions impacting the governance of billion dollar publicly held corporations.'"[108] The distinction is important: Patriarchs like Lear and Sumner Redstone should not have the power to manage and dispose of business assets once it is clear that they cannot act with ordinary prudence.

To be clear, requiring that incumbents have the functional ability to make informed business decisions is not a high bar. Only by comparison with the standard for testamentary capacity does business judgment rule deference resemble heightened scrutiny. Some level of cognitive decline is a normal part of aging and may be compensated for with the wisdom that comes from experience.[109] In most cases, even if there is cause for concern, the issue of capacity will not be sufficiently clear to warrant judicial intervention. Increased judicial scrutiny of the capacity of family business owners is not a panacea. Accordingly, the best remedy is for incumbents to begin succession planning early, reducing the risk that their judgment will be clouded by the time they are ready to make decisions about how to transfer ownership and control.

7.3 THIRD-PARTY INFLUENCE

The governance of a family business impacts nonfamily stakeholders. In particular, when a family business enters into long-term economic relationships with other parties, they are exposed to the risk that the family business will fail to meet its obligations. For many family businesses, succession is the greatest threat.[110] Thus, the extent to which a family business

he has an iPad loaded with snippets of his voice, connected to buttons for words or phrases including 'yes,' 'no' and 'f— you.'").

[108] Lisa Richwine, *Sumner Redstone Has Capacity to Make Trust Decisions, Says Doctor*, REUTERS (June 2, 2016), https://tinyurl.com/57hnde6h.

[109] *See* Lisa Zaval et al., *Complementary Contributions of Fluid and Crystallized Intelligence to Decision Making Across the Life Span*, *in* AGING AND DECISION MAKING: EMPIRICAL AND APPLIED PERSPECTIVES 149, 154 (Thomas Hess et al. eds., 2015) (stating that accumulated experience may "offset the declining ability to process and manipulate new information").

[110] *See* ANDREA COLLI, THE HISTORY OF FAMILY BUSINESS: 1850–2000 66 (2008) (identifying "leadership succession" as the "crucial issue" for a family-owned business); ROBERT B. THOMPSON, O'NEAL & THOMPSON'S CLOSE CORPORATIONS AND LLCS: LAW AND PRACTICE § 1:13 (rev. 3d ed. 2004) ("[P]erhaps most important of all, the managers of a close corporation or LLC are often so busy that they neglect to make definite plans for

has a reasonable succession plan in place may be important to lenders, suppliers, distributors, customers, nonfamily key employees, and private equity companies that specialize in acquiring and managing portfolios of family-owned businesses.

If a family business has not adopted an adequate succession plan, potential counterparties may refuse to do business or demand a more favorable price to account for the risk. Alternatively, counterparties may negotiate for the type of succession plan they believe is needed to protect the value of the deal.[111] Either way, whether counterparties choose "exit" or "voice," they send a signal to the management of a family business that there is a problem that needs to be corrected.[112] For example, even if they are otherwise impervious to advice, incumbent owners will listen if they are told that they must draft a succession plan and a buy-sell agreement in order to qualify for financing.

In a case study published by the *Harvard Business Review*, the CEO and chairman of Caterpillar, a major vendor of construction and mining equipment, explained the steps it takes to ensure the reliability of its sales distribution network.[113] Caterpillar sells its products through independent dealers, the majority of which are closely held and family owned.[114] From Caterpillar's standpoint, independent dealers provide "knowledge of the local market and … close relations with customers."[115] But Caterpillar's reputation is tied up with its dealers, and it conducts regular reviews of each dealer to ensure that "they are well run."[116]

In particular, Caterpillar takes a number of proactive steps to manage the risks associated with family business succession:

management succession and to develop younger participants capable of eventually taking over control of the business.").

111 *See* HAGEY, *supra* note 75, at 151 (noting that a major investor demanded a succession plan as a condition for funding Sumner Redstone's acquisition of Paramount. Although the succession plan was never binding, the plan nevertheless created family dissension because it named a nonfamily CEO as heir apparent: "[I]n some ways, the real news was that Sumner had passed over his own children, who were then in their forties, both lawyers, both on the board of Viacom, and both actively working in the family business." *Id.*).

112 *See* ALBERT O. HIRSCHMAN, EXIT, VOICE, AND LOYALTY: RESPONSES TO DECLINE IN FIRMS, ORGANIZATIONS AND STATES 4–5 (1970).

113 *See* Fites, *supra* note 3, at 157–60.

114 *See id.*

115 *Id.* at 162.

116 *Id.* at 175 ("Every year, we review all our dealers' performance – in terms of sales, market position, service capability, organizational structure, and plans for ownership and management continuity – to establish the areas that each dealership needs to work on during the next year.").

> We actively help dealers keep the business in the family. For example, when the principal of a privately held dealership is about 50 years old, we hold seminars for the family on tax issues and succession planning – both financial and management. These seminars are held two or three times during the principal's active working life to ensure that the next generation is ready.[117]

Caterpillar also pays attention to the next generation: "We also encourage owners to involve their kids in their dealerships from an early age."[118] In some cases, Caterpillar provides very specific advice about how the children should be integrated into the business, and it sponsors seminars to educate them.[119] Ultimately, Caterpillar reserves to itself the right to make succession decisions for its dealerships, stepping in where necessary to block next-generation leaders that Caterpillar believes are not up to the job.[120]

Caterpillar's level of involvement in the family dynamics of its independent dealerships may be unusual, but Caterpillar is not alone in recognizing the importance of business continuity and the risk factors associated with family ownership. One entrepreneur who has co-owned several businesses with her spouse explained that she has been on both sides of the issue:

> We were often asked to provide details of our succession plan and we always asked closely held asset managers for details on their succession plans. Although more than a few older business owners viewed it as an insult, it is simply a risk factor that needs to be assessed. Specifically, we always wanted to know 1) ownership structure and any transfer obligations, 2) who would fill senior roles when they were vacated, and 3) if plan A fails, what is plan B for succession. We would also include an ability to cancel the contract for cause with departure of key players being a stated cause.[121]

Admittedly, there may be downsides to having governance decisions influenced by third parties who are more interested in stability than fairness. For example, an outside investor might insist on a clearly identified control person, rejecting shared-control structures that better suit the talents and interests of family members. On the whole, though, private ordering should be seen as beneficial if it induces family businesses to engage in succession planning.

117 *Id.* at 179.

118 *Id.*

119 *See id.* ("We recently held a conference … that was attended by 20 to 25 sons and daughters, who ranged in age from 15 to 23. The idea was to introduce them to Caterpillar, to get them interested in the business, and to allow them to meet their peers.").

120 *Id.* (stating that by the time the incumbents "are ready to retire, we have seen enough of their children to know what they can do and which ones are capable of taking over the business").

121 E-mail from Karen Wells to author (Dec. 7, 2020, 8:10 AM EST) (on file with author).

7.4 THE ROLE OF COUNSEL

No standard business form can replace the vital role lawyers play in helping the parties to identify and negotiate appropriate solutions to a variety of business planning issues, including external regulatory requirements, financing needs, and desired tax treatment.[122] Default governance rules need tailoring to fit the parties' particular circumstances:

> Within each form of business, the lawyer must help the client create a working structure that accommodates the participants' interests and abilities .... It will establish who has what authority to legally bind the enterprise and lay out how business decision making will be accomplished. The structure should further define the financial relationships of the participants and how to parcel out the fruits of the endeavor. The structure will provide the means for accepting new participants and allow[] an exit mechanism for those who wish to leave.[123]

In order to craft provisions that meet a client's needs, a lawyer must first appreciate what the client seeks to accomplish: "For example, an estate planning attorney may be puzzled by a client's reluctance to implement the most rational distribution plan, until she considers the client's conflict between his desires as a parent (to treat each offspring equally) and as a business owner (to consolidate control in one successor)."[124] Lawyers advising family businesses should take special care to explore questions, such as succession and estate planning, that are critical to the success of the venture.[125]

Experienced business lawyers learn to work effectively with family businesses but methodological training in legal analysis and issue spotting does not provide lawyers with the tools they need to appreciate the influence of family dynamics. To supplement their skill set, lawyers may find that other professionals, such as business counselors and psychologists, are invaluable in helping families to avoid conflict. For instance, helping the parties to negotiate a buy-sell agreement will require a lawyer to respect the importance of trust and to take care to avoid the possibility that an arms-length agreement could undermine broader family dynamics.[126]

[122] *See* Steven H. Hobbs & Fay Wilson Hobbs, *Family Businesses and the Business of Families: A Consideration of the Role of the Lawyer*, 4 TEX. WESLEYAN L. REV. 153, 164 (1998).

[123] Steven H. Hobbs, *Toward a Theory of Law and Entrepreneurship*, 26 CAP. U. L. REV. 241, 257–58 (1997).

[124] KELIN E. GERSICK ET AL., GENERATION TO GENERATION: LIFE CYCLES OF THE FAMILY BUSINESS 5 (1997).

[125] *See* Hobbs & Hobbs, *supra* note 122, at 165.

[126] The buy-sell agreement bears some structural similarity to a marital prenuptial agreement and an absence of bargaining in both contexts may be explained by a need to preserve trust and a

Lawyers who advise family businesses might also collaborate with or learn from well-established counseling firms: Cambridge Family Enterprise Group;[127] the Family Firm Institute;[128] the Center for Family Enterprises, Kellogg School of Management;[129] and the Family Business Network.[130] At least one organization seeks to bring together legal professionals who specialize in representing family businesses: Attorneys for Family-Held Enterprises.[131] At present, with the possible exception of trust and estate lawyers, the legal profession does not seem to be well represented in the mix of counselors who advise family businesses on a regular basis.

Although this is not the place for a comprehensive analysis of possible changes to the structure of the legal profession, two considerations seem particularly relevant to a possible underrepresentation of lawyers in family business counseling. First, legal representation assumes positional conflict rather

perceived inconsistency of trust and contractual protection. *See* Margaret M. Blair & Lynn A. Stout, *Trust, Trustworthiness, and the Behavioral Foundations of Corporate Law*, 149 U. PA. L. REV. 1735, 1805 (2001) ("The phenomenon of trust behavior suggests … that sometimes participants in closely held corporations may deliberately choose not to draft formal contracts, even when they could do so.").

[127] *About CFEG*, CAMBRIDGE FAMILY ENTERPRISE GROUP, https://cfeg.com/about/ (last visited Mar. 10, 2025). According to its website: "For over 30 years, Cambridge Family Enterprise Group (CFEG) has helped enterprising families – those with a family company, family foundation, family office or with significant family wealth – to address and transcend the important, often complicated, and sensitive family business, ownership, and financial issues they face."

Id. "Dr. John A. Davis is the Founder and Chairman of Cambridge Family Enterprise Group, and has taught at Harvard Business School since 1996. He is recognized globally as a pioneer and foremost authority on family enterprise, family wealth, leadership, and succession, and as one of America's leading wealth advisors." *Id.*

[128] FAMILY FIRM INSTITUTE, INC., www.ffi.org/ (last visited Mar. 10, 2025) ("For more than thirty years, the Family Firm Institute (FFI) has been engaged in educating, connecting, and inspiring professionals who serve family enterprises.").

[129] *Family Business Programs*, NORTHWESTERN KELLOGG, https://tinyurl.com/4wxsyusv (last visited Mar. 10, 2025) ("The John L. Ward Center for Family Enterprises at Kellogg has developed a comprehensive curriculum that will help established, new and aspiring family business leaders master the concepts and skills required to navigate the intricacies of these complex organizations.").

[130] THE FAMILY BUSINESS NETWORK, www.fbn-i.org/ (last visited Mar. 10, 2025) ("The Family Business Network (FBN) is the world's leading organization of business families. Founded in 1989 and headquartered in Lausanne, FBN is a federation of Member Associations spanning 65 countries. A vibrant community, FBN brings together 4,500 business families – encompassing 20,000 individual members of which 8,000 are Next Generation (between 18 and 40 years old).").

[131] ATTORNEYS FOR FAMILY-HELD ENTERPRISES, https://afhe.com/ (last visited Mar. 10, 2025). The website states that "AFHE's mission is to be the leading resource for the on-going advancement, collaboration and education of practicing attorneys and other professionals who provide multi-disciplinary counsel to family-held enterprises." *Id.*

than cooperation; even in transactional practice, lawyers may help clients garner a higher percentage of existing value rather than find creative ways to enhance value for all parties.[132] Consequently, professional ethics rules prohibit conflicts of interest to ensure that clients receive independent advice. The agency cost concerns behind these prophylactic rules are real, but they may also inhibit creative problem solving.

Second, the desire to make effective use of psychologists, social workers, accountants, financial planners, and other professionals, can conflict with the rules of professional responsibility that police the boundaries of the practice of law and the ability of lawyers to partner with nonlawyers.[133] For lawyers who advise family businesses, the value of collaborating with professionals from other disciplines is both obvious and consistent with broader calls for reform to the structure of the legal profession.[134] As a number of legal commentators have observed, lawyers can no longer afford to insulate themselves from competition when other professionals can combine to meet client needs in a less adversarial, more cost-effective way. In the United States, slumping demand for traditional legal services suggests that change may be inevitable.[135]

There are a variety of ways that lawyers might approach these challenges within the confines of existing rules of professional ethics. For instance, lawyers who regularly advise family businesses might seek additional training in order to incorporate a broader, multidisciplinary perspective. Also, family business lawyers could make a practice of consulting with other professionals, though such arrangements could run afoul of existing rules concerning

[132] Obviously, a single negotiation can include value-claiming and value-creating elements, and a party that focused only on creating value would be in serious jeopardy of coming away with a disadvantageous bargain. *See* Ronald J. Gilson, *Value Creation by Business Lawyers: Legal Skills and Asset Pricing*, 94 YALE L.J. 239 (1984).

[133] *See* ABA MODEL RULES OF PROFESSIONAL CONDUCT R. 5.4 (prohibiting fee sharing and partnerships with nonlawyers); Tanina Rostain, *The Emergence of "Law Consultants,"* 75 FORDHAM L. REV. 1397 (2006); Janet Weinstein, *Coming of Age: Recognizing the Importance of Interdisciplinary Education in Law Practice*, 74 WASH. L. REV. 319 (1999).

[134] *See, e.g.*, Larry E. Ribstein, *Practicing Theory: Legal Education for the Twenty-First Century*, 96 IOWA L. REV. 1649, 1664 (2011).

[135] Some universities have already taken advantage of the need for a more interdisciplinary, collaborative approach: "Often family businesses reach for help at university-based family business centers, where they have access to the expertise of scholars and practitioners and can learn how to address succession issues in a holistic manner." *See* Steven H. Hobbs, *Entrepreneurship and Law: Accessing the Power of the Creative Impulse*, 4 ENTREPRENEURIAL BUS. L.J. 1, 19 (2009). Universities may in some cases garner substantial revenues from the provision of counseling and general education services to family businesses. For instance, the Harvard Business School charges 18,000 dollars for a week-long program. *See Families in Business*, HARV. BUS. SCH., EXEC. EDUC. (2025), www.exed.hbs.edu/families-business.

fee sharing.[136] More creatively, in appropriate circumstances, family business lawyers could borrow aspects of the collaborative model developed for dispute resolution in the context of divorce.[137] Lawyers who practice collaborative law seek to minimize the adversarial nature of the process and to avoid litigating matters that can be resolved through open dialogue and reasonable negotiation.[138] To incentivize cooperation, the parties agree that "the lawyers may act as settlement counsel but not as litigation counsel."[139] A collaborative model, if cleared by the state courts or bar ethics committees, could be extended to family business counseling and dispute resolution.[140]

Even if multidisciplinary advice or creative collaborations are not realistic for a particular representation, lawyers counseling clients involved in a family business should appreciate that their clients are unlikely to approach the investment in anything like a rational actor's frame of mind. In the first instance, this means that lawyers need to take special care to safeguard their clients from opportunism that they may be inclined to overlook, and that lawyers should be proactive in raising questions about business succession and estate planning that can cause problems if left unaddressed. However, lawyers should not view their role as forcing clients to adopt a "rational" market orientation; clients' goals whether market or nonmarket are equally entitled to respect.

136 *See* Steven H. Hobbs, *The Ethics and Professional Norms of Family Business Centers, in* FAMILY BUSINESS GATHERING 17 (Greg McCann & Nancy B. Upton eds., 2000). The client's willingness to pay a premium for additional advisors could also be an impediment.

137 *See* Elizabeth Z. Strickland, *Putting "Counselor" Back in the Lawyer's Job Description: Why More States Should Adopt Collaborative Law Statutes*, 84 N.C. L. REV. 979 (2006).

138 *See* Hobbs, *supra* note 135, at 19 ("The clients and each of their lawyers meet together and may call in experts such as counselors or financial experts to handle any issues that may arise during the divorce.").

139 E. WENDY TRACHTE-HUBER & STEPHEN K. HUBER, MEDIATION AND NEGOTIATION: REACHING AGREEMENT IN LAW AND BUSINESS 516 (rev. 2d ed. 2007).

140 *See id.* ("Collaborative law has arisen largely in the family dissolution context, but the same principles could be applied to many other types of disputes."). In 2009, the National Conference of Commissioners on Uniform State Laws drafted a Model Collaborative Law Act which has been adopted in four states, and eight state bar ethic committees have approved the use of collaborative law. *See Collaborative Law Act*, UNIF. LAW. COMM'N, https://tinyurl.com/yeyt8dft (last visited Mar. 10, 2025).

8

Dispute Resolution

Although family businesses benefit from the trust and loyalty characteristic of healthy family relationships, they can also be damaged by dysfunctional family dynamics. Some problems can be anticipated and provided for before they occur, but no amount of advance contracting can forestall every dispute that might arise. Business ventures involve relationships, not specific, bargained-for exchanges.[1] For family businesses, relational aspects are particularly significant: The time horizon stretches across generations, objectives often include more than simple profit maximization, and business dealings involve emotional consequences for the participants that also need to be acknowledged.[2]

Some disagreements can be resolved out of court. For example, if the parties are willing to make the effort, a good mediator can give space for the expression of grievances and then help the parties to generate a constructive compromise. Inevitably, though, other family business disputes will lead to litigation. In those cases, often involving a petition for dissolution brought by minority shareholders, courts should proceed carefully, mindful of the extent to which a family business is both a market institution and an extension of a broader family system. A narrow focus on family or business expectations will not do, because market and nonmarket values cannot be evaluated in the same way.[3] A more comprehensive legal approach to adjudicating governance problems in family businesses should address both sides of the equation.

1 *See* Robert B. Thompson, *The Law's Limits on Contracts in a Corporation*, 15 J. CORP. L. 377, 394 (1990).

2 Judicial monitoring remains important as a backstop to prevent opportunism and oppression. *See id.* at 394 ("A fully contingent contract cannot be drafted, so some *ex post* settling up by courts is used to support these [unstated] assumptions.").

3 ELIZABETH ANDERSON, VALUE IN ETHICS AND ECONOMICS 70 (1993) ("Two goods are incomparable in intrinsic worth if they are not candidates for the same mode of valuation.").

To that end, this chapter begins with a typology of family business conflict, identifying common types of disagreement, the intersections where those disagreements are most likely to arise, and the legal causes of action they implicate. In any area of overlap, dissension may result either when family values are given precedence or when a refusal to credit the existence of family obligations stirs resentment. Another common feature of family business disputes is a lack of exit opportunities. Often, family businesses are meant to be permanent and prevent shareholders from cashing out or selling to third parties. Lock-in rules can offer significant tax benefits, especially in the context of estate planning, but they exacerbate the minority's vulnerability to mistreatment. A legal structure premised on family harmony can create serious problems when family members turn on one another.

When family conflicts are brought into the courtroom, a threshold question is whether the plaintiffs can prove that they have an ownership stake to contest. Otherwise, they will lack standing to challenge any alleged mistreatment. Although the disgruntled family members may have considered themselves to be business owners, and they may have been treated as such, the actual business records may indicate otherwise. If they can avoid the snares of that threshold issue, the plaintiffs in a family business dispute will typically allege abuse of control by the majority owners. Claims alleged often include minority shareholder oppression, requiring a showing that the majority has violated the reasonable expectations of the minority. Again, the presence of family dynamics can make this assessment especially difficult. What is reasonable for a minority investor to expect when the majority owner is a parent, child, or sibling?

8.1 SHAREHOLDER OPPRESSION IN FAMILY BUSINESSES

Investing in a closely held corporation is a risky proposition unless the shareholder holds a controlling stake or has bargained for additional protections. Otherwise, the shareholder is in the minority and is vulnerable to abuse by the majority, who have the power to make decisions. The close corporation structure lends itself to abuse of minority shareholders. Their investment is likely to be a large percentage of their total wealth,[4] and, although they may rely upon family relationships or friendships with the majority owners, those are not legal protections. Indeed, family quarrels and soured friendships often lead to punitive business consequences. The minority shareholders may be removed from the board of directors; if they are employees, they

[4] Mary Siegel, *Fiduciary Myths in Close Corporate Law*, 29 DEL. J. CORP. L. 377, 384 (2004).

may be fired. Dividends may be withheld while the majority takes compensation in the form of salary. Under the business judgment rule, ordinary personnel and dividend decisions are not subject to judicial review. The minority shareholders could try to sell their stock, but who would step into their shoes, and at what price?[5] They might advocate for their interests, but who would listen?[6]

Most shareholder oppression claims in family businesses driven by conflict within family relationships appear to fit one of two general patterns: either a "spillover" family dispute in which the intersection of work and family is not itself a causal factor; or a problem concerning the prioritization of family and business values. In the latter case, it helps to identify whether family–management, family–ownership, or management–ownership intersections are at issue.

8.1.1 *"Spillover" Oppression*

A family business creates a feedback mechanism in which the strength of family bonds can provide support for the business and a successful business can help the family to thrive. However, feedback loops can be negative as well as positive. Breakdowns in family relationships can cause havoc in the workplace.[7] Marital dissolution represents one clear example, but damaged families come in all varieties. For example, in part because of deep-seated family grievances, the Murdoch family engaged in litigation over control of a family

5 *See* Donahue v. Rodd Electrotype Co. of New Eng., 328 N.E.2d 505, 515 (Mass. 1975) ("No outsider would knowingly assume the position of the disadvantaged minority. The outsider would have the same difficulties.").

6 *See In re* Kemp & Beatley, Inc., 473 N.E.2d 1173, 1179 (N.Y. 1984) (stating that the minority shareholder "may be without either a voice in protecting his or her interests or any reasonable means of withdrawing his or her investment"). In a public corporation, shareholders can always take the "Wall Street walk" and sell stock, a power that, in aggregate, gives managers reason to keep shareholders content. *See generally* Albert O. Hirschman, Exit, Voice, and Loyalty: Responses to Decline in Firms, Organizations and States 4–5 (1970) (identifying economic pressure ("exit") and political influence ("voice") as the two primary mechanisms a firm's members or customers may have available to protect their interests).

7 *See* Robert B. Thompson, O'Neal & Thompson's Close Corporations and LLCs: Law and Practice § 2:2 (rev. 3d ed. 2004) ("[B]usiness relationships often overlap family relationships so that a squeeze often reflects dysfunctional family relations or is exacerbated by family relations."); Donella Caspersz, *CEO Resilience in Family Firms in Times of Crisis*, 38 Fam. Bus. Rev. 58, 59 (2025) ("Conflicts occurring in the family domain can spill over to the business, and vice versa, thus 'triggering critical downward spirals.'") (citation omitted).

trust that will, in turn, have the power to oversee the operation of Fox News.[8] A dispute among siblings and their father may affect the shape of news coverage in future decades and the extent to which that coverage is influenced by a conservative political agenda. In this case, admittedly to an unusual extent, the terms of a private family trust have clear public significance. Even in smaller corporations, a family's disputes can have wider implications. However they start, family problems can become business problems and business disagreements can further sour family relations.[9]

Many examples could be cited. In one case, the court observed that the minority shareholder was excluded from the business possibly as "retaliation for the problems occurring between the siblings."[10] In another case, the plaintiff's marriage "resulted in problems with the relationships with his parents [that] affected the family's operations of its business and resulted in … litigation."[11] Or consider the total breakdown in relations among the members of the Shoen family that controlled U-Haul: Adult children alienated by their father's hasty remarriage after their mother's death, false insinuations that a family member who served as CEO had murdered his wife, fistfights among brothers, and other assorted mayhem all contributed to an atmosphere of dissension and distrust that led to protracted shareholder litigation.[12]

Spillover disputes do not fall within any plausible model of rational behavior, let alone the refined assumptions of rational-choice economic theory. If corporate law scholars proceed as though business participants are unfailingly rational and businesses can be analyzed without any appreciation of their social context, then corporate scholars can offer little insight or guidance in disputes that stem from family grievances. A narrow focus on how economically rational actors would allocate risk in an ongoing business venture illuminates neither the potential sources of conflict for a venture situated within family relationships nor the potential methods for resolving such conflict.[13]

8 Subject to inevitable appeals, Rupert Murdoch's effort to revise the trust has been rejected in court. *See* Jonathan Mahler & Jim Rutenberg, *Rupert Murdoch Fails in Bid to Change Family Trust*, N.Y. TIMES, Dec. 9, 2024.

9 *See id.*

10 Mueller v. Cedar Shore Resort, Inc., 643 N.W.2d 56, 65 (S.D. 2002).

11 Berger v. Berger, 592 A.2d 321 (N.J. Super. Ct. Ch. Div. 1991).

12 *See* GRANT GORDON & NIGEL NICHOLSON, FAMILY WARS: STORIES AND INSIGHTS FROM FAMOUS FAMILY BUSINESS FEUDS 192–208 (2010). The authors conclude: "In short, the Shoen family dynamic was totally dysfunctional." *Id.* at 199.

13 Exit, the standard answer to business conflict, assumes that the damage to relationships is irreparable. *See* Z. CHRISTOPHER MERCER, BUY-SELL AGREEMENTS FOR CLOSELY HELD AND FAMILY BUSINESS OWNERS (2010).

8.1.2 *Incompatible Values*

Conflicts can also arise at the intersection of business and family values rather than from a rupture within either of those two systems. The three-circle model described in Chapter 2 helpfully illustrates the main areas of overlap, in which family values affect share ownership and business management. Many shareholder disputes stem from a prioritization of family needs over business interests, for instance by dividing control equally among siblings, regardless of ability, or expropriating business assets and distributing them to members of the family to the exclusion of nonfamily or more distantly related minority shareholders.[14]

Hard feelings can also be created when business values take precedence and those in control of a family business give no consideration to family allegiances. For instance, if a family member's competence as a member of the business is judged without regard to family status, that individual may feel that they have been singled out for mistreatment.[15] Likewise, decisions to withhold dividends can cause turmoil, especially if not all family members receive a salary.[16]

Tensions between business goals and family values are likely to be exacerbated if only some family members work for the business. According to one commentator, the key to avoiding ownership–management conflict and aligning interests is making sure that all family shareholders are also active participants in the business:

> As a general principle, countless problems can be avoided if family members who do not intend to be active in the business are not left stock in it. The interests of inactive members are antithetical to those of active family members. *Simply stated, inactive owners usually want cash.*[17]

Nowhere are the difficulties of balancing family and business values more formidable than in the transfer of control from one generation to the next:

[14] Professor Lansberg notes that these situations arise when a founder cannot reconcile the competing value systems and tries to split the difference. Ivan Lansberg, *Managing Human Resources in Family Firms: The Problem of Institutional Overlap*, 12 ORGANIZATIONAL DYNAMICS 39, 44 (Summer 1983) ("These compromises, however, often lead to decisions that are suboptimal from a management point of view.").

[15] *See id.* at 43 ("It is not surprising … that a founder faced with having to assess the managerial competence of his or her own offspring experiences a great deal of stress because it is not possible simultaneously to do justice to the norms and prescriptions that operate in the family and in the business systems.").

[16] *See* Paul G. Mahoney, *Trust and Opportunism in Close Corporations*, *in* CONCENTRATED CORPORATE OWNERSHIP 189 (Randall K. Morck ed., 2000).

[17] DAVID BORK, FAMILY BUSINESS, RISKY BUSINESS: HOW TO MAKE IT WORK 129 (1986) (emphasis in original).

"Succession is the ultimate test of a family business."[18] As discussed more fully in Chapter 6, the transition may be difficult psychologically for individuals who have devoted their full energies to the business and now face decline and eventual death.[19] Yet, "[i]nevitably, individual and company life cycles must diverge."[20] To effect a transition, many considerations are involved:

> The owners must formulate a vision of a future governance structure and decide how to divide ownership to conform with that structure. They must develop and train potential management successors and set up a process for selecting the most qualified leaders. They must overcome any resistance to letting go that the senior may have and help the new leadership establish its authority with various stakeholders.[21]

One of the most important decisions is whether to transfer ownership control to a single person or divide it equally among heirs. In the Murdoch trust battle, the issue is whether Rupert Murdoch has the power to shift away from a shared-control model and to give one child sole authority to act as trustee. The choice may be affected by the pull of family and business ownership values. For instance, strong family values concerning equal treatment of children may lead to a variety of strategies for shared management and ownership in succeeding generations. In some cases, however, co-ownership may not be a successful business strategy, even if it affirms important family values concerning the equal worth of each child.[22] As the number of owners expands, the prospects for consensus-based decision-making decline. Yet, selecting a single leader while treating other family members fairly becomes more difficult with each generation the business survives.[23]

18 Kelin E. Gersick et al., Generation to Generation: Life Cycles of the Family Business 193 (1997).

19 Blake E. Ashforth, Role Transitions in Organizational Life: An Identity-Based Perspective 13 (2001) ("[T]he more the individual is involved in and identifies with work, the more consequential and potentially taxing the transition process tends to be for the individual.").

20 Gersick et al., *supra* note 18, at 193.

21 *Id.* at 194.

22 On the other hand, "[t]he idea that one and only one individual should be the leader is steeped in the rich imagery of the hero in Western culture." *Id.* at 204. In fact, "[f]amilies that choose a Controlling Owner structure for the next generation are betting the store and the family fortune on the leadership talent, business acumen, and emotional maturity of one person." *Id.* at 205. This risk must be weighed against the management benefit that follows from clear control – "[i]t permits decisive action, often critical when a company must move quickly to capture markets or beat competitors." *Id.* at 204.

23 To be effective, the choice of leadership must be combined with "a mechanism for concentrating the stock in the single successor's hands." *Id.* at 205. However, if "the business is the primary asset, this raises fundamental questions of fairness in distribution of the family's wealth."

In sum, family relationships have a habit of intruding on business matters. For example, if a married couple owns a corporation, either spouse can petition for divorce, triggering an equitable division of assets overseen by a family court judge who is not bound by the existing allocation of stock between the spouses. In a "no-fault" divorce proceeding, it is irrelevant whether the petitioning spouse could have sought corporate dissolution by alleging shareholder oppression, let alone demonstrated an ownership stake that would have provided the spouse standing to assert such a claim.[24] Whether the issue is divorce, inheritance, or the operation of a family trust that owns business assets, family law can have a considerable influence on business law outcomes.

Consequently, the recognition of family businesses as a distinctive form of commercial activity situated in the context of broader family systems would help courts to resolve shareholder disputes consistent with the parties' own expectations – their contractual bargain, broadly understood. Although value conflicts in family businesses might also be addressed through legislation or tailored business planning, the potential destructiveness of family disagreements is an unavoidable feature of doing business with one's family members. Through an appropriate monitoring role, courts can address these disputes when they occur.

8.2 TAX CONSIDERATIONS

In closely held businesses, family owned or not, minority investors are vulnerable to mistreatment at the hands of the majority.[25] Unless they have bargained for veto rights, board representation, or other checks on majority power, the practical ability of minority investors to earn a return on their investment depends upon the majority's decisions regarding dividends, employment, and other distributions of assets. The minority's vulnerability is exacerbated if the

Id. Splitting the difference by designating a successor but "dividing ownership among the sibling group and instructing them … to support the business leader" is a recipe for disaster. *Id.* at 206.

24 A petition for corporate dissolution, by contrast, is more akin to a divorce based on fault. *See* John H. Matheson & R. Kevin Maler, *A Simple Statutory Solution to Minority Oppression in the Closely Held Business*, 91 MINN. L. REV. 657, 691 (2007) ("[B]ecause there is no concept of no-fault divorce (or even irreconcilable differences) for business dissolutions, the mud of mistreatment allegations must be slung, and litigants (and courts) must muddle through the quagmire.").

25 *See* Benjamin Means, *A Voice-Based Framework for Evaluating Claims of Shareholder Oppression in the Close Corporation*, 97 GEO. L.J. 1207, 1217 (2009). Many classic cases of shareholder oppression involve family-owned businesses. *See* GRANT GORDON & NIGEL NICHOLSON, FAMILY WARS: CLASSIC CONFLICTS IN FAMILY BUSINESS AND HOW TO DEAL WITH THEM 3–4, 10 (2008).

business-entity form provides no right of exit.[26] Unless investors need assurances regarding the stability of their capital investment,[27] limited exit rights are puzzling from an internal governance perspective.[28]

Yet, as a matter of tax law, the minority's vulnerability has value because it enables a family to transmit wealth between generations while claiming a substantial reduction in value for lack of control and lack of marketability. Family members who receive shares of a business from loved ones as a gift may have less reason to worry about oppression – and, in any case, the shares do not represent an investment bargain. In order to accommodate family tax planning through closely held businesses, most jurisdictions restrict exit rights in limited partnerships, limited liability companies (LLCs), and trusts.[29] Indeed, default LLC rules that once provided for easy exit were altered to suit the needs of family businesses.[30]

The default no-exit rule can be defended on efficiency grounds, even if it turns out that most closely held businesses would be well advised to adopt more liberal exit rules. Crucially, the Internal Revenue Code calculates discounts for lack of control and marketability based upon the language of the business statute and may disregard private ordering that cuts back on exit rights that the statute would otherwise provide.[31] Business owners can

[26] *See* Means, *supra* note 25, at 1217.

[27] *See* Edward B. Rock & Michael L. Wachter, *Waiting for the Omelet to Set: Match-Specific Assets and Minority Oppression in Close Corporations*, 24 J. CORP. L. 913, 915 (1999) (arguing that "the close corporation form is best suited to companies that require extensive investments in match assets. In such cases, the close corporation acts as an incubator and the lock-in is a benefit, not a cost").

[28] *See* Larry E. Ribstein, *The Important Role of Non-organization Law*, 40 WAKE FOREST L. REV. 751, 772 (2005) ("[R]estricting exit may involve significant costs in closely held firms by subjecting members who have neither management power nor exit rights to potential oppression by the managers and controlling owners."); J. A. C. Hetherington & Michael P. Dooley, *Illiquidity and Exploitation: A Proposed Statutory Solution to the Remaining Close Corporation Problem*, 63 VA. L. REV. 1, 44–45 (1977).

[29] *See* Robert H. Sitkoff & Max M. Schanzenbach, *Jurisdictional Competition for Trust Funds: An Empirical Analysis of Perpetuities and Taxes*, 115 YALE L.J. 356, 360–61 (2005); Kenneth P. Brier & Joseph B. Darby, III, *Family Limited Partnerships: Decanting Family Investment Assets into New Bottles*, 49 TAX LAW. 127, 128 (1995).

[30] *See* LARRY E. RIBSTEIN, THE RISE OF THE UNCORPORATION 179–80 (2010).

[31] *See* Ribstein, *supra* note 28, at 771 ("Family members cannot avoid receiving full market value simply by a partnership agreement provision restricting transfers because only state statutory restrictions matter under the IRC.") (citing I.R.C. § 2704(b)(1) (2000)); 2 HOWARD M. ZARITSKY, TAX PLANNING FOR FAMILY WEALTH TRANSFERS DURING LIFE: ANALYSIS WITH FORMS ¶ 10.03[2][b][i] (5th ed. 2013) (noting that § 2704(b) ignores "limitations on the ability to liquidate the partnership that are more restrictive than those generally extant under applicable state law" if the limitations "will lapse or if the transferor or his or her family can remove [the limitations] after the transfer").

include exit provisions at relatively low cost; however, families that want the lock-in rule for tax planning are much better off relying on a statutory default rule.[32] Thus, an opt-out approach helps all business investors to maximize the value of their investment.

A possible compromise position – tailoring the no-exit defaults more narrowly to qualifying family businesses that have elected to be treated as such under special statutory provisions – would not necessarily lead to better outcomes.[33] First, while creating a separate set of statutory provisions for family businesses has some appeal, it would also require a more precise articulation of which businesses qualify, and any defined boundary would be both under- and over-inclusive. Unlike a fixed statutory definition, the contractual approach has enough flexibility to respond to family-controlled businesses with widely varying features.

Second, even if it were possible to identify "qualifying" family businesses in a satisfactory manner, those businesses would then have to elect the special family coverage. That is, if investors in nonfamily businesses behave irrationally by failing to include exit rights, it seems likely that family business owners will make similar mistakes. For a separate family business designation to serve its purpose, we must be able to assume that family owners will, in fact, elect that status when appropriate.[34] Also, although the lock-in rule applies to family and nonfamily businesses alike, family businesses are a significant percentage of all businesses.[35] Accordingly, while it is true that only a subset of businesses can take advantage of the tax benefit, that number is far from trivial.

In any event, whether no-exit rules can or should be tailored to family businesses, the risk of abuse of control exists even in those family businesses that have the most to gain from favorable treatment. Thus, the selection of an appropriate statutory default rule regarding exit rights should be coupled

32 *See* ZARITSKY, *supra* note 31, at ¶ 10.03[2][b][I] (noting that the Internal Revenue Code "causes the partnership interest to be valued without regard to the restrictions on liquidation contained in the partnership agreement").

33 *See* Douglas K. Moll, *Minority Oppression & the Limited Liability Company: Learning (or Not) from Close Corporation History*, 40 WAKE FOREST L. REV. 883, 974 (2005) ("[E]ven if family-business tax concerns are viewed … as issues of paramount importance, the elimination of default exit rights in *all* of a particular business structure seems unnecessarily overbroad.").

34 Family businesses may be reluctant to make an election that segregates them from other businesses – a problem that has limited the usefulness of optional supplements to corporate codes designed to address the needs of close corporations. *See, e.g.*, CAL. CORP. CODE § 158(a) (West 2012) (defining "close corporation" as "a corporation … whose articles contain … a provision that all of the corporation's issued shares … shall be held of record by not more than" thirty-five persons); DEL. CODE ANN. tit. 8, §§ 341–356 (2014) (offering "special provisions" in subchapter for qualifying close corporations that make the election).

35 *See* DWIGHT DRAKE, BUSINESS PLANNING: CLOSELY HELD ENTERPRISES 314 (5th ed. 2018).

with consideration of the judicial role: When asked to adjudicate a claim of oppression in a closely held business with no bargained-for exit rights, a court could conclude that capital lock-in default must have been important to the investors, or they would have bargained around it.[36]

However, in family businesses – at least those that fall outside the realm of the high-technology-driven, entrepreneurial startup – an explanation based upon the supposed desirability of capital lock-in for business purposes is generally unpersuasive.[37] Rather, tax considerations supply the obvious reason for retaining the no-exit rule. While the existence of a tax-driven rationale does not mean that courts should provide, after the fact, a right that the parties chose to exclude, neither should courts reinforce the no-exit rule by inventing an implausible rationale for it. Instead, the absence of a statutory exit right should feature only as background that explains the majority's power; whether the majority has abused its power is a separate matter to be resolved according to a jurisdiction's shareholder-oppression law.

8.3 STANDING

In addition to the complexity of exit limitations, the informality of a family business can lead to a lack of documentation of ownership interests. A friend of mine who is a lawyer once told me that it didn't matter to her whether she was an employee of the business her husband ran, whether she was a co-owner, or whether her contributions were valuable simply because they contributed to the assets of the marriage. As far as she was concerned, the money was going to the same place, regardless. The lack of concern regarding formalities is not unusual, but it can lead to a surprising threshold issue if there is ever a dispute. That is, the court's first task may be to determine whether the plaintiff has an ownership interest that would give them standing to sue.

36 *See, e.g.*, Rock & Wachter, *supra* note 27, at 920 (discussing the needs of a high-tech startup company: "If participants can trigger dissolution at will, they will be unwilling, ex ante, to make investments in match for fear that, ex post, they will be held up.").

37 However, if business owners anticipate a messy inheritance dispute, they may prefer a locked-in structure that avoids the dissipation of capital. For instance, I.M. Singer & Company incorporated in the late 1800s, not to raise capital or limit shareholder liability, but because it came to light that one of the two principals, Mr. Singer, had many children by several women. *See* Margaret M. Blair, *Locking in Capital: What Corporate Law Achieved for Business Organizers in the Nineteenth Century*, 51 UCLA L. Rev. 387, 446 (2003) ("Singer's heirs, however many of them there might be, would all have some legal claim to some share of the business, and it would probably require years of court battles to establish who was to get what."). After incorporation, "[h]eirs could be given equity shares in the business out of Singer's estate without disturbing or breaking up the assets and governance structure of the business." *Id.*

In some cases, there will be no formal evidence of ownership or the evidence may be inconsistent. This is particularly true when the allegation is that the parties were in a general partnership, a form of business organization that requires no formal registration and exists if the parties agree to co-own a business for profit.[38] Professors Alan Bromberg and Larry Ribstein describe the evidentiary problem: "Aspects of the relationship that would otherwise resemble partnership take on a different coloration in the family setting. The exercise of control by a spouse may be simply that of a helpmate in marriage rather than that of a partner; one spouse may share proceeds of the business in order to satisfy a support obligation."[39]

Even in a registered form of business organization, such as a corporation or LLC, it is possible that the parties will not have allocated shares or recorded them and that they will then state very different views of the situation once a dispute arises. In adjudicating such disputes, courts should attempt to parse the meaning of legal documentation, if it exists, in the full context of family relationships that may guide the interpretation.[40]

Consider, for example, the contrasting views in *Reichman v. Reichman*, in which a New York appellate court overturned the trial court's finding that the son lacked an ownership stake in the LLC and remanded without deciding what percentage interest the son actually held.[41] The father, Paul, exercised effective day-to-day control over the business, an online retail supplier of bed and bath products.[42] In an injunction action alleging oppression

38 *See* Rev. Unif. P'ship Act § 101(6) (1997).

39 1 Alan R. Bromberg & Larry E. Ribstein, Bromberg & Ribstein on Partnership § 2.10 (2d ed. 2014); *see also In re* Lampe, 331 F.3d 750, 756–57 (10th Cir. 2003) (rejecting argument for business partnership when traditional indicia could not be distinguished from the context of a marriage); McGregor v. Crumley, 775 N.W.2d 91, 99 (S.D. 2009) (same).

40 For instance, in *Berger v. Berger*, 592 A.2d 321 (N.J. Super. 1991), the court had to decide whether a plaintiff who held no shares of stock could petition for dissolution based on his beneficial interest in a voting trust controlled by his father. *Id.* at 323. The court held that, despite the lack of legal ownership, the son had standing to sue. *Id.* at 325–26 (relying on precedent concerning dissenters' rights in mergers where multiple stockholders leave legal title in the "street name" of a brokerage house); *see also* Chiu v. Chiu, 832 N.Y.S.2d 89 (N.Y. App. Div. 2007) (holding that "trial court's determination that the defendant Winston Chiu 'was never a member of the … LLC' was against the weight of the documentary and testimonial evidence" including tax returns that listed Chiu as a 25 percent owner).

41 Reichman v. Reichman, 930 N.Y.S.2d 262 (N.Y. App. Div. 2011); *see also* Peter A. Mahler, *Father May Not Know Best: Appeals Court Grants Injunction in Son's Bid to Establish Majority Ownership of LLC*, N.Y. Bus. Divorce (Oct. 17, 2011), https://tinyurl.com/5y3f6pp5.

42 The online bedbathstore.com LLC business was the successor to a retail establishment, Mildred's For Fine Linens, in Borough Park, Brooklyn. *See* Reichman v. Reichman, No. 000158-11, at 4 (N.Y. Sup. Ct., Mar. 15, 2011), www.nybusinessdivorce.com/uploads/file/ReichmanTrialCt.PDF [hereinafter Trial court].

and seeking an accounting and the imposition of a constructive trust, the son, Michael, claimed that he had an 80 percent ownership interest.[43] The father's response, which the trial court accepted, was that he held a 100 percent interest and that the son was merely an employee of the business.

The trial court noted that when the domain name was registered the plaintiff "was still in college"[44] and credited the father's explanation of the initial business dealings:

> Paul Reichman met with counsel to determine the ownership of the LLC.[45] Originally, Paul planned for a total of 100 shares to be issued, with Michael to own 80 shares. Paul explained credibly that, in sum and substance, he wanted Michael to feel like he had some ownership in a company, particularly given that Michael had had some difficulties in college. Paul wanted to have some ownership, nevertheless, because he put his life savings into the LLC.
>
> Almost immediately after forming the initial plan, Paul thought better of it given his extensive financial contribution, and determined that Michael should receive 15 shares, and Paul should receive the other 85. Paul also admitted that part of his motivation in granting shares to Michael was to shield assets from Paul's wife, as Paul and his wife had marital difficulties at that time.[46]

The documentation concerning the parties' respective ownership interests indicates that there were further alterations over time. The parties signed an LLC operating agreement that stipulated that Paul would have sixty shares and Michael would have the remaining forty shares. Finally, when the business applied for a loan from the Small Business Administration, it learned that the loan would be denied if Michael held an ownership stake because he had been arrested in college. The trial court accepted Paul's testimony that Michael had agreed to transfer his ownership stake to Paul, stating, "Whatever it takes, Dad."[47]

The trial court observed that the documentation of ownership was "far from atypical in a small, family run business"[48] and concluded that "the

[43] *Id.* at 4.

[44] *Id.*

[45] That the initial allocation of ownership interests was devised with the assistance of counsel should give the reader pause and, albeit anecdotal, suggests that lawyers will not always find drafting solutions to potential governance problems in closely held family businesses, even if they are consulted in advance.

[46] Trial court, *supra* note 42, at 4–5.

[47] *Id.* ("The Court credits this testimony, as it is consistent with Michael's age, relative inexperience in the industry compared with Paul, and Paul's capital contribution to the LLC which dwarfs any contribution by Michael.").

[48] *Id.*

actions of the parties are most telling as to their intent regarding ownership of the LLC."[49] Reviewing the evidence, the court found that Paul had acted in a manner consistent with ownership while Michael acted like an employee.[50] Moreover, Michael had never received tax returns indicating an ownership interest, received free health care typical for an employee, and had no familiarity with many of the important aspects of business ownership.[51] In sum, the trial court viewed the evidence through the perspective of the family relationship, giving significant weight to the son's relative youth and inexperience and citing background context to discount the import of documentation that seemed to indicate the son held a controlling stake.

In a summary order reversing the trial court and awarding temporary injunctive relief to prevent dissipation of assets, the appellate court held that the son established a likelihood of success on the merits "by submitting evidence tending to show that he is a member of the LLC, including a copy of the LLC operating agreement, which states that he owns a 40% share of the LLC."[52] As one commentator summarized the trial court's job going forward: "While the appellate court clearly views Michael as having some ownership interest, it left open what percentage he owns and gives little or no clue how the lower court is supposed to weigh and resolve the conflicting documentary evidence and testimony in reaching a determination whether Michael owns 15%, 40% or 80%."[53]

Although the appellate court did not fully explain its reasoning, it rejected the trial court's use of family context to trump properly executed business documents. It is not entirely clear from the appellate court's opinion whether analysis of the family relationships would be relevant to determining the status and proper interpretation of the relevant legal documents. Family context does not give a court license to ignore the entity form selected and any other formalities followed by the parties, but evidence that family relationships have created mutually understood expectations among the parties should be considered in order to place the formal legal materials concerning the business into proper context.

[49] *Id.*

[50] *Id.*

[51] *Id.* at 6. Although the ruling was not a final disposition on the merits, the court held that any damages Michael might establish either as an employee or possibly as a "limited shareholder" could be addressed through money damages, and the court took note of the fact that the business provided employment for approximately twenty people and that a transfer of control could jeopardize the financial health of the company. *Id.*

[52] Reichman v. Reichman, 930 N.Y.S.2d 262, 263 (N.Y. App. Div. 2011).

[53] Mahler, *supra* note 41.

8.4 PRINCIPLES FOR ADJUDICATION

An understanding of the common sources of conflict in family businesses can help courts to apply the law. When assessing the merits of allegations brought by a plaintiff in a family business dispute, a court should first determine whether there is an improper motive for challenged business decisions. In a spillover dispute, for instance, the business justification defendants might offer would merely disguise what is more a family grievance than an independent decision concerning the best deployment of economic resources. Especially when the source of conflict seems unrelated to business operations, the courts should scrutinize the challenged transactions closely for the possibility of abuse of control.

For example, in *Meiselman v. Meiselman*,[54] the complaining shareholder sought dissolution and alleged that he had been excluded from the business by his brother, who was the controlling shareholder.[55] The court concluded that the controlling shareholder's defense – that his brother suffered from mental illness – was not well supported and reflected family tensions stemming from "an argument [plaintiff] had with his father which took place about 20 years ago during which Mr. Meiselman castigated [plaintiff] for having a non-Jewish woman at a family function."[56] Nor was the court persuaded by testimony concerning "another fight which occurred between [the brothers] after [the controlling shareholder] had failed to invite [plaintiff] to a football game to which all of the males in the family traditionally had been invited."[57] Although family relationships may properly inform a court's understanding of the business arrangements that have been agreed upon, family grievances do not create a business justification for oppressive conduct against a minority shareholder.

Conversely, courts should be wary of claims that are motivated by family grievances and that fail to respect appropriate standards for business decisions. Family ties should not be treated as more important than business norms. A family member who participates in a business venture lacks a reasonable basis to expect to receive financial or control rights merely because of the existence of a family relationship. Unless the facts and circumstances indicate a bargained-for expectation otherwise, the fact that a family member's

54 Meiselman v. Meiselman, 307 S.E.2d 551 (N.C. 1983).

55 *Id.* at 553. The relevant statute authorized courts "to order dissolution or another appropriate remedy when 'reasonably necessary' for the protection of the 'rights or interests' of the complaining shareholder." *Id.* (citing N.C. GEN. STAT. § 55-125(a)(4) (currently located at § 55-14-30(2)(ii)).

56 *Id.* at 556.

57 *Id.*

personal interest conflicts with a business norm has no bearing on the appropriateness of an ordinary business decision, whether from a practical, moral, or legal standpoint:

> In private life, one may of course give the interests of the beloved priority over those of strangers. But in public life, as in assigning jobs, one may not weight the interests of the beloved more heavily than the interests of a random applicant. Nepotism is prohibited by the demands of respect, and it is not required by the forms of love compatible with life in modern liberal societies. No single weighted preference ranking can explain a person's choices across all of her social roles.[58]

For a family value to be implicated by a business decision, it must be part of the parties' understood business relationship. Somewhat akin to the statutory framework that authorizes the establishment of the business entity and sets its default rules, a family's value system also provides background principles against which the parties can order their affairs. A broadly contractual approach to interpreting and enforcing the parties' bargain advances the parties' purposes as to matters which – for reasons of transaction costs, social costs, or sheer inadvertence – they have left unspecified. This approach is consistent with the reasonable expectations analysis for resolving shareholder oppression claims adopted in an increasing number of states.[59]

It might be objected that judicial analysis cannot go beyond the formalized business arrangements without losing its objective character and becoming a vehicle for a court to impose its own values on the parties. Although this objection identifies a real concern, it is one that applies with equal force to the traditional economic approach to gap filling. When the parties have not bargained over a term, contract is always a metaphor. Courts seek to fill the gap with the term that, hypothetically, the parties would have chosen.[60] In traditional economic analysis, efficiency serves as a guiding principle, both predictive and normative, clarifying the role of the courts. Thus, courts assume that the parties would have selected the rule best designed to maximize the economic value of their investment.[61]

[58] ANDERSON, *supra* note 3, at 72. Although the anti-nepotism norm would not apply (at least as rigorously) in a family business set up in part to provide an employment vehicle for family members, neither would higher family obligations trump neutral consideration of merit.

[59] *See* Matheson & Maler, *supra* note 24, at 679.

[60] *See* JONATHAN R. MACEY, CORPORATE GOVERNANCE: PROMISES KEPT, PROMISES BROKEN 28 (2008) ("In other words, the provision of non-contractual corporate law rules is a creative exercise that only uses the contractual paradigm as a metaphor.").

[61] *See* FRANK H. EASTERBROOK & DANIEL R. FISCHEL, THE ECONOMIC STRUCTURE OF CORPORATE LAW 34 (1991) (contending that courts should assume that the parties are

Yet, the efficiency hypothesis may ignore the parties' actual intentions in entering the business relationship and supply a term that they would not likely have chosen for themselves. The gap between reality and the hypothetical, economically rational actor looms particularly large in a family business. If courts consult only economic values in completing the parties' contract, they will ignore an important dimension of the actual business arrangement, setting aside the parties' own understanding of their bargain. Admittedly, when family values and business values point in different directions, it may be hard to ascertain which rule the parties would have chosen.[62] However, this is a feature of long-term, relational contracts in general, and the lack of a perfect interpretive approach should not counsel in favor of retreating to a reductionist account of the parties' bargain. Without an appreciation of context, a court cannot hope to identify the parties' true bargain. To ignore enmeshed family values is to disregard the nature of a family business.

8.4.1 *Oral and Implied Agreements*

The nexus of contracts that defines a family business includes the parties' various written and unwritten contracts, connections, and understandings, all of which bear upon the parties' expectations and can guide the adjudication of disputes. Accordingly, unless the parties have a written agreement that excludes collateral provisions and expressly requires that modifications be in writing, evidence of oral agreements and implicit understandings among family business participants should be admissible. While an economically rational actor negotiating at arm's length might insist upon reducing important terms to writing, the participants in a closely held business, especially one that is family owned, are unlikely to pay scrupulous attention to niceties of documentation.

A jurisdictional split concerning the enforceability of oral LLC agreements highlights the importance of the issue. Notwithstanding the fact that participants often rely upon unwritten understandings, some jurisdictions require LLCs to have a written operating agreement.[63] For instance, New York

rational, economic actors and choose the term that they "would have bargained for had they anticipated the problems and been able to transact costlessly in advance").

62 When contract analysis is unhelpful, fiduciary duties could be a way of giving weight to family expectations that would fall outside even a broad understanding of the parties' contractual bargain. *See, e.g.*, Sandra K. Miller, *The Role of the Court in Balancing Contractual Freedom with the Need for Mandatory Constraints on Opportunistic and Abusive Conduct in the LLC*, 152 U. PA. L. REV. 1609 (2004) (arguing that fiduciary duties offer more protection than contractual obligations of good faith and fair dealing).

63 *See, e.g.*, N.J. STAT. ANN. § 42:2B-27(b)(1) (2009); WIS. STAT. ANN. § 183.0102(16) (2014).

provides that "the members of a limited liability company shall adopt a written operating agreement" and makes no provision for unwritten obligations.[64] In the absence of a written agreement, New York courts abandon the effort to understand the parties' actual bargain and resort instead to a statutory default operating agreement.[65]

Yet, the statutory default rules applicable to all LLCs describe a hypothetical bargain among generic investors and will miss many of the important features of family businesses. Not only will the default rules depart from the parties' intentions in significant respects, but a retreat to false simplicity may not even save judicial resources. If a jurisdiction's LLC law lacks the capacity to address the parties' comprehensive bargain, the excluded elements might be raised in collateral proceedings or causes of action, such as when a spouse alleges an economic partnership that enfolds the assets of the business entity,[66] or a trust beneficiary alleges that the fiduciary obligations of trust administration supersede the discretion that a business manager might otherwise have. Business statutes should, instead, facilitate coherent evaluation of the parties' mutual expectations.

In Delaware, and a majority of jurisdictions, the LLC operating agreement is more helpfully defined to include "any agreement … written, oral or implied, of the member or members as to the affairs of a limited liability company and the conduct of its business."[67] Even though this more permissive approach can generate litigation and uncertainty, the alternative would effectively exclude many family business bargains, thereby violating the parties' own expectations.[68] In other words, predictability at the adjudication

[64] N.Y. Limited Liability Company Law § 417(a) (McKinney 1996); *see also* Peter Mahler, *The Oral LLC Agreement: Boon or Bane?*, N.Y. Bus. Divorce (Feb. 3, 2014), www.nybusinessdivorce.com/2014/02/articles/llcs/laurel-hill/ [http://perma.cc/DZJ5-2WT7] ("My own view, perhaps reflecting my New York home pride, favors the relative certainty provided by the judicially imposed, statutory operating agreement that comes into play when the parties fail to enter into a written agreement.").

[65] Spires v. Casterline, 778 N.Y.S.2d 259, 266 (N.Y. Sup. Ct. 2004) ("When there is no written Operating Agreement, these statutory default provisions become the terms, conditions, and requirements for the conduct of the members for the operation of the limited liability company.").

[66] *See* Penley v. Penley, 332 S.E.2d 51, 63–64 (N.C. 1985).

[67] Del. Code Ann. tit. 6, § 18-101(7) (2014). The work of the National Conference of Commissioners on Uniform State Laws, which captures the majority view, provides similarly that an operating agreement can be "oral, in a record, implied, or in any combination thereof." Revised Unif. Ltd. Liab. Co. Act, § 102(13), 6B U.L.A. 429 (2006).

[68] In general, then, "[t]he benefits of certainty must be balanced against the potential costs of frustrating the parties' intent by refusing to enforce oral agreements, particularly in informal firms." Larry E. Ribstein, *An Analysis of the Revised Uniform Limited Liability Company Act*, 3 Va. L. & Bus. Rev. 35, 45 (2008).

stage should not be achieved by undermining settled expectations crucial to the overall business relationship. Instead, courts can protect against abuse by requiring adequate evidence to establish the alleged terms of an oral or implied agreement.

8.4.2 *Equity's Role*

In order to develop a coherent set of rules for family businesses, courts invoking the equitable dimension of family law should note a corresponding interest in business predictability. Without forcing all contracts into a single template, equitable considerations should be applied more evenhandedly to reduce the chance for confusion or manipulation. For instance, if family courts reviewing marital agreements apply a high degree of scrutiny in order to achieve an equitable result after the fact, that judicial scrutiny can produce unintended consequences within a family business involving overlapping obligations.[69] The business and family arrangements are contingent upon one another and can be adjusted accordingly.[70] For example, if a parent doubts that a child's marital agreement will be enforceable, the parent can exclude the child from any direct business ownership and rely on generation-skipping trusts rather than risk the dissipation of family business assets in a divorce.[71]

Divergence in the scrutiny of family and business contracts may have a historical explanation. Until fairly recently, for instance, courts rejected the idea of marital agreements.[72] Even today, a prenuptial bargain in some

[69] *See* Katharine B. Silbaugh, *Marriage Contracts and the Family Economy*, 93 Nw. U. L. Rev. 65, 75 (1998) (stating that many jurisdictions use a strict unconscionability review to police the fairness of marital bargains).

[70] *See* Steven L. Winter, *Human Values in a Postmodern World*, 6 Yale J.L. & Human. 233, 244 (1994) (noting original definition of contingent, from the Latin *contingentem*, means "touching together or on all sides") (citation omitted). As one scholar observes, restrictions on premarital agreements could also affect the willingness of individuals to enter marriages in the first place. *See* Brian Bix, *Bargaining in the Shadow of Love: The Enforcement of Premarital Agreements and How We Think About Marriage*, 40 Wm. & Mary L. Rev. 145, 169–70 (1998).

[71] Nor is this a fanciful scenario. In a high-profile divorce case involving a Canadian family business, the court threw out a postnuptial agreement that was drafted by the founder for the signature of his daughter-in-law in order "to pass on his wealth through generations of his bloodline, not fragmented by marital breakups." Joseph Brean, *"Over-Reaching" Marriage Contracts: McCain Divorce Case Shows Pitfalls of Keeping Fortune in the Family*, Nat'l Post (Jan. 13, 2013, 9:17 PM), https://tinyurl.com/4f7nba2t [http://perma.cc/3SCM-978U] (quoting affidavit of Michael McCain).

[72] Unif. Premarital & Marital Agreements Act, prefatory note, 9C U.L.A. 12–14 (Supp. 2014) ("Forty years ago, state courts generally refused to enforce premarital agreements that altered the parties' right at divorce, on the basis that such agreements were attempts to alter the terms of a status (marriage) or because they had the effect of encouraging divorce.").

jurisdictions will be subject to enhanced scrutiny, and a judge can set aside the bargain as coercive if the spouse in a superior bargaining position failed to disclose material information, took advantage of their position, or if enforcement of the bargain as written would produce a result beyond the parties' contemplation at the time it was entered into.

By contrast, although shareholder bargains were also considered void at one time, corporate law now permits shareholders wide freedom to modify the rules to suit their interests. The same principle of contractual freedom applies generally to other types of business organization. As long as the terms are clear, a party to the bargain will be hard-pressed to persuade a court to rewrite or disregard it. This remains true even if, viewed after the fact, the agreement leads to a one-sided outcome based upon events that could not easily have been anticipated at the time the agreement was signed.

The Uniform Premarital and Marital Agreement Act, adopted in some form in more than half of US jurisdictions, splits the difference between these positions in a way that could be useful for family businesses. The Act creates a presumption of enforceability and places the burden on the objecting party to show that the agreement was the product of duress, undue influence, or other bargaining defect.[73] However, the Act also provides a clear mechanism for raising such challenges and identifies important factors, including aspects of procedural due process.[74] Further, because a "significant minority of states authorizes some form of fairness review based on the parties' circumstances at the time the agreement is to be enforced, [the uniform act] offers the option of" adding a "substantial hardship" provision.[75] Thus, the Act recognizes the importance of contract without ignoring the context of family relationships that may make arm's-length bargaining more difficult.

The consistency that the Act aims to achieve across marital agreements could be extended to other kinds of agreements among family members – particularly, shareholder agreements and similar business arrangements.[76]

[73] *Id.* ("The general approach of this act is that parties should be free, within broad limits, to choose the financial terms of their marriage.").

[74] *Id.* § 9(a) (stating that a "marital agreement is unenforceable if a party against whom enforcement is sought proves" duress, lack of access to independent legal counsel, or lack of "adequate financial disclosure").

[75] *Id.* prefatory note.

[76] Further, the Act contemplates that "[w]hile most … marital agreements will be stand-alone documents, a fragment of a writing that deals primarily with other topics could also constitute a … marital agreement." *Id.* § 2 cmt. *Cf.* Lily L. Batchelder, *What Should Society Expect from Heirs? The Case for a Comprehensive Inheritance Tax*, 63 Tax. L. Rev. 1, 57 (2009) (discussing segregation of shareholder and marital agreements in *Colclasure v. Colclasure*, 295 P.3d 1123 (Okla. 2012)).

In family businesses, many of the same concerns about power and information disparities apply to business dealings, and the bargains are often between the same individuals. Thus, it would be helpful for courts to operate from a common set of interpretive principles. All bargains should come with a presumption of enforceability. However, to the extent courts take into account gross unfairness in substantive terms, disparate bargaining positions, or other equitable considerations, the equitable analysis properly applies to business and family bargains alike.

8.5 CASE STUDY: MARKET BASKET

While no single case study can represent the wide variety of family businesses, a dispute concerning the Market Basket supermarket chain illustrates some of the benefits and the perils of family ownership from a societal standpoint. Market Basket's experience shows that it is possible for family values to affect business operations, contributing to the profitability of the business while also taking into account the interests of other stakeholders. But Market Basket also illustrates how family businesses can be destroyed by conflicts rooted in family grievances, and how employees, suppliers, and customers may all be caught in the crossfire.

In 1917, Arthur and Efrasine Demoulas opened a grocery store in Lowell, Massachusetts.[77] In time, they sold the business to their sons, George and Telemachus,[78] and the single grocery store eventually became a chain "with 71 stores and 25,000 employees across Massachusetts, Maine, and New Hampshire."[79] However, soon after George's death in 1971, relations between the two sides of the family broke down over allegations that Telemachus had used his control to siphon assets and deprive George's heirs of an equal stake in the business.[80] Litigation dragged on for more than a decade.[81]

Conflict flared anew in 2014 because a family member who had aligned herself with the heirs of Telemachus shifted her vote, giving Arthur S. Demoulas (son of George) and his side of the family the majority needed to remove his cousin Arthur T. Demoulas (son of Telemachus) from his position as CEO. According to some news accounts, the Arthur S. side of the Demoulas family wanted to make Market Basket more profitable, disapproved of overly generous wages and benefits, and was concerned about

77 *See* Demoulas v. Demoulas Supermarkets, Inc., 424 Mass. 501, 504 (Mass. 1997).

78 *Id.*

79 Evan Horowitz, *The Saga of Demoulas' Market Basket*, BOSTON GLOBE, July 15, 2014, at A1.

80 *See Demoulas*, 424 Mass. at 501.

81 *Id.*

self-dealing transactions between Market Basket and entities controlled by Arthur T. or his family. In response, Market Basket's employees and customers staged a highly vocal protest, involving "work slowdowns, protests, and boycotts," in order to convince the board to retain Arthur T. as CEO.[82]

Public pressure delayed[83] but did not prevent Arthur T.'s removal, which created further turmoil threatening the company's survival.[84] As the dispute dragged on, Market Basket's revenues dropped precipitously and the company's struggles impacted employees, distributors, suppliers, and customers.[85] The dispute may have "cost the Demoulas family as much as $10 million per day while the stores remained closed or disrupted."[86] In the end, Arthur T. was able to buy out the other side of the family and to assume full control over the business.[87] Within a year, the business appeared to have recovered from the disruption; it opened several new branches and was "on pace to do nearly $5 billion in sales … according to company officials."[88]

Whatever the merits of the dispute among the Demoulas family members, the business thrived under Arthur T.'s leadership, and he appears to have adhered to a set of values associated with family ownership: "Family businesses are closely knit, with an integrated structure that makes employees feel as though they're not just numbers."[89] Despite Market Basket's size, Arthur T. carefully maintained the ethos of family in his stewardship of the business:

[82] *See* Ben Mathis-Lilley, *New England Supermarket Employees, Customers (!) Take Sides in Corporate Power Struggle*, SLATE (July 28, 2014, 12:21 PM), https://tinyurl.com/9y2jahv7.

[83] *See* Casey Ross, *Market Basket CEO Gets Reprieve*, BOSTON GLOBE (July 18, 2014), https://tinyurl.com/3hsmz2h4.

[84] *See* Callum Borchers, *Constant Challenges, No Certainties for New CEOs at Market Basket*, BOSTON GLOBE, Aug. 6, 2014, at A1 ("As the Demoulas family supermarket spectacle drags through a fourth week, Gooch and Thornton, who were appointed in June, are trying to return Market Basket's 71 stores to normal operations while ownership of the company hangs in limbo, shelves are bare, and thousands of workers continue their crusade to bring back the ousted president, Arthur T. Demoulas.").

[85] Editorial, *Market Basket's Only Solution Is to Bring Back Arthur T. Demoulas*, BOSTON GLOBE, Aug. 7, 2014 ("The family feud that led to Arthur T. Demoulas's dismissal may make for fascinating theater, but it's time to bring down the curtain. The showdown threatens to destroy thousands of jobs, a great local brand, and a community asset with it.").

[86] Margaret M. Blair, *Boards as Mediating Hierarchs*, 38 SEATTLE U. L. REV. 297, 303 (2015) (citing grocery store analysts).

[87] *See* Kevin Cullen, *A Way of Life Prevails in Market Basket Saga*, BOSTON GLOBE, Aug. 31, 2014.

[88] Adam Vacarro, *A Year Later, Things Are Going Pretty Well for Market Basket*, BOSTON.COM (Aug. 22, 2015), https://tinyurl.com/2a2zturn; Tom Moroney, *A Year After Upheaval, Market Basket Looks Stronger than Ever*, TELEGRAM.COM (July 31, 2015, 11:39 AM), https://tinyurl.com/3m9d4nje.

[89] Eric Andrew et al., *Playing Their Hand: U.S. Family Businesses Make Their Bid for the Future*, https://tinyurl.com/yr33jxhf (quoting Robert Simon, CFO Contractors Steel Company).

"Employees have said he remembers their family members' names and has helped those who need it."[90] Without losing sight of the need to earn a profit, it appears that Market Basket's business practices have been as enlightened as any advocate for corporate social responsibility could hope – it treats its employees (known as "associates") fairly, sets its prices lower than would maximize profits, not just to build its brand but also to be a responsible member of the community.[91] Market Basket has also been entrepreneurial in its efforts to put stores in underserved, poorer neighborhoods.[92]

Perhaps overstating his case, one reporter compared Arthur T. to a benevolent character in a Charles Dickens novel:

> Artie T. Demoulas is a modern-day Fezziwig, the big-hearted warehouse owner in Dickens's "A Christmas Carol." Fezziwig was a capitalist, but he prided himself on not maximizing profits at the expense of his employees, or his own soul. When the man who eventually buys him out makes a bid, suggesting he'll never get a better offer, Fezziwig's response could be lifted right out of the Market Basket story: "It's not just for money alone that one spends a lifetime building up a business," Fezziwig says. "It's to preserve a way of life that one knew and loved."[93]

Yet, even if Arthur T.'s public image was shrewdly cultivated, it remains true that he used his position as CEO to advocate for the interests of his employees, customers, and the communities in which the Market Basket stores operate. Market Basket managers are brought up in the ranks and learn the company's values before they are entrusted with supervisory responsibilities.[94] The

[90] Grant Welker, *Sun Man of the Year Arthur T. Demoulas Puts Workers, Customers Ahead of Profits*, LOWELL SUN (Massachusetts) (Jan. 14, 2014), https://tinyurl.com/3r2m8628; *see also* Galen Moore, *Market Basket List: 11 Management Tips from "Artie T.,"* BOS. BUS. J. (Oct. 9, 2013, 8:25 AM), https://tinyurl.com/mw3rmh2y (observing that while Arthur T. glanced at employee name tags, "nowhere does the Market Basket name tag say, 'my daughter just went to college,' or, 'my dad just died.' Arthur T. knew details like these").

[91] Welker, *supra* note 90 ("My interest is in continuing the legacy of my father, T.A. Demoulas, who built Demoulas Super Markets into what it is today on the simple principles of respect, fairness, honesty and sharing.") (quoting Arthur T. Demoulas).

[92] That members of the Demoulas family appear to disagree about the value of these practices is a useful reminder that family ownership is no guarantee that a business will behave more ethically than a nonfamily business. At most, the identification of the business with the family and with family values may make it more likely that a business will operate responsibly and with concern for all its stakeholders.

[93] Cullen, *supra* note 87.

[94] *See* Moore, *supra* note 90 ("We do all of our promoting from within. We start out bagging groceries and shagging carriages and cutting boxes in the back room and doing the things you do in a supermarket – 99 percent of our people come from within the ranks.") (quoting Market Basket CEO and third-generation family owner Arthur T. Demoulas).

sale of Market Basket to Arthur T. was remarkable because loyal employees and customers were prepared to destroy the company to prevent anyone else from running it. Had it been otherwise, a number of outside companies might have been able to outbid Arthur T. because they saw opportunities to increase revenue by operating Market Basket along more traditional lines.[95]

Reportedly, Market Basket's governance crisis arose in part because some Demoulas family shareholders were unhappy with Market Basket's failure to focus on profitability, complaining for instance that Arthur T. "unilaterally rolled out a 4 percent discount on goods within the store late last year, arguing that customers could use the money more than his fellow shareholders."[96] However, even from a profit-maximizing perspective, one might hesitate to critique a management philosophy that can generate annual sales of 4.6 billion dollars while creating a loyal workforce and customer base.

As Market Basket illustrates, family businesses can provide wider benefits, even though dependence upon family stability also has risks.[97] Scholars will no doubt continue to investigate the factors that promote healthy family business enterprise, as well as the factors that can signal trouble. Concerns about concentrated wealth and inequality should not cause us to caricature the contributions of family business or to ignore the disruption that would ensue if fortunes were fragmented each generation. Any form of business that can, on a good day, bring together owners, employees, customers, and other stakeholders has something of value to teach us.

[95] *See* Katherine Q. Seeleye & Michael J. de la Merced, *Grocery Chain Reels as Employees and Customers Rally for an Ousted President*, N.Y. Times, Aug. 6, 2014, at A12 ("Some prospective bidders have said that they could squeeze more profits out of the company, since management under Arthur T. Demoulas has shown little inclination to maximize profitability.").

[96] *Id. Cf.* Dodge v. Ford, 170 N.W. 688 (Mich. 1919) (involving allegations that Henry Ford improperly withheld dividends from shareholders). In a pre-trial interview, Henry Ford stated, "I do not believe that we should make such an awful profit on our cars. A reasonable profit is right, but not too much." *Id.* Although Ford lost the case, commentators have noted that this was also brilliant public relations. *See* M. Todd Henderson, *Everything Old Is New Again: Lessons from* Dodge v. Ford Motor Company, *in* Corporate Law Stories 37 (J. Mark Ramseyer ed., 2009).

[97] Even during the period of apparent quiet preceding the latest legal battle for control, Market Basket board meetings were far from cordial: "Arthur S. and the board member appointees from his side of the family continually challenged Arthur T.'s authority to enter into sizeable real estate transactions without approval from the board, and were generally fearful and distrustful that the Arthur S. side of the family was being taken advantage of." Blair, *supra* note 86, at 335 (citing board meeting transcripts obtained by *The Boston Globe*).

PART IV

SOCIETAL IMPACT

When family members work together, the intimacy of family life cannot be separated from the expectations of the marketplace. When families own businesses, the overlap means that lawyers who represent family businesses or individual participants need to ensure that governance arrangements meet family expectations, that business assets are protected in the estate planning process, and, when appropriate, that business assets are accounted for in marital agreements.

If the question is whether we should preserve the stability of family businesses, so that they can contribute to the economy, provide resources for the families that run them, and infuse personal values into an impersonal marketplace, the answer may seem obvious. In my role as Director of the Family and Small Business Program at the University of South Carolina Joseph F. Rice School of Law, I have had the opportunity to meet and learn from family business owners, many of whom I admire greatly. Protecting family businesses strikes me as a basic goal for economic development that should be accepted in South Carolina and elsewhere on a bipartisan basis.

Yet, from a broader perspective, there are unanswered questions about the role of family businesses in society. We should not allow the "family business" label to substitute for analysis. In a brilliant law review article, Professors Noa Ben-Asher and Margot J. Pollans examine the rhetoric of family in the context of immigration law and with respect to a constellation of issues primarily affecting businesses. They point out that the identification of family concerns sometimes turns on preexisting beliefs that are not politically neutral: "Liberals emphasize the sacredness of the family when attempting to defend immigrants from Muslim-majority countries and Central America against exclusionary policies. Conservatives turn to family values to empower family farms and closely held corporations."[1] Moreover, as Professors Ben-Asher and Pollans observe, the concept of family can be invoked for rhetorical advantage, as when advocates for changes to estate tax rules use family farms as their central example, even though the rules they propose would have much broader application.

The two chapters that follow consider issues of scale and distribution. First, do the values that we ascribe to family businesses hold true for larger-scale enterprises that are family controlled? That is, are family owners more likely to act as responsible stewards, managing a business for the long term, rather than seeking to extract short-term profits, potentially at the expense of employees, communities, and the environment? Relatedly, are the interests of controlling owners adverse to minority shareholders so that benefits for the control group come at the expense of other investors? If the stewardship we associate with family ownership can be sustained, even in larger-scale businesses, this may affect ongoing debates concerning dual-class stock and other mechanisms for perpetuating founder control rights.

Second, what impact does family business ownership have on the distribution of wealth in society? Scholars like the French economist Thomas Piketty have argued that rising levels of wealth inequality threaten our democratic institutions. Depending on the circumstances, family businesses can ameliorate inequality by creating new opportunities or solidify existing hierarchies. In formulating and refining principles of family business law, the goal should be to support long-term stewardship, balance competing interests among stakeholders, and address systemic challenges, such as wealth inequality and environmental responsibility, while safeguarding the unique values and relationships that define family enterprises.

[1] Noa Ben-Asher & Margot J. Pollans, *The Right Family*, 39 Colum. J. Gender & L. 1, 59 (2019).

9

Stewardship

Many of the nation's largest corporations are family controlled. Some, like Cargill, Koch Industries, and Publix Super Markets, remain entirely in family hands. Others, like Walmart, Berkshire Hathaway, and Estée Lauder are family governed even though they have also issued shares of stock to the public. The persistence of family ownership and control in multi-billion-dollar corporations requires an explanation because it contradicts conventional models of corporate governance. Controlled companies have been characterized as outmoded "relics of an earlier era."[1] According to this view, prevalent since the middle of the twentieth century, evolution from small "Mom and Pops" toward "widely held distribution of stock ownership and control" is "inevitable."[2] And yet real-world practices remain stubbornly resistant to expert forecasts.[3]

Indeed, the phenomenon of founder control is not limited to family businesses, even if pioneered by them. Google, Facebook, and Snapchat have all offered low-vote or no-vote stock to the general public while reserving effective voting control to company founders.[4] These maneuvers are legal under state corporate law codes that do not require each share to have a single vote,

1 *See* Alex Stewart & Michael A. Hitt, *Why Can't a Family Business Be More Like a Nonfamily Business? Modes of Professionalization in Family Firms*, 25 FAM. BUS. REV. 58, 58 (2012) (citing ALFRED D. CHANDLER, JR., SCALE AND SCOPE: THE DYNAMICS OF INDUSTRIAL CAPITALISM (1990); David S. Landes, *French Entrepreneurship and Industrial Growth in the Nineteenth Century*, 9 J. ECON. HIST. 45 (1949)).

2 Ronald J. Gilson, *Controlling Shareholders and Corporate Governance: Complicating the Comparative Taxonomy*, 119 HARV. L. REV. 1641, 1647 (2006) (characterizing argument as "teleological").

3 *See id.* at 1643; Rafael La Porta et al., *Corporate Ownership Around the World*, 54 J. FIN. 471, 471 (1999).

4 *See* Kirby Smith, *The Agency Costs of Equal Treatment Clauses*, 127 YALE L.J. F. 543, 544 (2017).

and they have been embraced by investors eager to acquire equity and apparently unconcerned by the lack of voting influence. Thus, unless regulators or stock indices change the rules to preclude stock classification, the trend seems likely to continue.

Why has insider control proved so durable?[5] According to most law and finance scholars, the answer is plain: Controlling owners enjoy private benefits of control.[6] For example, controlling owners may devise stratagems to expropriate economic resources. Alternatively, if the law stands in the way of self-dealing, controlling owners might still find intrinsic value in the enhanced social status and political access that ownership brings.[7] Either type of private benefit can be said to compensate controlling owners for the risk of an undiversified investment and the cost of monitoring it. Therefore, even if a widely dispersed ownership structure would be more efficient, controlling owners might prefer the status quo.[8]

In a *Yale Law Journal* article, Zohar Goshen and Assaf Hamdani question the prevailing view and offer a competing explanation that does not depend on private benefits of control. They argue that founders might instead seek to safeguard an "idiosyncratic vision."[9] By maintaining control, founders avoid the risk of being overruled by impatient or skeptical public investors. However, the value of the controlling owners' entrepreneurial strategy affects all shareholders equally – that is, minority investors receive a pro rata share of any value added as a consequence of the controlling owners' idiosyncratic vision.

The various rationales law and finance scholars offer for controlled ownership are not mutually exclusive – any or all of them could be true – but they lack a broader explanatory framework. A complete account of corporate control must include consideration of the identity of the controlling owners. In this regard, for the vast majority of controlled companies that are family

5 In a controlled structure, "a large blockholder owns a majority or large plurality of a company's shares." Lucian Arye Bebchuk et al., *Stock Pyramids, Cross-Ownership, and Dual Class Equity: The Mechanisms and Agency Costs of Separating Control from Cash-Flow Rights*, *in* CONCENTRATED CORPORATE OWNERSHIP 295 (Randall K. Morck ed., 2000).

6 *See* Gilson, *supra* note 2, at 1652.

7 *See, e.g.*, *id.* at 1666.

8 *See* Lucian Arye Bebchuk & Mark J. Roe, *A Theory of Path Dependence in Corporate Ownership and Governance*, 52 STAN. L. REV. 127, 130 (1999). On the other hand, investors might prefer the level of self-dealing associated with controlling owners to the agency costs inherent in managerial control. *See* Bernard S. Sharfman, *A Private Ordering Defense of a Company's Right to Use Dual Class Share Structures in IPOs*, 63 VILLANOVA L. REV. 1, 7 (2018) (citing Zohar Goshen & Richard Squire, *Principal Costs: A New Theory for Corporate Law and Governance*, 117 COLUM. L. REV. 767 (2017)).

9 *See* Zohar Goshen & Assaf Hamdani, *Corporate Control and Idiosyncratic Vision*, 125 YALE L.J. 560, 617 (2015).

owned, the family business literature supplies a plausible framework for analysis. In particular, the concept of family stewardship illuminates the ways in which private economic benefits, noneconomic benefits, and an entrepreneurial vision might coalesce.

9.1 THE LAW AND FINANCE OF CONTROL

To the extent control rights are commensurate with financial commitment, those who have control are, in effect, putting all their eggs in one basket.[10] Their investment is hostage to the uncertain fortunes of a single enterprise.[11] Moreover, the controlling owners must share earnings on a pro rata basis with minority shareholders who do not bear the same burden and may know little about a company other than its stock price. So why is control appealing? The dominant explanation that law and finance offers for the persistence of controlled business structures is that they enable controlling owners to extract private benefits at the expense of other investors.[12]

Empirical studies confirm that controlled companies are most common when minority investors lack meaningful legal protections against expropriation of wealth by controlling owners.[13] For example, controlling owners might cause a controlled company to engage in transactions with other entities wholly owned by the controlling owners on terms favorable to the wholly owned entities. Such maneuvers siphon wealth from minority owners who stand on the losing side of each transaction.

Yet, an explanation for controlled structures premised on expropriation by the controlling owners accounts for only half the puzzle – we still need to ask why outside investors would contribute capital without adequate safeguards against self-dealing. Unless outside investors are systematically uninformed, irrational, or bereft of other options, every increase in the prospects for controlling owner expropriation should drive down the market price for controlled company stock. Private benefits of control are illusory if they are offset by a higher cost of capital. That is, if self-dealing behavior has already been

[10] The size of the bet depends on the strategy for maintaining control. For example, the use of dual classes of stock separates voting rights from cash-flow rights, allowing founders to maintain control even if outside investors contribute most of the equity capital.

[11] Individual investors typically seek to acquire a diversified portfolio so that they are less exposed to company-specific or industry-specific risks. *See* BURTON G. MALKIEL, A RANDOM WALK DOWN WALL STREET: THE TIME-TESTED STRATEGY FOR SUCCESSFUL LIVING 235–40 (6th ed. 1996) (describing modern portfolio theory).

[12] *See, e.g.*, Vladimir Atanasov et al., *Law and Tunneling*, 37 J. CORP. L. 1 (2011).

[13] *See* Rafael La Porta et al., *Law and Finance*, 106 J. POL. ECON. 1113, 1145–51 (1998).

"priced in," controlling owners who operate in reasonably efficient capital markets should end up more or less where they started. Selling company stock at a discount in order to preserve the ability to misbehave is self-defeating from an economic standpoint, much like paying to stock a pond with fish to increase the chance of catching a fish. In the latter circumstance, at least the enjoyment of a day spent fishing might be worth the cost. Also, setting aside the controlling owners' motivation in any particular case, an increased cost of capital for controlled businesses would seem to put those corporations at a significant disadvantage to noncontrolled businesses.[14] Over time, one might expect those increased costs to motivate an evolutionary shift toward public corporations with widely dispersed ownership.[15] As a matter of logic, then, expropriation does not seem to offer a convincing explanation for the prevalence of controlled business structures.

Some law and finance scholars contend that controlled structures are not necessarily detrimental to the interests of outside investors, even if there is self-dealing by controlling owners. Rather, the desirability of a controlled business entity structure depends upon a "tradeoff."[16] With more capital at risk, controlling owners have a strong incentive to monitor the performance of management, thereby reducing managerial agency costs to the benefit of all shareholders. The tradeoff is that "[b]ecause controlling shareholders must bear the direct costs of monitoring, liquidity, and nondiversification from holding a concentrated position, some private benefits of control likely are necessary to induce a party to play that role."[17] Thus, the value of the tradeoff depends on the importance of shareholder monitoring and the amount of implicit compensation demanded by the controlling owners.[18]

[14] *See* WILLIAM A. KLEIN ET AL., BUSINESS ORGANIZATION AND FINANCE: LEGAL AND ECONOMIC PRINCIPLES 373–74 (11th ed. 2010) (explaining why someone solicited to invest in a restaurant business controlled by two owner-managers "might exact a high price for the investment, by demanding a larger portion of the total equity than would be appropriate in the absence of the possibility of opportunistic behavior by the owner-managers").

[15] *See* Henry Hansmann & Reinier Kraakman, *The End of History for Corporate Law*, 89 GEO. L.J. 439, 460 (2001) ("If, as the developing consensus view holds, the standard shareholder-oriented governance model maximizes corporate value, controlling shareholders who are motivated chiefly by economic considerations may not wish to retain control of their firms.").

[16] *See* Ronald J. Gilson & Jeffrey N. Gordon, *Controlling Controlling Shareholders*, 152 U. PA. L. REV. 785 (2003).

[17] Gilson, *supra* note 2, at 1652.

[18] The need for shareholder monitoring will depend on several factors, including the nature and volatility of the business and the existence of other sources of monitoring, such as "institutional lenders or government regulators." *See* Edward B. Rock, *Shareholder Eugenics in the Public Corporation*, 97 CORNELL L. REV. 849, 856 (2012) (citing Edward M. Iacobucci & George G. Triantis, *Economic and Legal Boundaries of Firms*, 93 VA. L. REV. 515, 552–57

Finally, it is worth observing that private benefits of control are not always financial. The availability of nonpecuniary benefits may explain why concentrated ownership is common even in jurisdictions that prohibit many forms of economic opportunism. Controlling owners might value enhanced community status, political influence, or other perquisites.[19] According to one commentator, it follows "[a]lmost tautologically" that "nonpecuniary benefits must play a prominent role in regimes in which functionally good law keeps pecuniary private benefits low."[20] Whatever the form of compensation, in dollars or social status, the prevailing law and finance explanation assumes that controlling shareholders must be paid for the risks they bear and the excess value of the monitoring they provide.

9.2 ENTREPRENEURIAL VISION

An alternative explanation for the persistence of controlled companies does not assume that controlling owners expropriate private benefits. Zohar Goshen and Assaf Hamdani argue that founders who refuse to surrender control may have in mind an entrepreneurial strategy that, if successful, will benefit majority and minority investors alike.[21] By accepting the burden of control, those with confidence in their own strategy for increasing the value of a business earn the right to follow that strategy without deviation.[22]

For example, in 1903, Henry Ford insisted upon sole control of the Ford Motor Company, his third entrepreneurial venture. He had learned the hard way that his financial backers could otherwise thwart his entrepreneurial vision in favor of a safer return on investment. In two previous ventures, co-investors refused to defer to Ford's judgment and insisted that he move from development into production before he was ready to do so. By establishing uncontested control of the Ford Motor Company, Ford was able to take the time necessary to develop a revolutionary assembly line process and the design

(2007)); Harold Demsetz & Kenneth Lehn, *The Structure of Corporate Ownership: Causes and Consequences*, 93 J. POL. ECON. 1155, 1159 (1985).

19 *See* Demsetz & Lehn, *supra* note 18, at 1162 (observing that certain firms have a higher "amenity potential" than others: "Winning the World Series or believing that one is systematically influencing public opinion plausibly provides utility to some owners even if profit is reduced from levels otherwise achievable.").

20 Gilson, *supra* note 2, at 1664.

21 *See* Goshen & Hamdani, *supra* note 9, at 617.

22 Although controlling owners would prefer to capture all the economic returns from their labor, the presence of outside investors may be unavoidable if the founders lack sufficient capital and cannot accomplish their entrepreneurial vision without taking on additional equity owners.

for the Model T automobile.[23] His vision paid off handsomely, and the Ford Motor Company became one of the world's most successful companies.

More recently, when Google offered shares to the public, it used a dual-voting structure to preserve the control of its founders, Sergey Brin and Larry Page, as well as its chairman, Eric Schmidt. In a disclosure required by securities law, Google explained that control was necessary to protect the entrepreneurial vision of its founders:

> We are creating a corporate structure that is designed for stability over long time horizons. By investing in Google, you are placing an unusual long-term bet on the team … and on our innovative approach.
>
> We want Google to become an important and significant institution. That takes time, stability and independence. We bridge the media and technology industries, both of which have experienced considerable consolidation and attempted hostile takeovers.
>
> In the transition to public ownership, we have set up a corporate structure that will make it harder for outside parties to take over or influence Google. This structure will also make it easier for our management team to follow [a] long term, innovative approach ….
>
> The main effect of this structure is likely to leave our team … with significant control over the company's decisions and fate, as Google shares change hands. New investors will fully share in Google's long term growth but will have less influence over its strategic decisions than they would at most public companies.[24]

Goshen and Hamdani do not purport to demonstrate that private benefits are irrelevant to the question of control.[25] Rather, they argue that there is a strong, alternative explanation – "control allows entrepreneurs to pursue business strategies that they believe will produce above-market returns by securing the ability to implement their vision in the manner they see fit."[26]

Perhaps the most significant limitation of Goshen and Hamdani's theory is that it provides a useful explanation for control only so long as the controlling owners can be said to have a distinctive entrepreneurial vision. Yet, most controlled businesses have no mechanism for transitioning toward a widely

[23] For a fuller account, see M. Todd Henderson, *Everything Old Is New Again: Lessons from* Dodge v. Ford Motor Company, *in* Corporate Law Stories 37 (J. Mark Ramseyer ed., 2009).

[24] Google, Inc., Registration Statement (Form S-1) (Apr. 29, 2004), https://tinyurl.com/5fvr3k44.

[25] Goshen & Hamdani, *supra* note 9, at 576 ("We do not argue that control offers no private benefits …. Nor do we rule out the possibility that … private benefits will motivate some controllers to hold a control block.").

[26] *Id.* at 565.

dispersed model.[27] An investor who accepted Google's justification regarding the value of controlled ownership might still be concerned about Google's lack of concrete plans for an eventual succession of control.

For this reason, some commentators have argued that insider control achieved via dual-stock classification should be subject to time limits of no more than ten or fifteen years unless reapproved by independent directors.[28] Consistent with this argument, at least one company has adopted a sunset provision premised on the diminishing value of insider control once the distinctive entrepreneurial vision of the founder is no longer a factor. Facebook (now Meta) adjusted its corporate structure to provide for a transition to widely dispersed ownership when Facebook's founder, Mark Zuckerberg, steps away from an active role in management:

> [T]he new automatic conversion triggers … provide for the unwinding of the multi-class stock structure and the relinquishment of Mr. Zuckerberg's majority voting control of us in certain circumstances …. The Special Committee and the board of directors believe that without these new terms (i.e., if Mr. Zuckerberg or his descendants could maintain majority voting control indefinitely after he is no longer in a leadership role at the company, which is currently the case), it could be exceedingly difficult to attract and retain a high-quality replacement for Mr. Zuckerberg. These new terms thus ensure that we will not remain a founder-controlled company after we cease to be a founder-led company.[29]

While Facebook continues to value Zuckerberg's leadership, just as Google relies upon its founders, Facebook's structure guarantees that Zuckerberg cannot transition control to a family heir. Facebook's time-limited approach to control is appropriate assuming that the justification for control depends on the founder's idiosyncratic entrepreneurial vision. Investors are invited to surrender voting protections ordinarily applicable to a publicly traded corporation in order to gain the alleged benefits of the founder's entrepreneurial vision. In doing so, however, they are not asked to accept the vicissitudes of permanent family ownership.[30]

[27] *See* Steven Davidoff Solomon, *Lessons from the Viacom Dispute*, N.Y. TIMES, Aug. 22, 2016 (arguing that "[a] public corporation is not necessarily a family business to be run forever by that founder and his family. And putting an expiration date on dual-class stock to the extent it is used may be prudent. Other companies should consider such a mechanism, and prospective shareholders should consider demanding it before they invest.").

[28] *See* Lucian A. Bebchuk & Kobi Kastiel, *The Untenable Case for Perpetual Dual-Class Stock*, 103 VA. L. REV. 585 (2017).

[29] Facebook, Inc., Proxy Statement Pursuant to Section 14(a) of the Securities Exchange Act of 1934 (Schedule 14(a)) (June 2, 2016) (Mitigating Succession Risk), 62, https://tinyurl.com/yc3ha68k.

[30] *See* Bebchuk & Kastiel, *supra* note 28, at 590 (stating that "as time passes, the potential costs of a dual-class structure tend to increase while the potential benefits tend to erode").

9.3 STEWARDSHIP

So far, I have canvassed several law and finance explanations for control: expropriation of private financial benefits, access to the perquisites of control, and idiosyncratic entrepreneurial vision. Yet, financial explanations do not fully account for the motivations of controlling owners, especially in family businesses. What is missing is stewardship – the sense that control comes with obligations, to the business, to one's own family, employees, and community.

Financial explanations of behavior presume that self-interest alone is what counts – hence the widely accepted view that the greater costs and risks borne by controlling owners must be compensated for with private benefits. Even Goshen and Hamdani accept that founders pursue an entrepreneurial vision because they believe, rightly or wrongly, that they will be able to maximize the value of the business.[31] But when individuals are part of institutions they have reason to care about, they do not necessarily make choices based solely on self-interest.[32] Indeed, there is evidence that family owners sometimes engage in "propping" behavior – devoting their own resources to sustain the viability of a business in a downturn, although the benefit of that investment will be shared with public investors.[33]

The expectation of stewardship may explain the appeal of controlled companies to outside investors, notwithstanding the concerns raised by law and finance scholars. As one commentator explained:

> If you buy New York Times stock, you are buying into the notion that you'll let the family run the show, as it has done for more than a century. And the Sulzbergers will put The Times's journalism ahead of all else, because that is what is in the family's DNA.[34]

Notably, stewardship implies a long-term relationship. Unlike Facebook, most controlled companies do plan for a succession of control from

[31] *See* Goshen & Hamdani, *supra* note 9, at 617.

[32] *See, e.g.*, Joe Nocera, Opinion, *How Punch Protected* The Times, N.Y. TIMES, Oct. 1, 2012 ("As many other well-known newspaper families have abandoned the business – most recently, the Bancrofts of Dow Jones and The Wall Street Journal – the Sulzbergers have remained steadfast in their belief that they were put on this earth to preserve and protect The New York Times.").

[33] *See* Belen Villalonga & Raphael Amit, *Family Control of Firms and Industries*, 39 FIN. MGMT. 863, 865 (Autumn 2010) ("[C]ontrolling shareholders, such as families, may use their private funds to 'prop up' (i.e., provide temporary support) to financially troubled firms, thereby benefiting minority shareholders in these companies.").

[34] Nocera, *supra* note 32.

generation to generation.[35] For this reason, the owners typically see themselves as stewards of the business enterprise, "which comes to satisfy their needs both for security, as well as for social contributions, sharing, belonging, and even standing within the family."[36] According to one recent study, public corporations run by their founders or by family owners reflect the values of their controlling owners.[37] The founders and family owners state that they are more inclined to give weight to the interests of all stakeholders.[38]

Stewardship can affect business strategy in several important respects. First, because family business owners tend to take a longer-term view, they may prioritize sustainability over profits. Family owners "exhibit much care about continuity, community and connection: specifically, about the long term preservation and nurturing of their business and its markets."[39] Other types of entrepreneurs are more likely to adopt "strategies of rapid growth through quick expansion rather than more gradual means such as substantive innovation, social contribution or reputation building."[40]

Second, family business owners often seek "to 'enlarge' the family concept sufficiently" to encompass workers and other important stakeholders.[41] The desire to include others within the family's ambit may reflect a perceived ethical obligation but also can strengthen the business. For example, family business owners engender loyalty by protecting workers even when it would be economically rational to engage in layoffs and outsourcing to

35 *See* Marianne Bertrand & Antoinette Schoar, *The Role of Family in Family Firms*, 20 J. ECON. PERSP. 73, 74 (2006).

36 Danny Miller et al., *Stewardship vs. Stagnation: An Empirical Comparison of Small Family and Non-family Businesses*, 45 J. MGMT. STUD. 51, 52 (2008); Donella Caspersz, *CEO Resilience in Family Firms in Times of Crisis*, 38 FAM. BUS. REV. 58, 59 (2025) (stating that the potential benefits of family involvement "include a commitment to stewardship to retain the business across generations and non-financial socioemotional wealth (SEW) or 'affective endowments' of the family that stems from family relations, networks, and ties") (citations omitted).

37 *See* William Mullins & Antoinette Schoar, *How Do CEOs See Their Roles? Management Philosophies and Styles in Family and Non-family Firms*, 119 J. FIN. ECON. 24 (2015) (reporting results of survey of more than 800 CEOs).

38 *Id.*

39 Miller et al., *supra* note 36, at 73; Danny Miller et al., *Family Ownership and Acquisition Behavior in Publicly-Traded Companies*, 31 STRATEGIC MGMT. J. 201, 202 (2010) ("[F]amily owners, preoccupied with corporate longevity, are said to pursue strategies of 'continuity' that avoid potentially destabilizing acquisitions and build enduring relationships with stakeholders inside and outside the firm to sustain the business and reduce risk." (citations omitted)).

40 Miller et al., *supra* note 36, at 54.

41 Andrea Colli, *Risk, Uncertainty, and Family Ownership*, *in* THE ENDURANCE OF FAMILY BUSINESSES: A GLOBAL OVERVIEW 104 (Paloma Fernández Pérez & Andrea Colli eds., 2013).

reduce labor costs.[42] In the short term, these commitments may come at the expense of profitability.[43] However, while corporate generosity might reduce revenue, the good will engendered gives family-controlled businesses better odds of weathering unforeseen challenges.[44] The decision by family owners "[t]o share some benefits [is] thus a way of safeguarding the survival of the company, as well as of enhancing the standing of the family within the community."[45]

Third, because of their identification with the business, family owners may be more willing than nonfamily owners to accept personal financial risk: "[T]he owners and managers of family businesses have an unusual amount at stake because of the deep connections between the family and the business."[46] In this respect, stewardship theory suggests that the family owners' commitment to the business may be stronger than economic analysis would otherwise predict.[47]

For example, Doug Corwin, the owner of a duck farm, is working to reopen the business after bird flu required the culling of all 100,000 ducks in January 2025.[48] The farm was established by his great-grandfather, and the land has been in the family since the 1640s. Although he had to lay off most of his employees, "his sister and niece, his brother and brother-in-law, and his son Pierce all work on the farm."[49] Even though it would be easier to quit, Mr. Corwin is resolved to do what it takes to restore the farm:

42 Timothy G. Habbershon & Mary L. Williams, *A Resource-Based Framework for Assessing the Strategic Advantages of Family Firms*, 12 FAM. BUS. REV. 1, 22, 24 (1999) ("Family firms have been described as having a unique working environment that fosters a family-oriented workplace and inspires greater employee care and loyalty."). For a case study, see BETH MACY, FACTORY MAN: HOW ONE FURNITURE MAKER BATTLED OFFSHORING, STAYED LOCAL – AND HELPED SAVE AN AMERICAN TOWN (2014).

43 *See* Pascual Berrone et al., *Family-Controlled Firms and Stakeholder Management: A Socioemotional Wealth Preservation Perspective*, *in* THE SAGE HANDBOOK OF FAMILY BUSINESS 179, 191 (Leif Melin et al. eds., 2014).

44 Colli, *supra* note 41, at 103; Berrone et al., *supra* note 43, at 191. To this end, family leaders may also "nurture employees who contribute to corporate health by creating a community culture populated by motivated, well-trained and loyal staff" and "create strong connections with outside stakeholders, especially customers who can sustain the business in times of trouble." Miller et al., *supra* note 36, at 52.

45 Colli, *supra* note 41, at 103.

46 Miller et al., *supra* note 36, at 51. *See generally* James H. Davis et al., *Toward a Stewardship Theory of Management*, 22 ACAD. MGMT. REV. 20 (1997) (distinguishing stewardship from other theories of managerial behavior).

47 Colli, *supra* note 41 (arguing that family owners "are often not acting on the basis of personal self-interest, but for the benefit of the organization and of its stakeholders").

48 *See* Chris Crowley, *Bird Flu Wiped Out His Entire Farm*, NEW YORK, Feb. 24, 2025.

49 *Id.*

> The USDA will apparently compensate the farm with $500,000, he estimates, for ducks he says were worth $1.5 million. He guesses he's spending $40,000 a week cleaning the farm and couldn't make any income until October 2026. After that, if there's another outbreak, he says he'll throw in the towel. But for now, he plans to keep going. "I'd be richer if I said 'Fuck it,' got a big concrete-crusher, brought in some equipment, tore this place apart, and marketed it as real estate," he says. "But I don't care about being the richest person. I like growing ducks."[50]

According to conventional wisdom, insider control of businesses is detrimental to the interests of noncontrolling investors. Family-run businesses, in particular, are seen as nepotistic and inefficient. Although commentators identify potential downsides of insider control, they overlook the significant benefits that controlled companies can offer. Notably, controlled companies can soften the harder edges of capitalism by bringing the values of controlling owners into the marketplace.[51] Unlike the managers of public corporations with widely dispersed shareholders, controlling owners have a personal stake that gives them reason to identify with their business and to care about its long-term success. A stewardship model signals commitment to other investors while also potentially benefiting employees, customers, and communities.

A news article entitled "Family Hands Off Its Business, and Its Philosophy" provides an interesting illustration of a closely held business that is, for its owners, more than an opportunity to make money.[52] The third-generation, self-described liberal owners of a family scrap metal company were reluctant to hand over the reins of their business to local managers who were politically conservative and perceived to be less worldly. The family views the business as an important part of the community with a philanthropic mission in addition to making money. So concerned were the owners over the future "soul" of the business, that they have – according to the *Times* – required their managers to read Thoreau, Sophocles, and Freud, and to attend cultural events, including a Shakespeare play. They have also provided each

[50] *Id.*

[51] One scholar argues that the standard narrative of impersonal public corporation should be replaced with a "more honest narrative" that would encourage "businesses to better reimagine and reengage with an uncertain world filled with complicated, interdependent shareholders and stakeholders." Tom C. W. Lin, *The New Corporate Political Governance*, 65 B.C. L. Rev. 833, 876 (2024) (citing Rebecca Henderson, Reimagining Capitalism in a World on Fire (2020)).

[52] *See* Jeff Bailey, *Family Hands Off Its Business, and Its Philosophy*, N.Y. Times, Feb. 24, 2007, at A1.

manager with a subscription to the Sunday *New York Times*. These are matters of, at most, indirect relevance to the effective management of a scrap metal company, and a family owner who was not involved in the business might not understand or approve. Precisely because the goals of shareholders in a close corporation are not always identical to the profit motive of investors in a public corporation, it is very helpful to make sure that all shareholders are included in forming and sustaining corporate values.

9.4 THE ROLE OF MARKETS

Family owners can provide effective stewardship, or they can fail to do so. Either way, the answer should be clear. Unlike inherited aristocratic privileges that are immune to challenge, the market mechanism itself provides a neutral test of merit. For a family business to survive, it must actually be the case that "family processes contribute to the efficient and effective functioning of the company."[53] Notably, very few family businesses continue into a second generation, let alone a third or fourth.[54] Thus, by rewarding merit, well-regulated markets can help to ensure that successful family businesses avoid the worst sorts of nepotistic abuses and that they contribute to society.

9.4.1 *How Markets Discipline Businesses*

In a family business, the concerns of family must be balanced against the demands of the marketplace. Properly harnessed, the discipline imposed by the marketplace provides a useful if imperfect mechanism for ensuring a sensible distribution of societal resources. The mechanism is imperfect because market outputs reflect inputs; if certain individuals or groups inherit unwarranted advantages, the state may be justified in undertaking redistributive measures.

Nevertheless, to the extent family owners internalize the consequences of their choices, they have a strong incentive to avoid unwise hiring and promotion decisions.[55] Over time, market pressures may cause family business

53 Harvey S. James, Jr., *What Can the Family Contribute to Business? Examining Contractual Relationships*, 12 FAM. BUS. REV. 61, 61 (1999).

54 *See* Michael Gilding, *Families and Fortunes: Accumulation, Management, Succession, and Inheritance in Wealthy Families*, 41 J. SOC. 29 (2005). For analysis of long-lived family businesses, see DENNIS T. JAFFE, RESILIENCE OF 100-YEAR FAMILY ENTERPRISES (2018).

55 On the other hand, family owners will want to avoid causing family dissension, and choices made to satisfy a family's expectation of equitable treatment may create business problems. *See* Ivan S. Lansberg, *Managing Human Resources in Family Firms: The Problem of Institutional Overlap*, 12 ORG. DYNAMICS 39, 41 (1983) ("Founders often find themselves in the difficult

enterprises to transition away from family control in order to raise capital or to benefit from highly skilled, professional management.[56] In any case, only a small fraction of family firms survive long enough to count as dynasties, and, from the standpoint of social equality, "shirtsleeves to shirtsleeves in three generations" may be more of a blessing than a curse.[57]

In light of market constraints, it should be unsurprising that many family businesses adopt hiring policies that require family members to develop adequate credentials in terms of education and experience before consideration for a position with the family business. Likewise, a business might require new employees to start on the proverbial shop room floor before moving into managerial positions.

In his novel *Gain* Richard Powers describes the implementation of a strict apprenticeship in a family-owned soap factory:[58]

> Though born to run the firm, Douglas Clare … came up through the ranks. While still a child, he cleaned and swept his father's offices. Learning to write, he spent a year as a copyist. At thirteen, he drove a horse-drawn dray back and forth between Roxbury and the Boston docks. Later, he shoveled rosin at the factory for his Uncle Resolve, eleven hours a day …. Douglas's patrimony was never in doubt. But the distance he traveled, from shoveler to president, never failed to impress those he did business with. Inside the firm and out, he emanated an authority grounded on calluses.[59]

Whether the heir apparent begins at the bottom, as in the fictional Clare Inc., or at a lower-level managerial position, familiarity with the business and establishment of merit seem essential as a precondition to effective leadership.[60]

situation of having to choose between either hiring (or firing) an incompetent relative or breaking up their relationship with some part of the family.").

56 *See* CHANDLER, *supra* note 1, at 335 (arguing that continued family ownership harmed "British organizational capabilities" and led those firms to underperform when compared to American rivals). However, some scholars argue that family businesses, in a variety of settings, can outperform nonfamily businesses. For present purposes, the answer is less important than the existence of a market mechanism capable of producing an answer.

57 George Stark & Henry Foley, *Avoid the Traps that Can Destroy Family Businesses*, HARV. BUS. REV. 25, 25 (Jan.–Feb. 2012) (citing "familiar aphorism").

58 RICHARD POWERS, GAIN (1998) (tracing the fortunes of several generations of the fictional Clare family and the soap company that they establish as a private partnership, later incorporate, and eventually take public).

59 *Id.* at 247.

60 *See* Galen Moore, *Market Basket List: 11 Management Tips from "Artie T.,"* BOSTON BUS. J. (Oct. 9, 2013, 8:25 AM), https://tinyurl.com/y5ehj4df (describing how a CEO seemed to know each of his employees and also "knew intimate details of the 138,000-square-foot store – like the price of a special, the length of the chicken case (at 84 feet, a yacht among refrigerators)

When the expectations of family life conflict with business needs, some accommodation must be reached if the business is to remain viable.[61] In one case, an uncle's dislike for his nephew undermined the potential for a smooth transition of control and led the nephew to found a competing business, taking with him key customers and employees.[62] Ironically, a clearer commitment to continued family ownership might have saved the business by assuring the nephew that he would eventually assume control.[63] Instead, the uncle warned his nephew that the nephew's right to inherit the business would depend upon whether the uncle or his brother, the nephew's father, lived longer.[64] Evidently, the uncle intended to fire his nephew at the first opportunity, and the nephew's incentives altered accordingly.[65]

Market considerations also apply when a business transitions from one generation to the next, because the older generation needs to find an economic exit strategy. If the business is to stay in the family, that means the capital demands of the retiring generation must be in keeping with what the business can afford to pay. There are, of course, many insurance and tax strategies for managing these transitions.[66] For present purposes, it is enough to observe that continued family ownership is possible only if each generation can generate sufficient profits through the business for a succession strategy to work.[67]

and the weekly revenue from a new kind of snack-food display piloted there"). As the CEO explained: "Dad taught us, God rest his soul, my dad Mike Demoulas, you know, he carried a notebook and a pad of paper and a pencil, and you walk around the store – just what we're going to do. We're going to talk to customers, talk to our great associates here and make a note of things that happen and you follow up on it." *Id.*

61 *See* MANFRED F. R. KETS DE VRIES ET AL., FAMILY BUSINESS ON THE COUCH: A PSYCHOLOGICAL PERSPECTIVE 25 (2007) ("Unresolved personal conflicts, lack of trust, difficult interpersonal relationships, sibling rivalry, generational issues, the family's demands on the business – any or all of these issues can affect a family firm's success.").

62 *See* Hamburger v. Hamburger, 1995 WL 579679 (Super. Ct., Mass., 1995) (included in CHARLES O'KELLEY ET AL., CORPORATIONS AND OTHER BUSINESS ASSOCIATIONS: CASES AND MATERIALS (6th ed. 2010)).

63 Moreover, as a matter of equity, the child who had done the work building the business would seem to have a legitimate claim as against outsiders, even meritorious outsiders.

64 *See Hamburger*, 1995 WL 579679, at *1.

65 *See id.*

66 Several tax provisions are also designed to "protect family businesses from forced sales." Lily L. Batchelder, *What Should Society Expect from Heirs? The Case for a Comprehensive Inheritance Tax*, 63 TAX. L. REV. 1, 57 (2009).

67 MARK RUSS FEDERMAN, RUSS & DAUGHTERS: REFLECTIONS AND RECIPES FROM THE HOUSE THAT HERRING BUILT 87 (2013) ("Contrary to what most people assume, I didn't simply 'inherit' Russ & Daughters. After years of working six days a week, ten hours a day, I earned the right to buy the business from the preceding generation of Russes."). The parents "actually seemed relieved; they had no other exit plan." *Id.* at 69. And, in turn, the third

When a family falters, the markets will wrest control away, one way or another. For example, if a family business squanders its capital, it will need to obtain more, either by taking on debt or bringing in equity investors.[68] In either case, the contributors of capital will take steps to protect their investment, thereby diminishing the benefits of family control.[69] Unless there are barriers to entry that permit undue market power, kinship preferences within an organization do not preclude others from establishing competing firms: "[D]eveloping a business ... may require only that one learn the relevant skill, obtain some capital, and find willing customers; no particular decision-maker or small set of decision-makers has authority over the question of who can pursue that path."[70] A business that fails to make room for outside talent may be forced to compete with it.

9.4.2 *The Competitiveness of Family Businesses*

Conventional wisdom once held that family businesses were nothing more than a first step on the path toward professional management.[71] In a family business, "policy and direction are subject to significant influence by one or more family units through ownership and sometimes through the participation of family members in management."[72] In a nonfamily business, by contrast, the "managers and key decision makers come from the professional labor market rather than the family."[73] The distinction is often significant. Even though they are governed by the same formal legal rules, "[f]amily firms differ from nonfamily businesses in that the norms, principles, and obligations of the family overlap with those of the business."[74]

For several reasons, scholars have long considered family to be a relatively undesirable form of economic organization. First, when other

generation has sold the business to the fourth: "In the Russ family, every generation inherits the right to buy out the preceding generation." *Id.* at 73.

68 Ronald J. Gilson, *Controlling Shareholders and Corporate Governance: Complicating the Comparative Taxonomy*, 119 HARV. L. REV. 1641, 1677 (2006) (noting that for poorly managed businesses, "internally generated funds will be insufficient, requiring recourse to the capital market").

69 *Id.* ("[E]xternal suppliers of debt or equity can be expected to insist on a means to dissipate the controlling shareholder's influence if poor performance threatens the new investment.").

70 JOSEPH FISHKIN, BOTTLENECKS: A NEW THEORY OF EQUAL OPPORTUNITY 130 (2014).

71 *See* DAVID S. LANDES, DYNASTIES xii (2006) ("[T]he current economic orthodoxy sees family enterprise as inappropriate, ineffective, and essentially finished as a major economic engine ....").

72 Peter Davis, *Realizing the Potential of the Family Business*, 12 ORG. DYNAMICS 47, 47 (1983).

73 James, *supra* note 53, at 61.

74 *Id.*

stakeholders are involved, there is reason to worry that family owners will find ways to benefit from control, putting family interests ahead of the business.[75] Second, if managerial leadership must be drawn from the family's ranks, the talent pool may be too thin to replicate the successes of a first-generation entrepreneur.[76] Third, in seeking to placate family concerns, business leaders may fail to maximize profits.[77] Finally, if a family ethos becomes associated with a particular way of doing business, the family may find it difficult to innovate.[78]

However, empirical investigations suggest that these concerns are overstated and often invalid: "Much research concludes that family businesses not only last longer, but drive greater profits than their non-family counterparts."[79] Studies have shown that family ownership can produce significant value, especially in founder-managed companies.[80] If family members are loyal to each other and appreciative of the business, they may work harder and take a flexible view of their role, contributing financial and human resources where needed. From an early age, family members have an opportunity to learn how the business works and to develop expertise that an outside manager could not hope to match.[81] Thus, a business embedded in a family system can leverage family support to lower the cost of capital and labor, thereby producing goods and services more efficiently.[82] Also, in industries where personal connections matter, there is often no effective substitute for the credibility that family ownership provides. Family businesses may seek to capitalize on their perceived virtues, advertising family

75 *See* Belen Villalonga & Raphael Amit, *How Do Family Ownership, Control, and Management Affect Firm Value?*, 80 J. FIN. ECON. 385, 387 (2006) ("The large shareholder may use its controlling position in the firm to extract private benefits at the expense of the small shareholders.").

76 *See* Jon I. Martinez et al., *Family Ownership and Firm Performance: Evidence from Public Companies in Chile*, 20 FAM. BUS. REV. 83, 93 (2007) (arguing that managerial professionalization helps family firms to achieve success).

77 *See* Lansberg, *supra* note 55, at 41.

78 *See* Sharon Belenzon et al., *Married to the Firm? A Large Scale Investigation of the Social Context of Ownership*, 37 STRATEGIC MGMT. J. 2611 (Dec. 2016).

79 AMY SCHUMAN ET AL., FAMILY BUSINESS AS PARADOX 2 (2010).

80 *See, e.g.*, Villalonga & Amit, *supra* note 75.

81 *See* Khai Sheang Lee et al., *Family Business Succession: Appropriation Risk and Choice of Successor*, 28 ACAD. MGMT. REV. 657, 658 (2003) (noting that family businesses often depend on "personal business contacts and networks" that an outsider to the business will have difficulty accessing).

82 *See* FRANK H. EASTERBROOK & DANIEL R. FISCHEL, THE ECONOMIC STRUCTURE OF CORPORATE LAW 232 (1991) ("[I]f family-owned ventures reduce the agency costs of management, there will be gains for all to share.").

stewardship as a signal of quality and trustworthiness.[83] Finally, family-owned firms may take a longer view of success than their peers, avoiding a counterproductive focus on quarterly returns.[84]

The sheer prevalence of family businesses should count as some evidence of their fitness. Otherwise, the continuation of a defective, fundamentally flawed institution would be hard to explain, at least in a society that has stable legal and market institutions to support business dealings among strangers as well as kin.[85] In such a legal environment, kinship-based business arrangements are a choice rather than a necessity. From the standpoint of economically rational choice, an investment in a family business makes sense only if other available investments do not present a better value.[86]

Admittedly, some of the claims made in favor of the competitiveness of family firms have been too anecdotal. Even if family businesses outperform their peers, as a general proposition, it is still important to understand whether family attributes matter and, if so, in what contexts and in what ways.[87] Analytic methodologies vary, in part, because family businesses have been studied by "[s]cholars trained in psychology, sociology, law, accounting, economics, organizational behavior, strategic management, entrepreneurship, and numerous other disciplines."[88] Empirical studies have begun to address

[83] *See* Isabel C. Botero et al., *Understanding Multiple Family Firm Identities: An Exploration of the Communicated Identity in Official Websites*, 4 J. Fam. Bus. Strategy 12 (2013); Ulrich R. Orth & Mark T. Green, *Consumer Loyalty to Family Versus Non-family Business: The Roles of Store Image, Trust and Satisfaction*, 16 J. Retailing & Consumer Servs. 248 (2009); Marylyn Carrigan & Joan Buckley, *What Is So Special About Family Business? An Exploratory Study of UK and Irish Consumer Experiences of Family Businesses*, 32 Int'l J. Consumer Studies 656 (2008).

[84] *See* Lawrence A. Cunningham, Berkshire Beyond Buffet: The Enduring Value of Values (2014) (describing how the legendary investor Warren Buffet likes to acquire family businesses whose owners have adopted a long-term perspective).

[85] *See* Adam Bellow, In Praise of Nepotism: A Natural History 469 (2003) ("[W]hile nepotism may indeed shelter some incompetent family members from the consequences of their failures, the record of family contributions to the history of capitalism has been overwhelmingly positive. If this hadn't been true, the American economy would be a basket case instead of a thriving engine of prosperity.").

[86] *See* Easterbrook & Fischel, *supra* note 82, at 231 ("Each organizational form presents its own problems, for which people have designed different mechanisms of control. At the margin the problems must be equally severe, the mechanisms equally effective – were it otherwise, investors would transfer their money from one form to the other until the marginal equality condition was satisfied.").

[87] Habbershon & Williams, *supra* note 42, at 5–6 (arguing that "generalizations beg certain questions – for instance, What family firms have advantages and when? How long do these advantages endure? Are they the result of internal or external factors? Under what conditions do family firms have an advantage?").

[88] *Id.* at 1–2.

these methodological concerns, for instance by distinguishing public corporations from smaller, closely held businesses.[89] In sum, not only are family businesses "the dominant form of organization in the world" but "largely negative portrayals" of their performance "do not seem to hold up."[90] Instead, "recent research … shows [family-owned businesses] outperform and outsurvive most companies."[91]

To the extent family businesses contribute to aggregate social welfare by boosting economic productivity, creating jobs, and benefiting consumers, legitimate worries about the distributive implications of family businesses should take into account their economic value. As discussed in the next section, the relevance of a market test depends upon whether the markets in question are fully competitive.

9.4.3 *Regulating Markets*

Markets depend upon legal rules to function properly. At the most basic level, that means a reliable method of identifying property rights and a court system capable of enforcing contractual claims. In addition, as this section describes, competitive markets may depend upon the regulatory structure of securities law, antitrust law, and licensing provisions. In some cases, legal rules can undermine market competition, and this section identifies potential problem areas involving family businesses, including protectionist set asides for particular industries and excessively generous tax exemptions for intrafamilial transfers.

9.4.3.1 Protecting Competition

The competitive environment family businesses must negotiate depends upon a number of overlapping bodies of business law. Taken together, securities law, antitrust law, and, where applicable, licensing regulations, limit the ability of family business owners to preserve economic advantages without facing effective competition.

Securities Law. A well-developed market for corporate securities can provide an important test of the competitiveness of family-owned businesses. Even if a family business itself avoids the capital markets, it must be prepared

89 *See, e.g.*, Miller, *supra* note 36, at 52 (observing that concerns about family-firm performance have often involved studies of public corporations to the exclusion of "more representative [family-owned businesses] in which there are multiple family members involved in owning and running the business, and where family ownership is complete or dominant").

90 *Id.* at 73.

91 *Id.*

to compete with other firms that will access public capital to grow. Thus, one author argues that "characteristics of the stock market help to explain how German and U.S. corporate experience began to diverge at the beginning of the twentieth century."[92] German law responded to an agrarian movement resentful of modern capitalism by restricting securities trading; meanwhile, the US began to develop "a securities culture."[93] The result was that German companies relied upon bank financing more than equity markets. By the time the German stock market rules were liberalized, "the damage had been done."[94] Instead of using markets to allocate resources efficiently, "[i]nstitutional arrangements, syndicate agreements, and cartels had been deployed to reorganize German business and had set it on a path where the capital market mattered less."[95] In an environment of business cooperation among a relatively small set of players, family continuity could be more important than efficiency.[96] Consequently, to the extent the past continues to influence the present, the prevalence of family-owned businesses in Germany may be explained by something other than their competitiveness.[97]

Antitrust Law. Laws designed to curb market power also have a role to play in protecting competition so as to test the fitness of family firms. That is, anti-collusion rules facilitate competition and therefore make close-knit, familial relationships among capitalists less important. Once again, Germany provides an interesting counterexample. At the beginning of the twentieth century, "German firms in the great industries began to work out sophisticated ways to cooperate in maintaining market share and profits."[98] While US firms had to comply with the Sherman Antitrust Act of 1890, which prohibits "every contract, combination, or conspiracy in restraint of trade" and any "monopolization, attempted monopolization, or conspiracy or combination to monopolize,"[99] German firms faced no such constraint.[100] Accordingly, "whereas the American story illustrated the emergence of competitive managerial

92 Harold James, Family Capitalism 117 (2006).

93 *Id.* at 118.

94 *Id.*

95 *Id.*

96 *See id.*; *see also* Chandler, *supra* note 1, at 501 (arguing that large, industrial "German firms differed from the American in that the family often continued to have a powerful, even a decisive, say in management").

97 Of course, the history of German corporate law cannot be summarized in a paragraph. For a more detailed review, see Peter Muchlinski, *The Development of German Corporate Law Until 1990: An Historical Reappraisal*, 14 German L.J. 339 (2013).

98 Chandler, *supra* note 1, at 501.

99 15 U.S.C. § 1.

100 Chandler, *supra* note 1, at 501 ("[A]greements between firms as to price, production, and markets were legally enforceable in courts of law.").

capitalism, the German story exemplifies the coming of cooperative managerial capitalism."[101] Although family ownership declined somewhat by the end of the twentieth century, it was still "a significant force" and revealed "the persistence of family ownership in Germany and the impact it has had on accumulated wealth."[102]

Entry Requirements. In addition to legal rules that structure markets, industry-specific licensing requirements create an external merit filter regardless of the family's own predilections. For instance, children can practice law with a family law firm only if they attain the qualifications necessary for admission to law school, graduate in good standing, pass the state's bar examination, and receive and maintain a license from the state. The same could be said of accounting, medicine, and other professions subject to licensing requirements. In certain sub-specialties – say, neurosurgery – the merit filter may be so stringent that family connections among practitioners become more a matter of curiosity than legitimate concern. Of course, licensing requirements create artificial barriers to entry and some argue that informed consumers can make better choices for themselves as to whether to use the provider of a particular service. Even if licensing can help markets to function better by ensuring minimum standards, incumbent businesses have reason to lobby for licensing rules in order to limit competition – in which case, licensing rules could squelch entrepreneurship and create some of the problems that the antitrust rules were designed to prevent. For example, the Institute for Justice Clinic on Entrepreneurship at the University of Chicago Law School has advocated on behalf of food truck vendors whose business is inhibited by regulations that, arguably, do more to insulate established restaurants from competition than to protect public health.[103]

9.4.3.2 Market-Insulating Rules

Sometimes, the law structures markets in ways that seem to undercut the competitive pressures that would otherwise require family businesses to

[101] *Id.*

[102] Caroline Fohlin, *The History of Corporate Ownership and Control in Germany*, *in* A HISTORY OF CORPORATE GOVERNANCE AROUND THE WORLD: FAMILY BUSINESS GROUPS TO PROFESSIONAL MANAGERS 235–36 (Randall K. Morck ed., 2005) (noting that nearly all of the largest German fortunes "derive from family-founded enterprises"). On the other hand, lax enforcement of antitrust rules can reduce the ability of smaller, mom and pop businesses to thrive. For example, large intermediaries may insist on taking too large a share of the profits and make it difficult for small businesses to forge relationships with customers. *See* KATHRYN JUDGE, DIRECT: THE RISE OF THE MIDDLEMAN ECONOMY AND THE POWER OF GOING TO THE SOURCE (2022).

[103] *See* Testimony of Beth Kregor About Proposed Amendments to Chicago Food Truck Legislation (July 19, 2012), https://tinyurl.com/3v87n8us.

create value in order to survive. Market exceptions may be justified on other grounds, but, as this section shows, the slackening of market constraints necessarily reduces our confidence in family businesses and increases our concern that family business wealth may simply reinforce existing inequalities.[104]

Protectionism. The most straightforward examples of market-insulating rules are those that involve the exemption of family businesses from ordinary competition. For example, in *Kotch v. Board of River Port Pilot Commissioners*, the Supreme Court upheld a Louisiana state law that allowed river pilots to restrict access to the profession to relatives and, occasionally, friends.[105]

In *Kotch*, the plaintiffs brought an equal protection challenge to Louisiana's requirement that pilots serve a six-month apprenticeship with a current pilot to receive a certification to pilot seagoing vessels along the stretch of Mississippi river that leads to the port of New Orleans.[106] Although the river boat pilots almost always restricted apprenticeships to kin, the court noted that the "history and practice of pilotage demonstrate that … it is also a highly personalized calling."[107] While acknowledging the nepotism at issue, the court was unwilling to declare the practice unconstitutional.[108] Even the *Kotch* dissent conceded the value of a family business culture while concluding that it violates equal protection for "blood" to be made "the crux of selection."[109]

Whether the Supreme Court was correct that Louisiana had a rational basis for believing that nepotism protected the quality of its river pilots, the

[104] *Cf.* Gilson, *supra* note 68, at 1674 (arguing in the context of inefficient controlling shareholder structures that when markets do not perform their role, there is reason to alter "legal rules and supporting institutions to increase the exposure of control to the market").

[105] Kotch v. Board of River Port Pilot Comm'rs, 330 U.S. 552 (1947).

[106] *Kotch*, 330 U.S. at 558 ("The pilot's job generally requires that he go outside the harbor's entrance in a small boat to meet incoming ships, board them and direct their course from open waters to the port. The same service is performed for vessels leaving the port. Pilots are thus indispensable cogs in the transportation system of every maritime economy.").

[107] *Id.* ("A pilot does not require a formalized technical education so much as a detailed and extremely intimate, almost intuitive, knowledge of the weather, waterways and conformation of the harbor or river which he serves."); *see also* MARK TWAIN, LIFE ON THE MISSISSIPPI (1883).

[108] *Kotch*, 330 U.S. at 563 ("Probably in pilotage more than in any other occupation in the United States the male members of a family follow the same work from generation to generation.") (internal quotation marks and citation omitted).

[109] *Id.* at 566 ("Conceivably the familial system would be the most effective possible scheme for training many kinds of artisans … from the viewpoint of securing the highest degree of skill and competence."). Later courts have distinguished the unique setting of river pilots and have found that similar restrictions are without rational basis and therefore unlawful. *See, e.g.*, Backlund v. Hessen, 104 F.3d 1031 (8th Cir. 1997) (holding that Minnesota fire department violated the Constitution's requirement of equal protection by failing to hire the best qualified applicant in order to hire relatives of current department employees).

Court's holding ensured that the insularity of the profession would not be challenged by external competitors. Also, the nostalgia for family business ownership seems misplaced because of the heavy involvement of the state in regulating the relevant market.[110] In an industry dependent upon public regulation to create a demand for its services, to set fees, and to forestall outside competition, there is no way to know whether the river pilots offer a value commensurate with what they are paid.[111] Moreover, when the law permits families to erect barriers to entry, as in the case of the Louisiana river pilots, worries about the distributional consequences of kinship preferences are heightened.

Likewise, there is reason to worry about corporate farming restrictions enacted in nine states that have limited the ownership of agricultural land to closely held entities and that specially privilege family ownership.[112] According to one commentator, such laws leave "the food consumer … vulnerable to the political machinations of agrarian interest groups."[113] The restrictions could be justified if family businesses are intrinsically valuable and merit extra protection. By contrast, "a large corporation operating without any local owners in a given area may care less about costs it imposes on neighbors in the form of, for example, environmental damage, than firms that are locally owned and operated."[114] However, again, the assumed benefits are locked in by legislation and no longer open to market verification, for instance whether consumers are willing to pay more for the benefit of a family-owned brand.[115]

110 *Kotch*, 330 U.S. at 566 ("[S]omething very worth while largely disappeared from our national life when the once prevalent familial system of conducting manufacturing and mercantile enterprises went out and was replaced by the highly impersonal corporate system for doing business.").

111 Interestingly, one commentator notes that traffic in the New Orleans port has declined sharply since 2008, a decline largely explained by price competition from other ports. The political power of the river pilots and the lack of direct competition for setting prices may have led to overreaching and, perhaps, to a political correction driven by a broader market impact. *See* Jeffrey Kenneth Prattini, Note, *Louisiana's 2004 River Pilot Reform Muddies the Water*, 52 Loy. L. Rev. 369 (2006).

112 *See* Anthony B. Schutz, *Corporate-Farming Measures in a Post-Jones World*, 14 Drake J. Agric. L. 97, 98 (2009). The nature of the family preference varies from state to state. *See id.* at 112 (citing Iowa Code § 9H.1(8)(a) (2007) (requiring that family hold majority of stock); Okla. Stat. tit. XVIII § 951(A)(1), (3) (2009) (creating exception to ten shareholder maximum for family members)).

113 Jim Chen, *The American Ideology*, 48 Vand. L. Rev. 809, 877 (1995).

114 Schutz, *supra* note 112, at 101.

115 It is possible that market failures make it difficult to price the intangible benefits of community or that these values lie outside the market and are worth pursuing. Ultimately, the agricultural laws might be justified, but they have a cost, which is the diminished incentive for family farms to ensure that kinship preferences are defensible on the merits.

The Trust-Fund Loophole. When business founders receive compensation in the form of stock, they do not pay capital gains tax until they sell the stock, as is generally the case with appreciated assets.[116] Moreover, if a founder leaves their stock to heirs rather than selling it, the transfer may qualify for a large estate-tax exemption. Below that threshold, currently 13.61 million dollars per individual, the heirs are not obligated to pay taxes when they receive the stock. Even if the heirs sell the stock later, they can exclude any appreciation of value that occurred between the time of the founder's initial investment and their death – the stock transfers to the heirs at a "stepped-up" basis and only further appreciation is subject to a capital gains tax. Hypothetically, if a founder turned a 100,000-dollar investment into a 10-million-dollar company, none of that appreciation would ever be taxed.[117]

For wealth that exceeds the estate-tax exemption, more sophisticated planning tools include grantor retained annuity trusts, intentionally defective grantor trusts, family limited partnerships, dynasty trusts, and spousal lifetime access trusts, all of which can be used to reduce or eliminate estate and gift tax liability in various circumstances. These strategies exploit tax exemptions and valuation rules. The ability to avoid taxation on business wealth is not a small matter: "Founders' stock – not high executive salaries and bonuses – accounts for a significant part of the growing inequality of wealth in the United States."[118]

As Professor Fleischer explained, defending President Obama's plan to subject inherited wealth to taxation:

> The White House proposal is … efficient …. By taking away the largest incentive to hold on to appreciated assets – the step up in basis at death – the proposal significantly reduces the lock in effect and will improve economic efficiency. In other words, if Junior is not the best person to run the business, taxing the founder's gains at death will make him more likely to sell the business earlier to someone who is.[119]

Some exemptions might nevertheless be warranted to protect the family owners of smaller scale businesses from incurring an unmanageable tax

[116] Victor Fleischer, *Taxing Founders' Stock*, 59 UCLA L. Rev. 60, 62 (2011). For an explanation of how ordinary income can be transformed into capital gains, see *id.* at 64.

[117] *Id.* at 66 ("As it stands, this entrepreneurial wealth is taxed at a low rate or not at all, allowing founders to leave behind a legacy of dynastic wealth subject only to the rather dodgy application of the estate tax.").

[118] *Id.* at 64.

[119] Victor Fleischer, *Echoes of Piketty in Obama Proposal to Address Income Inequality*, N.Y. Times (Jan. 20, 2015), https://tinyurl.com/39bmsfue. *But see* David A. Weisbach, *The Taxation of Carried Interests in Private Equity*, 94 Va. L. Rev. 715, 743 (2008) (arguing that business founders create jobs and economic productivity and should be incentivized to do so).

burden at a time – succession of ownership – that is already highly stressful. However, the continuation of a family business should reflect something other than tax arbitrage.

Dual-Class Stock. Controversy regarding the use of dual-class stock provides another example of legal rules that limit the corrective power of markets.[120] In a typical dual-class stock scenario, founders reserve to themselves a class of stock with enhanced voting rights, ensuring that the founders will always be able to outvote public shareholders.[121] Although not mandated by law, the practice is authorized by state statutes that set the permissible boundaries for stock classification and by national stock exchanges that permit listed firms to have a dual-stock structure.[122]

Dual-class stock is commonly employed in family-owned businesses that have nonfamily equity investors[123] but has also been adopted in more recent public stock offerings by major high-technology companies including Meta and Google. As I argued earlier in this chapter, family control can facilitate stewardship as well as the pursuit of an idiosyncratic entrepreneurial vision. However, because the founders reserve the voting power, among other things, to shut down any unwanted offer to buy the business, the market for corporate control cannot serve as a check on value-diminishing choices that may serve the private interests of the controlling family at the expense of other investors.[124] Nor can shareholders remove directors should the business underperform

[120] *See* Press Release, Elizabeth Warren, US Senator for Massachusetts, Senator Elizabeth Warren Urges NYSE, NASDAQ to Propose Rules Requiring "One Share, One Vote" Structures (June 5, 2013), www.warren.senate.gov/?p=press_release&id=145 ("'If a company goes to the public markets to raise money, long-term ordinary common stock investors – a category that includes directly or indirectly millions of retirees and workers – should be entitled to certain basic rights .... One of the most basic of those rights is one-share-one-vote.'"); *see also* Paul Lee, Note, *Protecting Public Shareholders: The Case of Google's Recapitalization*, 5 Harv. Bus. L. Rev. 281, 282–83 (2015) (describing efforts by institutional investors to force change, either by refusing to invest in companies with dual-listed stock or by lobbying the stock exchanges to exclude such companies). Legal academics have long debated the appropriateness of dual-class stock, *see, e.g.*, Joel Seligman, *Equal Protection in Shareholder Voting Rights: The One Common Share, One Vote Controversy*, 54 Geo. Wash. L. Rev. 687 (1986).

[121] *See* Jeffrey N. Gordon, *Ties That Bind: Dual Class Stock and the Problem of Shareholder Choice*, 76 Cal. L. Rev. 1, 4 (1988). Thus, insiders have voting rights that exceed their cash-flow rights. *See* Paul A. Gompers et al., *Extreme Governance: An Analysis of Dual-Class Firms in the United States*, 23 Rev. Fin. Stud. 1051, 1052 (2010).

[122] Gompers et al., *supra* note 121, at 1052.

[123] *See, e.g.*, *id.*

[124] *See* Deborah A. DeMott, *Guests at the Table?: Independent Directors in Family-Influenced Public Companies*, 33 J. Corp. L. 819, 822 (2008) ("Transactions in control occur only through processes of negotiation and consent, which heightens the importance of governance mechanisms within dual-class firms.").

market expectations. As one commentator observes, "The market for corporate control can force a widely held firm to internalize change; nothing plays a similar role in a controlling shareholder regime save the market mechanism."[125]

In theory, nonfamily investors price in the potential costs of value-reducing choices family owners might make, buying stock at an appropriate discount, and cannot be heard to complain when founders use the control they have bargained for. At the same time, if the justification for dual-class stock is that it insulates a public corporation from short-term market pressures, enabling the corporation to behave more like a family-owned venture, it should be noted that the economic circumstances are not identical. In particular, the family does not fully internalize the costs of decisions that harm the business while benefiting the family's private interests. Costs to the business are socialized among all investors, while the family enjoys the benefits. Kinship preferences may still provide value in businesses that also use a dual-stock structure, but the market context gives us less confidence that the family has the right incentives to make sure this is so.[126]

Religious Exemptions. In *Burwell v. Hobby Lobby Stores, Inc.*,[127] the Supreme Court held that three closely held family businesses could claim protection under the Religious Freedom Restoration Act, because of the religious scruples of their family owners, even though the businesses had been organized as for-profit corporations.[128] The court concluded that "Congress did not discriminate in this way against men and women who wish to run their businesses as for-profit corporations in the manner required by their religious beliefs."[129] The scope of the Court's ruling remains unclear, but it is difficult to imagine circumstances in which a public corporation with a diverse set of shareholders could plausibly assert an objection based on religious identity.[130] Therefore, the *Hobby Lobby* precedent seems to provide

[125] Gilson, *supra* note 68, at 1678.

[126] For discussion of possible solutions to the dual-stock issue, see *id.* at 1676.

[127] Burwell v. Hobby Lobby Stores, Inc., 134 S. Ct. 2751, 2759 (2014).

[128] *See id.* The court concluded that "Congress did not discriminate in this way against men and women who wish to run their businesses as for-profit corporations in the manner required by their religious beliefs." *Id.* However, the court did not state explicitly whether other kinds of for-profit corporations might be eligible under RFRA (Religious Freedom Restoration Act of 1993, Pub. L. No. 103-141, 107 Stat. 1488 (codified at 42 U.S.C.§§ 2000bb – 2000bb-4.).

[129] *Id.* The court observed that "[a] corporation is simply a form of organization used by human beings to achieve desired ends." *Id.* at 2768. However, since corporations have a separate existence at law and individual shareholders are not ordinarily exposed to liability for the debts of the corporation, it is not clear why the court thought that the corporate artifice should be ignored in this context but not others.

[130] *Id.* at 2774 ("These cases … do not involve publicly traded corporations, and it seems unlikely that … corporate … will often assert RFRA claims."). Apart from assertions of religious identity,

special competitive advantages to closely held businesses owned by religiously observant families, because those businesses can assert a religious objection to compliance with costly regulations if the regulations encroach upon the families' sincerely held religious beliefs.

As the preceding analysis illustrates, the presence or absence of market constraints matters; when multigenerational family businesses succeed in a competitive market, concerns about inequality may be muted, not because the family heirs fully deserve their advantages, but because the family's wealth can be tied to measurable, ongoing achievement. In this regard, it is notable that family business dynasties are rare and even great fortunes dissipate.[131] Indeed, the well-known pitfalls of family succession pose a challenge that motivates a prodigious academic literature focused on the management of family-owned businesses.[132] From a different perspective, though, the limited lifespan of most family businesses may be a feature rather than a bug. If unfortunate for the families involved, business failures can be viewed, from a broader perspective, as an appropriate limitation of family control.[133]

9.5 CASE STUDY: INMAN MILLS

An example may help clarify the distinction between stewardship and other explanations for insider control. Inman Mills is a fifth-generation family-owned business that has been weaving fabric in Spartanburg County for nearly 125 years. It is a notable survivor in a US textile industry decimated by price pressure from global competitors, especially in the wake of free trade agreements in the late 1990s. Unlike many other US textile mills that closed their doors or outsourced production, Inman Mills took business risks to protect its

however, there is no question that corporations of all sizes have become enmeshed in social policy debates that are, at most, indirectly related to the pursuit of profits for their shareholders. *See* Tom C. W. Lin, *Incorporating Social Activism*, 98 B. U. L. REV. 1535 (2021).

131 For instance, one commentator repeats "[t]he lament of the ancient Jewish retailer: 'The first generation founds the business, the second generation builds the business, and the third generation kills the business.'" FEDERMAN, *supra* note 67, at 199. In any case, the relatively small number of family-owned mega-firms have little to do with the local "bakeries and barbecue joints, funeral homes and furniture builders, cheesemakers, fishermen, [and] ferry boat drivers," *see* CARL COREY, FOR LOVE AND MONEY: PORTRAITS OF WISCONSIN FAMILY BUSINESSES 48 (2014), that may be more typical of family enterprise.

132 *See* FRED NEUBAUER & ALDEN G. LANK, THE FAMILY BUSINESS: ITS GOVERNANCE FOR SUSTAINABILITY 17 (1998) (stating that problems in "managing the process of ownership and management succession" are "the single most important reason for the fragility of family enterprises").

133 *See, e.g.*, Kerry A. Dolan, *How to Blow $9 Billion: The Fallen Stroh Family*, FORBES MAG., July 8, 2014, at 74–77.

customers and its community. To stay in business while staying local, Inman Mills pursued a strategy of reinvention and focused on specialized technical fabrics, such as flame-resistant materials. Inman Mills also acquired licenses to manufacture military fabrics that must be produced domestically. Those investments paid off. Today, Inman Mills employs several hundred people and operates three facilities. As Inman Mills illustrates, it is possible to run a successful business – even in challenging circumstances – without putting profits above every other consideration.

Family-Ownership Structure. In 1901, James A. Chapman raised 150,000 dollars to establish Inman Mills, leaving the practice of law to pursue an entrepreneurial venture. The corporation has been in family hands ever since. The family is represented both on the board of directors and in operations. Family control provides more freedom to experiment and take risks than is typical in a corporate setting. One aspect of this freedom is flexibility in job descriptions. Depending on what is needed, employees can take on new duties without worrying about crossing boundaries on an organizational chart. Also, because the family answers only to itself and not to public shareholders, Inman Mills can adopt a long-term perspective that allows for effective stewardship, rather than worrying about earnings on a quarterly basis.

Although Inman Mills is closely held and accountable only to family shareholders, it has implemented a governance structure to provide meaningful oversight. The shareholders elect the board of directors, offering what fifth-generation owner Ellis Fisher describes as "visibility into the business." The bylaws for the corporation give the board of directors "real power." Board dynamics can be tricky, because there are family and nonfamily members involved, but this approach offers substantial benefits. Without board input, family members might otherwise be "too confident in their license to make the decisions and know what is best because they're on the front lines." The board is designed to ensure that individuals "think critically about the way things are done." The board also oversees hiring and promotion decisions involving members of the controlling family. Ellis emphasizes that "fitting the generational demographic" alone does not guarantee employment with Inman Mills; prospective family members must be valuable and dedicated to the business to earn approval from the board.

The resilience of Inman Mills's governance structure survived a severe test in 2017. At that time, the corporation was in its fourth generation of family ownership and was controlled by two cousins, Rob and Norman Chapman. Norman held the position of President, while Rob managed the roles of Treasurer, CEO, and Chairman of the Board. Both had been with the company for many years. On August 3, 2017, after a decade in private law practice, Ellis Fisher, Rob's son-in-law, was hired to serve as General Counsel. In that capacity, he was responsible for compliance and risk management issues for Inman Mills, including insurance policies, human resources, and technology systems. However, just twenty days later, Rob unexpectedly passed away. In the wake of this profound loss, Norman stepped into Rob's shoes, assuming the responsibilities of CEO, Treasurer, and Chairman of the Board.

Norman had the experience necessary to lead the company and could seek advice from the board of directors, but he was grieving the loss of his cousin and needed help running the business. Accordingly, a partial transition to the fifth generation took place, even though Ellis was still new to the company. The new leadership model proved to be successful despite the rushed timetable. Today, Ellis still serves as Inman Mills's Executive Vice President and Secretary while continuing to oversee legal and compliance issues. Norman remains CEO and Chair of the Board. It is worth pointing out that this approach was not inevitable. Inman Mills's family owners could have hired outside professional managers to take over Rob's role and relinquished some of their direct managerial involvement. In many multigenerational family businesses, the family delegates day-to-day operations to professional management and is involved only at the board of directors level. Yet, the secret of Inman Mills's success over five generations has been the combination of ownership and management.

Resilience in the Global Market. The textile industry remained stable for nearly a century after Inman Mills's founding, and the company earned steady profits producing commodity goods. Aside from a brief expansion into carpet yarns in the 1970s, the company mostly focused on cotton, polycotton, and polyester for "print cloth" products. Like other textile companies, Inman Mills transitioned to production of military supplies during times of war, benefiting from industry-wide spikes in demand for such products. But these shifts were temporary; as Ellis explains, once a major war ended, "we'd go back to our commercial products."

Inman Mills had its best year in 1998. Immediately thereafter, however, the textile industry faced a significant downturn, driven by the passage of the North American Free Trade Agreement and by China's entry into the World Trade Organization. Greater exposure to foreign competition "essentially created a crater in the textile industry." In South Carolina, according to Ellis, the textile industry today "is maybe a tenth of what it once was." United States textile companies struggled to compete for market share in the global arena for commodity goods. This difficulty stemmed from the fact that commodities were being produced "around the world where labor is a lot cheaper, and the regulatory environment makes it a lot less expensive to manufacture." Domestic companies that survived often did so by outsourcing their production to lower-cost factories abroad.

Inman Mills prioritized staying local. To that end, the company adapted to global competition by moving away from commodity products and by concentrating on specialized technical fabrics, including flame-resistant materials, and expanding into the military sector. This approach allowed them to maintain their domestic workforce. Ellis notes that "the company's been constantly reinventing itself over the last twenty to twenty-five years, and before that, not a lot changed because it didn't need to. Business conditions were much better then." This reinvention has not been without its difficulties. As Ellis puts it, "There was such an impact from overseas pressure that you're constantly trying to just get ahead."

Today, Inman Mills operates a plant exclusively for yarn spinning and knitting, where raw materials – comprising up to thirty different fibers – are spun into yarn. This facility has enabled the company to develop a specialized line of flame-resistant fabrics. Some of this yarn is then knitted or woven into bedding products. Inman Mills has effectively carved out a niche in producing flame-resistant protective barriers for foam mattresses. In addition, Inman Mills spins yarn and then weaves it into fabrics for industrial and workwear uses. For example, Inman Mills weaves technical fabrics for personal protective equipment (PPE) such as for "electricians, shop technicians that are exposed to flame, and arc flash." By developing this product line, Inman Mills has been able to capitalize on barriers to entry posed by federal safety standards for producing flame-resistant products.

In addition to PPE, Inman Mills has developed a niche producing military uniforms. Ellis explains, "We have a significant amount of military business in a variety of uses, but largely uniform fabrics and flame-resistant fabrics." In recent years, Inman Mills has also expanded its operations to include printing and finishing. The company has started to employ rotary screen printing to apply designs, primarily camouflage, to fabrics. This printing process is predominately used for military applications. Ellis states, "We'll be weaving military fabrics for uniforms and then passing them through to our other facility; we will be vertical to where we are able to print camouflage." Ellis highlights that this business endeavor is "the biggest opportunity by far" but also warns that it "poses some execution risk, since we've made a huge investment in it." The risks have not deterred Inman Mills; it sees an opportunity for the first time in twenty years to shift from merely "surviving" to actively "growing."

Because United States regulations mandate that military products be produced domestically, Inman Mills has an advantage over global competitors in military products. Furthermore, the licensing requirements for military product printing involve considerable intellectual property, further benefiting Inman Mills. Ellis notes that "there are a lot of proprietary products where our customer sees us as an approved supplier, and they don't want to get too far out of their supply chain because what they are making is proprietary to them, and we have some nice exclusivity in certain situations, which has been beneficial to us." Rising to the challenge posed by global competition, Inman Mills has successfully reinvented its business model without losing touch with the community values that made it successful in the first place.

A *"Labor of Love."* Inman Mills contributes to the local community, not only by providing jobs but through involvement in service organizations, and Inman Mills attributes much of its success to the strength of these connections. The company's board of trustees directs its philanthropic efforts, allowing Inman Mills "to stay plugged in" to the community. Many family members are actively involved in various boards within their community. For instance, Ellis serves on the South Carolina Manufacturers Alliance board in Greenville. Ellis says, "Community service is sort of the hallmark of this family." For instance, the county's Center for Philanthropy is named after Rob Chapman, the former chairman, treasurer, and CEO of Inman Mills. Additionally, the Chapman Cultural Center in Spartanburg honors the Chapman family because, as Ellis explains, "[W]e are involved and supportive of the arts, and that was something our family always believed in."

Inman Mills's commitment to its community influences its decision-making. Ellis observes that "there have probably been lots of business decisions that a company that's not rooted in its community probably wouldn't have made. They're too risky." In particular, the corporation maintains a strong sense of responsibility toward its 600 employees. As Ellis puts it, "They drive a lot of what we do." The business is "a labor of love." Sometimes, tough decisions cannot be avoided. To remain competitive in the United States, for example, Inman Mills has had to close some facilities to ensure the overall stability of the business. A commitment to staying local is not a guarantee that nothing will change.

In a family business, personal connections matter. As Ellis points out, "It is not an invisible shareholder that has a piece of paper somewhere. These are people we know." He underscores the advantages of running a family-owned business, noting that the tradition of having family members – who also are coworkers – gathered at Christmas dinners fosters a deep sense of responsibility: "It's a driver because these are people we have to answer to for the rest of our lives; they are our family .... It drives you to be a little bit more dogged." Ellis says that this responsibility "kind of challenges you to really push internally and say, 'Are we doing everything we can to make sure we are setting ourselves up for continued success?'"

10

Wealth Inequality

Wealth inequality endangers democratic values and calls for a public response.[1] Janet Yellen acknowledged the problem during her tenure as Chair of the Federal Reserve Board, presenting evidence that "[t]he distribution of income and wealth has been widening more or less steadily for several decades, to a greater extent than in most advanced countries."[2] This gap, she observed, is as wide as it has been in 100 years and undermines efforts to achieve a meaningful equality of opportunity. The nation's top 0.1 percent alone is worth approximately as much as the bottom 90 percent.[3] In the intervening years, the distribution of wealth has gotten worse.[4]

How did we reach this state of affairs? Although the Constitution prohibits inherited titles and other perquisites of nobility,[5] nothing in the logic of

[1] *See* Joseph R. Fishkin & William E. Forbath, *The Anti-oligarchy Constitution*, 94 B.U. L. Rev. 669, 671 (2014) ("The constitutional problem of oligarchy is the danger that concentrations of economic power and political power may be mutually reinforcing – and that because of this, sufficiently extreme concentrations of power may threaten the Constitution's democratic foundations.").

[2] Janet L. Yellen, Chair, Bd. of Governors of the Fed. Reserve Sys., Perspectives on Inequality and Opportunity from the Survey of Consumer Finances, Keynote Address at the Conference on Economic Opportunity and Inequality (Oct. 17, 2014), www.federalreserve.gov/newsevents/speech/yellen20141017a.htm.

[3] *See* Emmanuel Saez & Gabriel Zucman, *Exploding Wealth Inequality in the United States* (Oct. 20, 2014), https://tinyurl.com/ywb7snyc ("The share of wealth held by the top 0.1 percent of families is now almost as high as in the late 1920s, when 'The Great Gatsby' defined an era that rested on the inherited fortunes of the robber barons of the Gilded Age.").

[4] *See Trends in the Distribution of Family Wealth, 1989 to 2022*, Cong. Budget Off. (Oct. 2024), www.cbo.gov/publication/60807 ("In 2022, families in the top 10 percent of the distribution held 60 percent of all wealth, up from 56 percent in 1989, and families in the top 1 percent of the distribution held 27 percent, up from 23 percent in 1989.").

[5] U.S. Const. art. 1, § 9, cl. 8 ("No title of nobility shall be granted by the United States.").

capitalism prevents the accumulation of vast, intractable disparities in wealth.[6] Indeed, concentrated economic power can be self-perpetuating.[7] Family businesses merit special scrutiny as a potential source of inequality because they combine two of society's most important economic institutions: family and business. As such, family businesses implicate concerns regarding both inherited wealth and the concentration of economic power made possible by the corporate form.

Typically, owners seek to increase family wealth, to provide employment for family members, and, ultimately, to transfer control to a new generation of family owners.[8] Nor are these kinship preferences inconsequential.[9] The ten wealthiest families in the US derive their fortune from a family business venture.[10] Also, the wealthiest Americans are much more likely than their fellow citizens to have shares in private, often family-owned businesses.[11] More general assessments of the prevalence of family ownership vary, but all commentators agree that family businesses play a major role in the economy.[12]

6 *See* THOMAS PIKETTY, CAPITAL IN THE TWENTY-FIRST CENTURY 21 (2014) ("[T]here is no natural, spontaneous process to prevent destabilizing, inegalitarian forces from prevailing permanently.").

7 *See id.* at 27 (arguing that "the process by which wealth is accumulated and distributed contains powerful forces pushing toward divergence, or at any rate, toward an extremely high level of inequality").

8 *See* Marianne Bertrand & Antoinette Schoar, *The Role of Family in Family Firms*, 20 J. ECON. PERSP. 73, 74 (2006); Peter Jaskiewicz et al., *Is Nepotism Good or Bad? Types of Nepotism and Implications for Knowledge Management*, 26 FAM. BUS. REV. 121, 121 (2013).

9 *See Business in the Blood*, ECONOMIST, Nov. 1, 2014, at 59 ("Founding dynasties run, or wield significant clout at, some of the world's largest multinationals, from Walmart to Mars, Samsung to BMW.").

10 *See* Nick Kirkpatrick & Justin Moyer, *Meet America's Richest Families, Courtesy of Forbes*, WASH. POST (July 11, 2014), https://tinyurl.com/4dnzs8p2 (summarizing data). The list includes the Walton family (Wal-Mart), the Koch family (Koch Industries), the Mars family (Mars, Inc.), the Cargill-MacMillan family (Cargill, Inc.), the Johnson family (Fidelity), the Hearst family (Hearst Corp.), the Cox family (Cox Communications), the Pritzker family (Hyatt hotel chain), the S.C. Johnson family (S.C. Johnson, Inc.), and the Duncan family (Enterprise Products Partners). *Id.*

11 Yellen, *supra* note 2 (reporting that "slightly more than half of the top 5 percent of households have a share in a private business"). By contrast, "[o]nly 14 percent of families in the next 45 have ownership in a private business, but for those that do, this type of wealth constitutes a substantial portion of their assets." *Id.* Yellen clarifies that "ownership of a private business … usually means ownership and sometimes direct management of a family business." *Id.*

12 *See, e.g.*, Joseph H. Astrachan & Melissa Carey Shanker, *Family Businesses' Contribution to the U.S. Economy: A Closer Look*, 16 FAM. BUS. REV. 211, 217–18 (2003) ("No matter what criteria are used, family businesses represent a substantial portion of the U.S. economy and have a massive impact on the economy as a whole.").

Despite their economic importance, little has been done to investigate whether family businesses contribute to wealth inequality.[13] Family businesses appear to play a double role. On the one hand, family businesses can entrench existing disparities in wealth and opportunity. Heirs, after all, stand to benefit from the hard work of previous generations. On the other hand, family businesses can be a powerful antidote to inequality. By facilitating the accumulation of capital, family businesses can disrupt entrenched class hierarchies and create opportunities for individuals, families, and ethnic communities.[14] As one court observed, "small businesses ... have been for many immigrant groups, and continue to be, the first rung on the ladder of American success."[15]

Consequently, whether family businesses produce net social costs or benefits depends crucially on two principal factors. First, to the extent there is a lack of public investment in social mobility, family businesses can increase the distribution of wealth by providing needed investments in human capital. Second, to the extent the rewards of capitalism are not widely shared, family businesses can offer a source of opportunity, not just for family members, but also for employees and the communities in which family businesses operate. Thus, family businesses should not be viewed in isolation; a comprehensive response to the problem of wealth inequality must involve the state, the family, and the market.[16]

10.1 SOURCES OF INEQUALITY

In the United States, the gap between rich and poor has widened to levels not seen since the 1920s.[17] More troubling, wealth inequality persists across

[13] *See* Paul Bingley et al., *Equality of Opportunity and Intergenerational Transmission of Employers*, *in* FROM PARENTS TO CHILDREN: THE INTERGENERATIONAL TRANSMISSION OF ADVANTAGE 441 (John Ermisch et al. eds., 2012).

[14] *See* JOSEPH FISHKIN, BOTTLENECKS: A NEW THEORY OF EQUAL OPPORTUNITY 146 (2014) (arguing that "[a]s far as possible, there should be a plurality of paths leading to the valued roles and goods, without bottlenecks through which one must pass in order to reach them").

[15] EEOC v. Consolidated Serv. Sys., 989 F.2d 233 (7th Cir. 1993).

[16] *See* Miles Corak, *Income Inequality, Equality of Opportunity, and Intergenerational Mobility*, 27 J. ECON. PERSP. 79, 80 (2013) ("The interaction between families, labor markets, and public policies all structure a child's opportunities and determine the extent to which adult earnings are related to family background."); HAROLD JAMES, FAMILY CAPITALISM 1 (2006) (identifying as a central theme "the interplay of three powerful social constellations, families, states, and markets").

[17] *See* Yellen, *supra* note 2. According to one commentator, a Nobel laureate in economics, "[W]e haven't just gone back to nineteenth-century levels of income inequality, we're also on a path back to 'patrimonial capitalism,' in which the commanding heights of the economy are controlled not by talented individuals but by family dynasties." Paul Krugman, *Why We're in a New Gilded Age*, N.Y. REV. BOOKS, May 8, 2014, at 15, 16 (reviewing PIKETTY,

generations; the social and economic status of a child's parents has a very strong influence on their prospects.[18] Such pervasive, entrenched inequality is inconsistent with central tenets of the American Dream – that merit will be rewarded and that anyone who works hard can hope to achieve success.[19]

Yet, even if economic inheritances were sharply curtailed, successful parents would continue to give many other valuable advantages to their children.[20] For example, the child of an entrepreneur has an excellent chance to learn firsthand the skill set necessary to run a business.[21] Short of abolishing families and raising children communally, we cannot prevent families from equipping their children for success in life, a task that they will perform more or less well with the economic, cultural, and social resources at their disposal.[22] Thus, to the extent families take primary responsibility for raising children, no liberal society can promise full equality of opportunity to each of its citizens.[23]

Only by appreciating this context can we usefully evaluate the impact of family businesses on wealth inequality. The relevant issue is not whether family businesses detract from an otherwise perfect meritocracy, but how family

supra note 6). Increased levels of wealth inequality are not just an American phenomenon. *See* Anupreeta Das, A *Wedding Puts India's Gilded Age on Lavish Display*, N.Y. TIMES, Jul. 12, 2024 (describing a wedding celebration involving "wedding invitations made of silver and gold" and observing that billionaires have become "overlords of the Indian economy, running the phone networks that connect millions of people, the hospitals that treat them, the supermarkets where they shop and the high-rises in which many live").

18 *See* HARRY BRIGHOUSE & ADAM SWIFT, FAMILY VALUES: THE ETHICS OF PARENT–CHILD RELATIONSHIPS 2 (2014).

19 The American Dream is not the only conception of equal opportunity. According to some scholars, intelligence, athleticism, beauty, and perhaps even mental dispositions constitute morally arbitrary advantages that should not entitle a person to claim more of society's resources. *See* John Rawls, A *Kantian Conception of Equality*, *in* COLLECTED PAPERS 254, 264 (Samuel Freeman ed., 1999).

20 As one scholar explains, "The basic problem arises because parents – and families more generally – act in ways that give their children advantages." FISHKIN, BOTTLENECKS, *supra* note 14. Yet, "[p]arents do this to different degrees and in different ways, creating inequalities of opportunity that begin early, run deep, and tend to persist." *Id.*

21 *See, e.g.*, Adam Bryant, Corner Office, *Three Keys to Hiring: Skill, Will and Fit*, N.Y. TIMES, Jan. 11, 2015, at BU2 (interview with Marla Malcolm Beck, Chief Executive of Bluemercury, a beauty products and spa services retailer) ("My dad was an entrepreneur. He started an insurance agency and a real estate company, and I worked in his office from the time I was 9. When I was in high school, I used to balance his books.").

22 *See* BRIGHOUSE & SWIFT, *supra* note 18, at 2 (arguing that the problem is to provide for equal opportunity in even "the limited sense that people's chances of achieving desirable jobs should reflect their own merits rather than their family background").

23 *See, e.g.*, JOHN RAWLS, A THEORY OF JUSTICE 64 (1971) (stating that "the principle of fair opportunity can be only imperfectly carried out, at least as long as some form of the family exists").

businesses affect our society's overall opportunity structure.[24] Framed this way, as an example of what economists call the theory of second best, it is plausible that family businesses reduce inequality by providing ladders of opportunity.[25] As a locus for entrepreneurship and social advancement, family businesses can offset inequalities that arise from other forms of inheritance, not to mention more pervasive background conditions of social inequality.

10.1.1 The Great Gatsby *Curve*

Inheritance practices contribute substantially to wealth inequality.[26] Moreover, the consequences of inheritance are likely to be cumulative, as invested capital outperforms the overall economy, a trend that shows no sign of abating.[27] Unfortunately, the most accurate predictor of a person's future earnings is the socioeconomic status of their parents.[28] Although inequality is a global problem, "there is now less social mobility in the United States than in other advanced countries."[29] Wealth inequality is disturbing, not only because of its magnitude, but because it often reflects family background more than individual merit.[30]

24 *See* Jon Elster, Explaining Social Behavior: More Nuts and Bolts for the Social Sciences 439 (2007) (arguing that it is false to believe that one necessarily achieves a better result by seeking "to approximate the optimum as closely as possible, on the apparently reasonable assumption that the more of the conditions for optimality that are satisfied, the closer one will get to the optimum").

25 The economic theory of the second best contends that in an imperfect world the best available outcome might result from fulfilling fewer of the conditions that would pertain in a perfect world. *Id.*

26 *See* Adam J. Hirsch, *Testation and Contract*, 95 Minn. L. Rev. 2180, 2183 (2011) (citing William G. Gale & John K. Scholz, *Intergenerational Transfers and the Accumulation of Wealth*, 8 J. Econ. Persp. 145, 146–47, 156–57 (1994)) ("Economic studies have found that a large fraction (possibly in the range of eighty percent) of household wealth in the United States traces to gifts and inheritances, as opposed to participation in the labor economy.").

27 Piketty, *supra* note 6, at 377–78 ("Whenever the rate of return on capital is significantly and durably higher than the growth rate of the economy, it is all but inevitable that inheritance (of fortunes accumulated in the past) predominates over saving (wealth accumulated in the present)."). Piketty describes the relation as $r > g$. *Id.*

28 *See, e.g.*, Karl Alexander et al., The Long Shadow: Family Background, Disadvantaged Urban Youth, and the Transition to Adulthood (2014) (summarizing results of a twenty-five-year study that tracked almost 800 individuals in west Baltimore from childhood to early adulthood).

29 Fishkin, Bottlenecks, *supra* note 14, at 42 (citing From Parents to Children: The Intergenerational Transmission of Advantage (John Ermisch et al. eds., 2012); Pew Charitable Trusts, Does America Promote Mobility as Well as Other Nations? 2 (2011)).

30 *See* Brighouse & Swift, *supra* note 18, at 2 ("The egalitarian challenge demands an account of why families should be permitted to create inequalities between children.");

In remarks presented at the Center for American Progress on January 12, 2012, Alan Krueger, then Chair of the American Council of Economic Advisors, explained the link between current income inequality and future opportunities:

> Higher income inequality would be less of a concern if low-income earners became high earners at some point in their career, or if children of low-income parents had a good chance of climbing up the income scales when they grow up. In other words, if we had a high degree of income mobility we would be less concerned about the degree of inequality in any given year. But we do not. Moreover, as inequality has increased, evidence suggests that … economic mobility has decreased.[31]

When grouped by nation, measurements of income inequality and "mobility across generations" align, creating what Krueger described as a *Great Gatsby* curve: "The points cluster around an upward sloping line indicating that countries that had more inequality across households also had more persistence in income from one generation to the next."[32] Put more simply, if your parents are poor, that fact speaks volumes about your own life prospects.[33] In the United States, income inequality has gone up considerably, and Krueger concludes that "[i]t is hard to look at these figures and not be concerned that rising inequality is jeopardizing our tradition of equality of opportunity."[34]

Recent survey data confirms not only that the rich are "getting richer" but that "[t]he typical American has been getting poorer, too."[35] In the wake

PIKETTY, *supra* note 6, at 241 ("[D]emocratic modernity is founded on the belief that inequalities based on individual talent and effort are more justifiable than other inequalities."). One commentator argues, however, that we should not assume that all lasting inequalities can be attributed to a lack of opportunity. *See* N. Gregory Mankiw, *Defending the One Percent*, 27 J. ECON. PERSP. 21, 25 (2013) ("[P]arents and children share genes, a fact that would lead to intergenerational persistence in income even in a world of equal opportunities …. Smart parents are more likely to have smart children.").

31 Alan B. Krueger, Chairman, Council of Econ. Advisers, The Rise and Consequences of Inequality in the United States, Remarks before the Center for American Progress 3 (Jan. 12, 2012), www.whitehouse.gov/sites/default/files/krueger_cap_speech_final_remarks.pdf.

32 *Id.* at 4 (citing the work of economist Miles Corak). The reference is, of course, to F. Scott Fitzgerald's 1925 novel, *The Great Gatsby*.

33 *See* JAMES S. FISHKIN, JUSTICE, EQUAL OPPORTUNITY, AND THE FAMILY 31 (1983) ("The basic intuition is that it seems unfair that we should be able to predict eventual positions in a society merely by knowing the strata into which children are born.").

34 Krueger, *supra* note 31, at 4 ("The fortunes of one's parents seem to matter increasingly in American society."). Or, in one journalist's pithy formulation, "The American Dream isn't dead – it just moved to Denmark." Matthew O'Brien, *"The Great Gatsby Curve": Why It's So Hard for the Poor to Get Ahead*, ATLANTIC, June 18, 2013; *see also* JOSEPH E. STIGLITZ, THE PRICE OF INEQUALITY: HOW TODAY'S DIVIDED SOCIETY ENDANGERS OUR FUTURE (2013).

35 Anna Bernasek, *The Typical Household, Now Worth a Third Less*, N.Y. TIMES, July 27, 2014, at BU6.

of the Great Recession, households at every income level lost wealth, but "households at the bottom of the wealth distribution lost the largest share of their total wealth."[36] According to some measures, wealth inequality "roughly doubled" in the decade from 2003 to 2013.[37] Taking a longer view, from 1984 to 2013, the picture looks even worse: Those in the 95th percentile saw their wealth double; in the 75th percentile, wealth increased by approximately a third; at the median, though, wealth declined by 20 percent; and, in the bottom quartile, wealth declined more than 60 percent.[38] In part, the differences may be attributable to the fact that the wealthy have more diverse investment portfolios and are better able to navigate market anomalies.[39]

This is not to suggest that only a radically egalitarian society will suffice, or even that inequality is always harmful. To the contrary, "[n]o one denies that it is important for society to have entrepreneurs, inventions, and innovations .... The problem is simply that the entrepreneurial argument cannot justify all inequalities of wealth, no matter how extreme."[40] At some point, the increased incentive for the already wealthy to work hard in order to accumulate more capital must be outweighed by the diminishment of opportunity for those in the bottom rungs of the economy, who may never have the chance to contribute to the full extent of their abilities. Moreover, to the extent that returns to capital outpace the overall economy, the wealth disparities produced by useful entrepreneurial activity can lead to entrenched inequality over generations, well beyond the initial justification for rewarding the entrepreneur.

10.1.2 *Family Autonomy*

The phenomenon of wealth inequality is clear, and yet it resists easy answers. In that regard, there is a "trilemma" identified by the philosopher James Fishkin and elaborated in a recent book by the law professor, Joseph Fishkin.[41]

36 Fabian T. Pfeffer et al., Russell Sage Found., Research Summary: Wealth Levels, Wealth Inequality, and the Great Recession 2 (June 2014), https://tinyurl.com/4uyrz5f8.

37 *Id.*

38 *See id.*

39 *See id.* at 1 ("Affluent households are more likely than other households to hold stocks and have large portfolios, which allowed them to benefit from the gains in the stock market.").

40 Piketty, *supra* note 6, at 443.

41 Given the subject of this book, the reader may not be surprised to learn that James is Joseph's father, and that Joseph credits the opportunities afforded by his upbringing for his own development as a scholar. Fishkin, Bottlenecks, *supra* note 14, at 260. In the spirit of disclosure, I should acknowledge the tremendous advantages provided by my own parents, including

In brief, it is not possible to stipulate simultaneously that social goods are to be awarded according to a principle of merit, that each individual will have a fair chance to compete, and that families are free to "pass on advantages to their children."[42] Nor is it clear whether society would benefit from more modest efforts to advance the principles of merit and equality by restricting economic inheritances without intruding upon the core principle of family autonomy. Such restrictions on inheritance would leave untouched the vast disparities in cultural and educational resources that replicate inequality across generations. Moreover, an incomplete approach could produce perverse results by reinforcing the existing class structure.

10.1.2.1 How Families Create Inequality

The horns of the trilemma may not always be apparent, because liberalism tends to focus on autonomous individuals and to ignore family life.[43] Thus, the familiar tension between liberty and equality has not "systematically incorporated ... the role of the family in generating inequalities."[44] For example, equality of opportunity might offer a useful compromise between liberty and equality, but it cannot be achieved without serious intrusions into the autonomy of family life.[45] Families are a crucial source of inequality, and inherited financial resources are only one aspect of this inequality.[46]

Consider a *New York Times* profile of Michael Brantley, a former professional baseball player.[47] At the time the article was written, Brantley played for the Cleveland Indians and had one of the best slugging percentages in the league, powered by a "smooth left-handed swing."[48] As it happens, Brantley's father was a hitting coach for the New York Mets, and so Brantley

legacy consideration for admission to an Ivy League college – whether or not that legacy status was decisive might be debated by the reasonable observer and my mother.

42 FISHKIN, BOTTLENECKS, *supra* note 14, at 53 (citing FISHKIN, JUSTICE, *supra* note 33, at 44).

43 *See* FISHKIN, JUSTICE, *supra* note 33, at 2 ("Liberalism presents us with a picture of isolated, atomic individuals who seem to spring from nowhere in order to experience utility or claim rights or enjoy rights and then vanish.").

44 *Id.* at 1.

45 *Id.* at 4 ("Once the role of the family is taken into account, the apparently moderate aspiration of equal opportunity produces conflicts with the private sphere of liberty – with autonomous family relations – that are nothing short of intractable."). The autonomy of family life includes a parental right "to substantially influence the development of ... children." *Id.* at 5.

46 *See id.* at 1 ("The family is the one crucial source of inequality in modern society that has gone largely unexamined in the theory of distributive justice.").

47 *See* Tyler Kepner, *A Paternal Touch Yields a Smooth Swing: Cleveland's Brantley Succeeds at the Plate with Help from His Father*, N.Y. TIMES, Aug. 10, 2014, at SP3.

48 *Id.*

grew up around professional players and had access to professional coaching. According to Brantley's account, the advantages went beyond the opportunity to perfect the mechanics of his swing: "Being around major league players at that young age, seeing how they acted, seeing how they prepared, it just made me want to get better and kind of showed me how to carry myself."[49]

The importance of connections and background extends to professions of every kind. The family acculturation that causes the daughter in one family to pursue acting or directing[50] may cause another to contemplate joining a family business selling used books.[51] Moreover, entry into a specialized business is easier when, for instance, you have spent half a lifetime watching your parents set prices for books[52] or select the right kind of herring.[53] And the same could be said for commercial fishing,[54] cheesemaking,[55] bookselling,[56] hardware,[57] jewelry,[58] or the operation of resort hotels.[59]

As long as family remains the institution primarily responsible for raising children, the odds that a talented child will realize their potential will depend

49 *Id.* (internal quotation marks omitted). Later, scouts took this background into account as a reason to take a chance on Brantley. *Id.* ("The Indians, notably the scout Don Poplin, liked Brantley for his swing, athleticism, *bloodlines* and, perhaps most of all, his approach to the game.") (emphasis added).

50 *See* Adam Bellow, In Praise of Nepotism 498 (2003) (noting the many members of the Coppola family, including Sofia, who have established careers in Hollywood).

51 *See* Janet Malcolm, *The Book Refuge, Three Sisters Keep a Family Business Going*, New Yorker (June 23, 2014), www.newyorker.com/magazine/2014/06/23/the-book-refuge.

52 *See id.* ("'To prepare my daughters for a bookselling career, I conducted classes in the bookstore by going over new acquisitions with them,' [the bookstore's founder] wrote in his autobiography.").

53 Mark Russ Federman, Russ & Daughters: Reflections and Recipes from the House That Herring Built 127 (2013) ("When I decided to stop practicing law and go into the family business full-time, I asked my father to teach me how to tell a good fish from a bad fish.").

54 Carl Corey, For Love and Money: Portraits of Wisconsin Family Businesses 48 (2014) ("At age eight, Alvin Anderson … was the first deckhand …. A generation later his son Dan … slept in a net box on the boat while his parents, Alvin and Sandy, worked. Dan … returns every spring to fish with his father in the original boat.").

55 *Id.* at 68 ("Master cheesemaker Sid Cook began making cheese as a child but his cheesemaking lineage goes back much further – more than 125 years.").

56 *Id.* at 88 ("Janke Book Store, run by Carl Janke's grandchildren, Jim Janke and Jane Janke Johnson, is known for its community involvement and knowledgeable staff members.").

57 *Id.* at 90 (noting that Lull of Hardware was established in 1920 and is today owned and operated by two sons and a grandson who "run a true old-fashioned hardware store, providing service and selling goods from washing machines to feed").

58 *Id.* at 54 ("Siblings Karen Nelson and Dale Nummi run Nummi Jewelers, which was founded by their father, Harry, a watchmaker.").

59 *Id.* at 98 (noting that the Afterglow Resort, established in 1949, is now owned and operated by the son and daughter-in-law of the founder).

in large part upon the economic, cultural, and social resources of the family. Thus, "unless we are willing to destroy the family and move to a system of collective childrearing, like the one contemplated in Plato's *Republic* or in mythologized versions of early Israeli kibbutz experiments, life chances will never be completely independent of circumstances of birth."[60]

Alternatively, if families are permitted to convey advantages to children, teaching the values and life skills necessary for professional success, then affirmative action programs undertaken as a corrective measure to preserve fair life chances would violate the merit principle "by placing individuals who have faced disadvantages based on their birth circumstances in educational places and jobs for which they are less formally qualified."[61] Accordingly, tradeoffs are unavoidable; we cannot guarantee simultaneously that merit will be rewarded, equal opportunities afforded, and family autonomy respected.

10.1.2.2 Tax Implications

The connection between business law and family law can also be inverted: In some cases, a family business offers a mechanism for preserving family wealth by recharacterizing it.[62] For instance, while there is no rule prohibiting family members from doing business together as partners, "a family partnership may represent no more than a thinly veiled attempt to fracture the personal income of a taxpayer in a high-income tax bracket between himself and related persons … in lower brackets."[63] Such allocations violate the basic principle that income should be assigned to the person responsible for generating it.

Before changes to the tax code were adopted to tax household income jointly, the assignment of income question could be particularly troublesome if a household allocated business income to a spouse in a lower tax bracket,

60 Fishkin, Bottlenecks, *supra* note 14, at 53.

61 *Id.* So-called "leveling up" strategies give additional resources to those who are disadvantaged but cannot fully compensate for the "rich, iterative early interactions between children and parents." *Id.* at 55.

62 *Cf.* Kerry Abrams, *Marriage Fraud*, 100 Cal. L. Rev. 1, 4 (2012) ("This Article approaches the issues of how to define marriage and its proper place in our legal landscape from a different perspective. Instead of asking the question of what marriage *is*, the Article tries to determine what marriage *is not*. It does so by examining when and why the law determines that a particular marriage is a 'sham' or a 'fraud.'"). As Professor Abrams observes, studying the legal restriction of a concept can help illuminate its core purpose: "The fraud doctrines, in other words, tell us what work the law is asking marriage to do." *Id.* at 5.

63 William S. McKee et al., *Development of the Family Partnership Rules*, Federal Taxation of Partnerships & Partners ¶15.01 (2012).

thereby reducing the family's overall tax obligation.[64] When the Internal Revenue Service (IRS) challenged the existence of a business partnership, courts had to decide whether both spouses were genuinely involved in a productive enterprise or whether business partnership designations had been made purely for tax purposes.[65]

Because family businesses are embedded in a family context, with overlapping economic considerations, such distinctions are not easily drawn. In *Commissioner v. Culbertson*, the Supreme Court held that the inquiry into partnership status for tax purposes was necessarily fact intensive and included an assessment of:

> [W]hether, considering all the facts – the agreement, the conduct of the parties in execution of its provisions, their statements, the testimony of disinterested persons, the relationship of the parties, their respective abilities and capital contributions, the actual control of income and the purposes for which it is used, and any other facts throwing light on their true intent – the parties in good faith and acting with a business purpose intended to join together in the present conduct of the enterprise.[66]

Rejecting the *Culbertson* approach, Congress amended the law to clarify that a partnership designation for tax purposes is valid if the partner "owns a capital interest in a partnership in which capital is a material income-producing factor, whether or not such interest was derived by purchase or gift from any other person."[67] The tax rules are complex,[68] and the requisite "ownership" can be debated, but it is enough for our purposes to see that Congress decided not to examine the details of family business structure, so that "questions regarding the business or tax avoidance motivation for a

64 *See, e.g.*, Lucas v. Earl, 281 U.S. 111, 114–15 (1930). By contrast, the current approach uses a "joint-return rate schedule" that awards a "marriage bonus" to single-earner families, because the rate schedule achieves the equivalent of income splitting by applying a lower rate than would apply to an individual's income, and imposes a "marriage penalty" on dual-earning families with equal incomes, because the rate schedule is higher than the equivalent split if each earner were taxed as an individual. *See* Lawrence Zelenak, *Marriage and the Income Tax*, 67 S. CAL. L. REV. 339, 340–41 (1994). For further discussion of the consequences of the joint-filing rules, see Dorothy A. Brown, *Race and Class Matters in Tax Policy*, 107 COLUM. L. REV. 790, 800–03 (2007) and Boris I. Bittker, *Federal Income Taxation and the Family*, 27 STAN. L. REV. 1389, 1395–96 (1975).

65 *See, e.g.*, Comm'r v. Tower, 327 U.S. 280, 283 (1946).

66 Comm'r v. Culbertson, 337 U.S. 733, 742 (1949).

67 26 U.S.C. § 704(e)(1) (2012).

68 One commentator observes that the US tax system actually relies upon two distinct conceptions of family, depending upon whether the objective is to facilitate the extension of benefits or to constrict abuses. *See* Tessa R. Davis, *Mapping the Families of the Internal Revenue Code*, 22 VA. J. SOC. POL'Y & L. 179 (2015).

transfer of a partnership capital interest to a family member are thus largely irrelevant."[69] Households are now taxed as a unit, but issues concerning the allocation of taxable income within a family continue to arise in partnership cases involving children or other relatives.

Tax considerations also explain the use of limited partnerships and limited liability companies (LLCs) as an estate-planning device. The crucial features for tax purposes are that the limited partners have no right to control the investment – only general partners or voting members of the LLC have that authority – and no right to exit the investment and to redeem their membership interest. Accordingly, the IRS accepts substantial deductions to account for a limited partner's lack of control and the absence of an available market for the partnership interest, even if those vulnerabilities are of no real consequence within a family context.[70] Thus, transferring limited-partnership shares to a child, instead of the equivalent cash value in a will, helps the transferor take advantage of the gap between family expectations and objective market value.

The notion that a limited-partnership interest would trade at all, apart from the family context, is unrealistic for reasons that Professor Brant Hellwig has explained:

> Because the transferee of a partnership interest is guaranteed only to receive distributions that would have been made to the transferor, an unrelated third party would discount the value of the transferred interest on account of the inability to participate in decisions affecting management of the partnership affairs. Furthermore, due to the transferee's inability to require the partnership interest to be redeemed and the absence of an established market on which an interest in a closely held partnership can be readily liquidated, the value of the transferred interest will be discounted to reflect its lack of marketability. While one may sense an air of fabrication relating to the asserted discounts, the discounts are genuine. The air of fabrication exists because the likelihood of an interest in a family owned partnership ever being sold in an arm's-length exchange to an unrelated third party is virtually nonexistent.[71]

Nevertheless, the law hypothesizes a bargain negotiated at arm's length, and limited-partnership interests can often claim a substantial deduction for

69 McKee et al., *supra* note 63, ¶ 15.01[2] (citing S. Rep. No. 82-781, at 38 (1951) and H.R. Rep. No. 82-586, at 32 (1951) (stating intent to "harmonize the rules governing interests in the so-called family partnership with those generally applicable to other forms of property or business")).

70 Brant J. Hellwig, *Revisiting* Byrum, 23 Va. Tax Rev. 275, 278 (2003).

71 *Id.* at 278 n.8.

supposed impairments of value.[72] Whether or not the use of limited partnerships as a family tax-planning device undermines the integrity of the estate tax through a kind of relationship arbitrage, the popularity of the technique highlights the overlap of family relationships and business choices.[73] In sum, the subtlety of family and business connections can create opportunities for tax reduction strategies that the law only imperfectly apprehends and sometimes chooses to ignore. The choice of business entity form reflects family and business considerations.

10.1.2.3 Curtailing Inherited Wealth

Conceding that our fundamental values conflict does not leave us powerless to enact policies that will improve our current circumstances. Rather than let the perfect be the enemy of the good, we can take concrete steps to create greater equality of opportunity where it is possible to do so without encroaching upon other important values. For example, some argue that we should reduce disparities in life opportunities by limiting the transfer of economic resources across generations. In his 2015 State of the Union address, President Obama called for Congress to "close the loopholes that lead to inequality by allowing the top one percent to avoid paying taxes on their accumulated wealth."[74] The president's proposal, which closely resembled arguments advanced by the tax scholar Victor Fleischer,[75] would have made the transfer of accumulated capital gains at death a taxable event – for capital held in a business, often the first time any taxes would have been paid.[76]

More aggressively, some legal scholars have argued that inheritance and estate taxes should be used to restrict or even abolish the transfer of economic

[72] *See id.*

[73] *See id.* at 279 (citing Laura E. Cunningham, *Remember the Alamo: The IRS Needs Ammunition in Its Fight Against the FLP*, 86 TAX NOTES 1461, 1466 (2000) ("It is apparent that the family limited partnership, as evolved, is in danger of making the estate tax truly voluntary.")).

[74] Barack Obama, *State of the Union Address*, TIME (Jan. 20, 2015), http://time.com/3675705/full-text-state-union-2015/.

[75] *See* Victor Fleischer, *Taxing Founders' Stock*, 59 UCLA L. REV. 60, 60 (2011) (arguing that "[t]axing founders at a low rate is a conspicuous loophole in the fabric of our progressive income tax system, uniquely undermining our shared commitment to equal opportunity and distributive justice").

[76] *Id.* Equally important, the proposed rules would have leveled the playing field by requiring heirs to pay taxes on all earnings that would have been taxable to the testator. Under existing rules, heirs take a "stepped up" basis so that their eventual tax bill, whenever the transferred asset is sold, includes only changes in valuation since the heirs acquired ownership.

resources.[77] Inheritance law might be restructured to achieve both a "leveling down" to reduce unequal private inheritances and a "leveling up" to ensure everyone receives adequate resources "to start adult life from a position of equality."[78] As these commentators observe, a society based on merit alone will not achieve substantial equality of opportunity since it "leave[s] uncorrected the brute luck that affects early development and the resources to which one has access."[79] Indeed, it might be argued that "[c]hildren lucky enough to have been raised, acculturated, and educated by wealthy parents need not be allowed the additional good fortune of inheriting their parents' property."[80] Embracing one horn of the trilemma, these scholars insist upon the priority of individuals, not families.[81]

However, setting aside the merits of achieving a formal equality of economic resources through obliterating levels of taxation,[82] such measures would prevent only direct transfers of financial resources and leave untouched the features of family life that make it easier for privileged children to replicate their parents' success. Whatever the merits of eliminating economic inheritances (which would, among other things, preclude the direct transfer of family businesses from generation to generation),[83] a system of taxation would

77 *See, e.g.*, Mark L. Ascher, *Curtailing Inherited Wealth*, 89 MICH. L. REV. 69, 71 (1990) (Rejecting metaphor of a level playing field: "For no particularly good reason, we allow some players, typically those most culturally and educationally advantaged, to inherit huge amounts of wealth, unearned in any sense at all.").

78 Anne L. Alstott, *Equal Opportunity and Inheritance Taxation*, 121 HARV. L. REV. 469, 472 (2007). In addition to the inheritance tax, Professor Alstott's approach to achieving equal opportunity would include "a social inheritance, meaning a government expenditure program that would pay a universal, public inheritance." *Id.*; *see also* BRUCE ACKERMAN & ANNE ALSTOTT, THE STAKEHOLDER SOCIETY 3–5 (2000) (proposing that each US citizen receive 80,000 dollars at adulthood to be used for any purpose).

79 Alstott, *supra* note 78, at 486.

80 Ascher, *supra* note 77, at 74; *see also* RAWLS, *supra* note 23, at 264 ("Those favored by social and natural contingencies regard themselves as already compensated, as it were, by advantages to which no one (including themselves) had a prior claim."); Alstott, *supra* note 78, at 488 ("Being born to rich (or poor) parents is a matter of brute luck, and so the conventional equal opportunity prescription is to tax material inheritance heavily, perhaps even to confiscate it.").

81 Alstott, *supra* note 78, at 518 (refusing to "view the family rather than the individual as the real unit").

82 For example, some scholars worry that estate taxation can create a disincentive for wealth creation and that wealth equality should be pursued through other means. *See* Edward J. McCaffery, *The Uneasy Case for Wealth Transfer Taxation*, 104 YALE L.J. 283, 288 (1994) (identifying "likely consequences of a strengthened transfer tax, such as reduced work, reduced savings, and increased inequality in consumption").

83 *See* Ascher, *supra* note 77, at 73 ("My major premise is that all property owned at death, after payment of debts and administration expenses, should be sold and the proceeds paid to the United States government."). Professor Ascher would resist the label "confiscation" as it is his position that property rights terminate at death. *Id.*

not purport to regulate directly "the core of parent-child relations, namely, consensual efforts to influence child development."[84] As long as the family endures in its current form, true social equality cannot be realized.

10.1.3 *The Risk of Piecemeal Reform*

Not only would policies designed to curtail economic inheritances fail to achieve their social goals, such policies would risk reinforcing the very inequalities they sought to combat. That is, even if those "lucky enough to have been raised … by wealthy parents need not be allowed the additional good fortune of inheriting their parents' property,"[85] it does not follow that taking away those inheritances would produce a more egalitarian society. Consider the implicit logic: (1) in a society governed exclusively by the principle of equality, children would inherit no special advantages from their parents; (2) given the importance of liberty in our society, it is not possible to intrude upon the parent–child relationship so as to block the transmission of all such advantages; (3) restricting economic inheritances does not violate any core interest of family autonomy; and (4) therefore, to best approximate conditions of equality, we ought to curtail economic inheritances. Or, more simply, doing something is better than doing nothing.

The fatal flaw in the logic is that it assumes that the best course of action is that which most closely approximates the outcome under ideal circumstances.[86] Yet, if the surrounding circumstances *also* depart from the ideal, the correct course of action may be quite different because of the influence of other variables. Jon Elster recounts that "when Mao Tse-tung decided to eliminate sparrows because they ate grain, he had to reimport them later from the Soviet Union when the pests they kept down flourished with catastrophic ecological results."[87] Mao Tse-tung's edict has a similar logic: (1) in a perfect world, crops intended for human consumption would never be eaten by birds,

[84] FISHKIN, JUSTICE, *supra* note 33, at 38. Professor Fishkin argues that the principle of family autonomy he espouses should "not be construed to protect nepotism, the buying of positions, or large-scale inheritance." *Id.* at 37 ("Such practices would raise obvious conflicts with any attempts to fully institutionalize merit.").

[85] Ascher, *supra* note 77, at 74.

[86] To be clear, the use of the term "ideal" refers to a society in which each person has an equal set of opportunities (however measured) and does not imply any endorsement of a society that would relentlessly pursue a single value at the expense of all others.

[87] ELSTER, *supra* note 24, at 441. While proofreading this manuscript, Inge Kutt Lewis added a personal comment in the margin that is worth preserving: "My father was in a business meeting in Beijing when all the participants in that meeting, including himself, were forced to go outside to hunt and kill sparrows."

insects, or animals; (2) it is not possible to destroy all such culprits; (3) it is possible to kill sparrows; and (4) to best approximate a world in which crops are eaten only by humans, we should kill the sparrows. Of course, Mao Tse-tung overlooked the fact that sparrows are one part of a complex ecosystem.

Piecemeal reforms enacted without consideration of their systemic context can make matters worse. In the formal language of economics, this is known as the problem of second best:

> The general theory of second best holds that where it is not possible to satisfy all the conditions necessary for an economic system to reach an overall optimum, it is not generally desirable to satisfy as many of those conditions as possible. Rather, the failure to satisfy optimality conditions on one variable means that other variables must take on suboptimal values as well, in order to compensate for the initial failure.[88]

If one or more variables outside our control are suboptimal, the variables that we do control may need to counterbalance those other variables. The goal is to make the overall system work as well as possible. Adjusting any particular variable – say, the taxation of inherited wealth – should not be an end in itself. Still, it could be the case that curtailing inherited wealth would be a highly desirable strategy for curbing wealth inequality. The theory of the second best does not tell us whether it is better to kill sparrows or let them live; the theory simply cautions us to base our judgment on real-world conditions.

By applying the theory of second best to family businesses, we can better appreciate why the advantages family businesses confer on family members (and, sometimes, members of a wider ethnic community) might compensate for other background conditions of inequality.[89] In particular, wealth amassed over generations may enable families to propel their children and grandchildren from wage labor into professional occupations. Family ties can help newer immigrants establish businesses when traditional bank loans and nonfamily labor would otherwise be impossible to secure.[90] Also, family

88 Adrian Vermeule, *Foreword, System Effects and the Constitution*, 123 HARV. L. REV. 4, 17 (2009).

89 In general, "[i]ndividuals' opportunities to pursue different combinations of forms of flourishing that they choose for themselves depend in a significant way on the structure of work and the broader structure of capitalism." FISHKIN, BOTTLENECKS, *supra* note 14, at 220.

90 Lan Cao, *Looking at Communities and Markets*, 74 NOTRE DAME L. REV. 841 (1999) [hereinafter Cao, *Communities and Markets*] (discussing informal systems of community credit); Lan Cao, *The Diaspora of Ethnic Economies: Beyond the Pale?*, 44 WM. & MARY L. REV. 1521, 1531 (2003) [hereinafter Cao, *Diaspora*] ("For members of these transitional or marginal groups especially, who may lack mainstream advantages, turning inward and utilizing available ethnic resources to engage in community ethnic preferences within the ethnic community will be crucial for their economic well-being.").

businesses may provide employment for those who lack conventional qualifications or who are discriminated against.[91] For these reasons, kinship and ethnic preferences in family businesses arguably amount to a form of private affirmative action that facilitates integration by moving families and communities into the middle class.

While it might be that redistributing wealth each generation would create a more level playing field, a ban on inherited wealth could also have the perverse effect of locking into place existing class distinctions. After all, the children of accountants, dentists, doctors, lawyers, and other professionals do not need to inherit their parents' wealth in order to replicate their accomplishments. Equally talented children from working-class backgrounds lack comparable opportunities for success, not just because they are poorer, but because they do not have access to the same educational, cultural, and social resources.[92] In this regard, the accumulation of capital facilitated by family businesses can reduce inequality by creating additional pathways for success.[93]

Perhaps, rather than restricting economic inheritances in order to better approximate the conditions of economic equality that would pertain in a perfect meritocracy, we ought to focus on a smaller set of outsized fortunes. Even if mom and pop businesses reduce wealth inequality, family-controlled capital beyond a certain scale may tend to entrench inequality rather than relieve it.[94] But this qualification only reinforces the point: We should not assume that economic redistribution will invariably produce a more equal society; instead, we should seek to identify policies that will, in fact, produce that result.

91 *See* Cao, *Diaspora*, *supra* note 90, at 1612 ("For non-English speakers … the barriers to entering the general labor force are often quite high."); Daina C. Chu, Comment, *The Cultural Defense: Beyond Exclusion, Assimilation, and Guilty Liberalism*, 82 CAL. L. REV. 1053, 1092 (1994) (arguing that "the American labor market … includes Asian Americans, but only in lower-tier jobs with poor pay and dim advancement prospects, and only while retaining structural barriers to exclude Asian Americans from primary-sector jobs with better compensation, benefits, and upward mobility").

92 *See, e.g.*, *America's New Aristocracy*, ECONOMIST, Jan. 24, 2015, at 9 (noting that "America is one of only three advanced countries where the government spends more on schools in rich areas than in poor ones").

93 Even when a family business is illegal, the founders may use their ill-gotten resources to support a "quiet and determined push toward respectability" for subsequent generations. Malcolm Gladwell, *The Crooked Ladder: The Criminal's Guide to Upward Mobility*, NEW YORKER, Aug. 11, 2014, at 36 (citing FRANCIS A. J. IANNI, A FAMILY BUSINESS: KINSHIP AND SOCIAL CONTROL IN ORGANIZED CRIME (1972)). By the fourth generation, most members of one family known for its involvement in organized crime "were firmly planted in the American upper middle class." *Id.* at 37.

94 For example, in South Korea, "[a]bout 20 families run the huge conglomerates or *chaebol* that make up 60% of the country's stockmarket value and most of its exports." *Special Report: Family Companies*, ECONOMIST, Apr. 18, 2015, at 13.

10.2 FAMILY VALUES

The problem of wealth inequality is not that some people have more money than others, even if by many orders of magnitude.[95] Rather, there is a growing consensus across the political spectrum that inequality deserves serious attention because of its impact on opportunities.[96] In today's society, it is unrealistic to suppose that someone born into poverty will have a fair chance at success in life.[97] Without a ladder of opportunity, whether provided by the state or cobbled together by families and communities, many members of society will continue to be trapped by the circumstances of their birth.[98] In order to succeed, individuals and families need stable economic circumstances, access to education, and support networks. Those who cannot save money or insure against risks cannot afford to take entrepreneurial risks, let alone defer income long enough to earn a professional degree.[99]

When the state fails to invest adequately in social mobility, family businesses offer a second-best solution by enabling a family to advance the interests of its members over multiple generations, thereby breaking down an exclusionary class structure. However, private entrepreneurship and public support should not be perceived as binary alternatives. Rather, we should recognize that the structure of opportunity depends upon the interrelationship of three institutions: the family, the market, and the state. For example, food stamp programs that strengthen the social safety net can also provide the conditions necessary for business entrepreneurship that, in the long run, lifts individuals and families out of poverty.[100] The mechanisms may be complementary.

[95] *See* Jedediah Purdy, *Wealth and Democracy*, 58 WEALTH 235 (2017) ("Inequality, as a merely formal or statistical feature of the economy, is not good or bad; it becomes good or bad only as it affects those things that people value and have reason to value.").

[96] *See* Amy Chozick, *Economic Plan Is a Quandary for Clinton '16*, N.Y. TIMES, Feb. 8, 2015, at A1 ("The debate [over income inequality] is extending beyond the Democratic Party as Republicans wade into the issues. 'If Americans are working harder than ever, earning less than they once did, our government and our leaders should step up, offer a plan, fix what's wrong,' former Gov. Jeb Bush of Florida said in a speech in Detroit last week as he laid the groundwork for his potential 2016 candidacy.").

[97] *See* Gary Solon, *Intergenerational Income Mobility in the United States*, 82 AM. ECON. REV. 393, 403–04 (1992).

[98] *See* Mankiw, *supra* note 30, at 24.

[99] *See* James R. Repetti, *Democracy, Taxes, and Wealth*, 76 N.Y.U. L. REV. 825, 839 (2001) (noting that an "inability to invest in human capital traps many families in intergenerational poverty, thus slowing the nation's economic growth").

[100] *See* Carmen Nobel, *Food Stamp Entrepreneurs: How Public Assistance Enables Business Bootstrapping*, WORKING KNOWLEDGE, HARV. BUS. SCH. (Sept. 2, 2014), http://

In some respects, family businesses offer an attractive vision of capitalism. A family's commitment to a business enterprise can reinforce family relationships, as family members work together to achieve a shared vision. Consequently, family businesses are notably resilient; family owners have reason to invest resources during hard times when investors with a less personal investment would walk away.[101] Sometimes, these investments follow from a view that the biological family is part of a broader economic family that includes various other stakeholders.[102] Just as public safety nets create economic stability, family businesses can do much the same, helping members of a community accumulate wealth and provide opportunities for their children.[103]

On the other hand, family businesses are vulnerable to family dysfunction. Irrational feuds can destroy businesses that would otherwise enjoy an enviable market position. In the long run, the market should correct business failures caused by family disputes. Other competitors will emerge and thrive. However, for the families and other stakeholders involved in a needless business failure, the disruptions can be considerable. Moreover, there can be no guarantee that the values a family business seeks to advance will promote social equality. Family owners have tremendous power over the lives of their employees. Whether driven by discriminatory animus or parochial religious conviction, family owners can exercise that power to impose their values on others.

hbswk.hbs.edu/item/7589.html (interviewing Professor Gareth Olds regarding his empirical research into food stamp programs and his own parents' experience using public assistance to form a business).

101 *See* BETH MACY, FACTORY MAN: HOW ONE FURNITURE MAKER BATTLED OFFSHORING, STAYED LOCAL – AND HELPED SAVE AN AMERICAN TOWN (2014) (reporting efforts of third-generation family owner to preserve business and hundreds of jobs); Susan S. Kuo & Benjamin Means, *Corporate Social Responsibility After Disaster*, 89 WASH. U. L. REV. 973, 977 (2012) ("Businesses are economic enterprises situated in a broader web of social networks. When business owners live where their customers live, these social networks strengthen as business ties overlap with other networks (school, church, recreation) that together form the fabric of place.") (citations omitted).

102 *See, e.g.*, Katherine Q. Seeleye, *Across a Grocery Chain, a Labor Protest in Support of a Manager*, N.Y.TIMES, July 18, 2014, at A11 (interviewing employees in connection with family business dispute involving control of the Market Basket supermarket chain and the removal of Arthur T. Demoulas, a third-generation family owner, from his role as President: "Several … employees spoke of Arthur T.'s generosity and compassion. 'He's been to my kids' weddings, my mother's funeral, his sisters came to my mother's funeral, to my brother-in-law's funeral,' said Michael King, 57, the company's controller.").

103 *See, e.g.*, Tom Moroney, *A Year After Upheaval, Market Basket Looks Stronger than Ever*, TELEGRAM.COM (July 31, 2015, 11:39 AM), https://tinyurl.com/3m9d4nje ("'[Arthur T. Demoulas, the family business CEO] gives more than you put in,' said Sean Morse, 45, assistant manager at the Market Basket in Londonderry, New Hampshire. 'He wants us all to have a better life. I can take care of my family, they're healthy and it's all because of him.'").

10.2.1 *Potential Social Benefits*

Family businesses have social significance and are more than just a vehicle for transferring family wealth across generations. They can affect social welfare by facilitating economic growth, distributing wealth more widely than would otherwise be the case, and by serving as "a model for creative, humane capitalism."[104] To the extent this is true, the involvement of multiple generations of a single family in the ownership and operation of a business offers social benefits that ought to be accounted for in any comprehensive assessment of wealth inequality.[105]

10.2.1.1 Reinforcing Kinship Ties

Family businesses often have special meaning for their family owners.[106] Just as we may respect the commitment to service of a fourth- or fifth-generation police officer or soldier, there is something ennobling about a new generation willing to take over a family business, even though higher paying jobs might have been available elsewhere.[107] For example, one family business owner left the practice of law at a major New York law firm to run his family's Lower East Side smoked fish establishment.[108] By continuing the family enterprise, family members embrace their own heritage and find meaning in commercial activity.[109]

[104] Benjamin Means, *Nonmarket Values in Family Businesses*, 54 WM. & MARY L. REV. 1185, 1191 (2013).

[105] The concentration of economic resources in a single family may still be undesirable, from the standpoint of wealth inequality, but that conclusion should follow from a full consideration of the pros and cons of family business ownership. *See* Purdy, *supra* note 95, at 2 ("To diagnose unequal wealth … one must disaggregate its effects and relate them to a scheme of values and the institutions that embody those values").

[106] The nonpecuniary benefits of ownership can sometimes explain the desire to maintain family control. *See* Ronald J. Gilson, *Controlling Shareholders and Corporate Governance: Complicating the Comparative Taxonomy*, 119 HARV. L. REV. 1641, 1666 (2006) ("[O]ne would expect to find controlling shareholders in major newspaper companies because running a major national newspaper puts one at the center of major public and cultural issues, with the potential to influence the outcome.").

[107] *See* BELLOW, *supra* note 50, at 16 ("Because we live in what might be called a 'postkinship' society, we have forgotten what we once knew about the intimate connections between kinship and human community.").

[108] FEDERMAN, *supra* note 53, at 68–69.

[109] *See, e.g.*, COREY, *supra* note 54, at 110 ("Owner and chef Jon Kaber says he is most proud of his grandmother's chilled beet recipe."); FEDERMAN, *supra* note 53, at xi–xii ("This is our yichis, the hard work and the satisfaction of selling herring: of getting the fish into the store each morning, of arranging the displays hundreds of times each day, of customers buying and

In order for the younger generation to make such a commitment, the older generation must first take pains to build something worthy of the commitment. Although kinship preferences might be viewed as selfish from the perspective of those who do not benefit, the continuation of a family enterprise can also be characterized as an expression of generosity:

> To the extent that nepotism takes place in the context of a family enterprise ... the spirit of it requires that its benefits be passed on to the next generation. We therefore express our gratitude to our parents in the form of generosity to our own children. This view of life as a multigenerational project was very apparent to our immigrant forebears.[110]

Put more formally, family businesses can create "generation-spanning continuities in the sociostructural position of families."[111] In this regard, the family business "can play a symbolic, identity-creating role."[112]

For a thoughtful exploration of one family's identification with a business enterprise, consider *Jiro Dreams of Sushi*, a documentary film concerning a master chef, Jiro Ono, who trained his eldest son to take over his renowned Tokyo sushi restaurant.[113] At the time of filming, Jiro's son was in his fifties, had long since completed his apprenticeship, and stood ready to carry on the family legacy. No one else had the requisite qualifications for the role at a restaurant so exacting that chefs must apprentice for years before they are entrusted to prepare the tamagoyaki egg omelet.[114]

Inherited resources are also "a material foundation for family continuity" and "even for the middle class, transfers of wealth provide at least a partial buffer against the vagaries of the market place."[115] Additionally, a family business can help achieve a "family's goal of keeping the family located within

counter-men selling, and, it is to be hoped, of making a profit in the process."), Steven H. Hobbs & Fay Wilson Hobbs, *Family Businesses and the Business of Families: A Consideration of the Role of the Lawyer*, 4 TEX. WESLEYAN L. REV. 153, 158 (1998) ("Socially and culturally, the family business offers the opportunity to unify work and family concerns for the benefit of succeeding generations.").

110 BELLOW, *supra* note 50, at 472.

111 JENS BECKERT, INHERITED WEALTH 18 (Thomas Dunlap trans., 2004); BELLOW, *supra* note 50, at 472 ("The more such generational transactions there are, the healthier for society as a whole.").

112 BECKERT, *supra* note 111, at 19.

113 JIRO DREAMS OF SUSHI (Magnolia Pictures 2012). For a review and synopsis, see Roger Ebert, *And Apparently of Nothing Else* (Apr. 4, 2012), www.rogerebert.com/reviews/jiro-dreams-of-sushi-2012.

114 Other employees, including a younger son, completed their apprenticeships and then opened restaurants elsewhere.

115 BECKERT, *supra* note 111, at 18. Thus, family wealth "allows a better education, a higher risk tolerance, and improved living conditions." *Id.*

close proximity of one another to accommodate their family values, one of which involves spending quality time together."[116] In a national economy that frequently requires family members to relocate, these are not trivial benefits.

For immigrants, family business ownership can provide an alternative pathway when other opportunities are limited. For example, Old Bay Seasoning was created by Gustav Brunn, "a German Jew who emigrated to Baltimore in 1938 – and, according to his son, was fired two days into a gig with McCormick & Co. because he was Jewish."[117] A version of the story recently published in the *New Yorker* attributed Brunn's termination to a statement "that his English was too poor."[118] Regardless, instead of working for someone else, Mr. Brunn "opened the Baltimore Spice Co. across from the city's wholesale fish market" and developed his famous seasoning blend.[119] Many years later, in 1990, the McCormick company acquired the rights to Old Bay Seasoning, "maintaining Old Bay's name, original recipe, and iconic packaging."[120] McCormick would, of course, have owned the recipe from the beginning had they kept Mr. Brunn employed.

Over time, a family business can create opportunities for children to succeed in the broader economy and not just as business heirs. As one third-generation owner explained regarding his early education in the business:

> At the time, I had no intention of growing up to be a fishmonger, nor, I'm equally sure, would my father have wanted me to "take over the business." The plan was for me to go to college and become a professional; that was the unstated but clearly understood trajectory for most Jewish boys growing up in the 1950s.[121]

The multigenerational continuity of family ownership in some industries may, therefore, reflect family pride and heritage rather than a lack of other options or the locking up of economic advantage.[122] The prevalence of family

[116] Bridget K. Mulder, *A Model of Organizational Nepotism*, *in* NEPOTISM IN ORGANIZATIONS 231 (Robert G. Jones ed., 2012) (noting as well that "an offer of nepotism" may not be forthcoming if the position would require the family member "to travel a great deal or live significant distances apart for the job").

[117] *The Spicy, Sultry Cult of Old Bay*, TAMPA BAY TIMES (Oct. 16, 2009), www.tampabay.com/archive/2009/10/16/the-spicy-sultry-cult-of-old-bay/ (reporting statements of Mr. Brunn's then-84-year-old son; McCormick did not deny the account but stated that it has no records of the firing).

[118] Casey Cep, *An Ode to Old Bay, the Great American Condiment*, NEW YORKER, Aug. 15, 2024.

[119] *Spicy, Sultry Cult*, *supra* note 117.

[120] Cep, *supra* note 118.

[121] FEDERMAN, *supra* note 53, at 62.

[122] *Cf.* Malcolm, *supra* note 51 (reporting that the Argosy bookstore owners "are proud of their success in carrying on the family business and aware of the mystique that attaches to the old-book trade. Children who inherit slaughterhouses or factories that manufacture incontinence products may not feel as blessed.").

ownership (and ethnic association) even in countries like the US with robust economic and legal institutions that support business dealings among strangers indicates the "resilience of informal, personalized exchanges and in-group preferences."[123]

10.2.1.2 Strengthening Communities

When family members work together on a daily basis, combining business and family values, they not only strengthen the family but may also make lasting contributions to their communities.[124] Family business can provide an anchor for widening circles of concern and responsibility. For example, by recognizing the connection between paid work and family life, family businesses may consciously include the families of employees who are not related to the owners.[125] As one family business owner explained, "[W]e're not just a family business in that we're family owned. We know and appreciate the needs of our employees and their families so we want to make sure we succeed for them as well."[126]

These connections are especially important when the community is tested by hardship: "When business owners live in the same community as their customers, they have a deeper stake in the success of disaster recovery and the ability to influence not only the economic aspects of recovery but also the social connections that determine a community's overall resilience – its spirit."[127] In this regard, family businesses "exhibit much care about continuity,

[123] Cao, *Diaspora*, *supra* note 90, at 1563.

[124] *See, e.g.*, Lizette Alvarez, *After 150 Years of Rolling Them, Tampa Is Close to No Cigars*, N.Y. TIMES, July 22, 2014, at A1 (reporting on the J. C. Newman Cigar Company, currently owned by the grandsons of the founder, and notable as the last cigar manufacturing factory remaining in the Tampa area after a "tide of owners … moved to the Caribbean and Central America"); Means, *Nonmarket Values*, *supra* note 104, at 1190–91 ("[B]usiness ownership can provide nonmonetary benefits to family members such as stable employment, status in the community, and agreeable working conditions.").

[125] *See* Teresa J. Rothausen, *Management Work-Family Research and Work-Family Fit: Implications for Building Family Capital in Family Business*, 22 FAM. BUS. REV. 220, 226 (2009) ("If [family] leaders include employees' families as well as their own families as members of the system, family businesses have the potential to play a prominent role in the policy arena on work-family in business.").

[126] Annie Pilon, *From Humble Beginnings in a Garage, Family Business Thrives for 60 Years*, SMALL BUS. TRENDS (Aug. 29, 2015), http://smallbiztrends.com/2015/08/family-business-through-generations.html (quoting Louis Kahn, founder of Perfection Spring & Stamping Corp.) (internal quotation marks omitted).

[127] Susan S. Kuo & Benjamin Means, *After the Storm: The Vulnerability and Resilience of Locally Owned Business*, *in* VULNERABILITY: REFLECTIONS ON A NEW ETHICAL FOUNDATION FOR LAW AND POLITICS 95, 97 (Martha Albertson Fineman & Anna Grear eds., 2013).

community and connection: specifically, about the long term preservation and nurturing of their business and its markets, the fostering of talent and effective deployment of employees, and an emphasis on growing and sustaining relationships with clients."[128]

During a speech accepting his party's nomination, President Barack Obama lauded a "family business in Warroad, Minnesota, that didn't lay off a single one of their 4,000 employees when the recession hit ... even when their competitors shut down dozens of plants, even when it meant the owner gave up some perks and some pay because they understood that their biggest asset was the community and the workers who had helped build that business."[129] Although an anecdote does not establish that family businesses are more likely to exhibit socially responsible behavior, the business cited by President Obama illustrates how family values could be extended to employees and communities.

In a similar vein, consider the Wisconsin Historical Society's book jacket description for a photography book about family-owned businesses in Wisconsin:

> The businesses portrayed here – bakeries and barbecue joints, funeral homes and furniture builders, cheesemakers, fishermen, ferry boat drivers – have survived against all the odds, weathering tough economic times and big-business competition. The owners are loyal to their employees, their families, and themselves. And they are integral to their local economies and social fabric. The services and goods they provide are usually for neighbors and friends. Generations serve generations, creating lasting relationships and strong, vibrant neighborhoods and rural communities.[130]

When family businesses successfully combine family and community values with a for-profit model, they can benefit a broader group of stakeholders.

10.2.2 *Dysfunction, Discrimination, and Parochial Values*

Unfortunately, when families own and operate businesses, family pathologies can adversely impact the lives of many other people who depend on those businesses. Family relationships are not invulnerable, and the overlap of business and family concerns can prove enormously destructive both to

[128] Danny Miller et al., *Stewardship v. Stagnation: An Empirical Comparison of Small Family and Non-family Businesses*, 45 J. Mgmt. Stud. 51, 73 (2008).

[129] ABC News, *President Obama's Full Acceptance Speech* (Nov. 7, 2012), https://tinyurl.com/yr7shzwy.

[130] Corey, *supra* note 54 (book jacket).

family interests and other stakeholders.[131] Business problems poison family relationships, and unhealthy family dynamics infect the business.[132] It is not uncommon for putative heirs to war for control, wreaking havoc along the way.[133] Sometimes, family disputes can be settled without permanently damaging the business asset.[134] Often, though, a family business will not survive the infighting. Thus, the destructive downside of family business ownership should be considered when evaluating the overall role of family business in society.

Also, for a society stratified along lines of race and class, the insular hiring practices of family firms are of particular concern because they can cement existing disparities in opportunity.[135] African Americans who are not considered for employment, let alone managerial responsibility, in family businesses often lack comparable avenues for success because of "low rates of black entrepreneurship."[136] The business ownership gap, in turn, can be explained in part by poor credit traceable to segregated housing patterns, to say nothing of the lasting effects of slavery and de jure discrimination.[137] Past discrimination continues to matter because "[b]usiness startups depend heavily on personal and family wealth, which is leveraged into lines of credit."[138]

131 *See* F. Hodge O'Neal & Robert B. Thompson, O'Neal and Thompson's Oppression of Minority Shareholders and LLC Members § 2:2 (rev. 2d ed. 2012) (noting that "business relationships often overlap family relationships so that a squeeze often reflects dysfunctional family relations or is exacerbated by family relations").

132 Means, *Nonmarket Values*, *supra* note 104, at 1191–92.

133 See Roxanne Roberts, *The Darcars Family Drama: Cut Out of the Auto Business, a Daughter Sues*, Wash. Post, Apr. 1, 2015.

134 For example, the New Orleans landmark restaurant Brennan's nearly collapsed as a result of family dissension. *See* Michael Kunzelman, *Brennan's Family Squabble over New Orleans Eatery Scheduled for Court on Monday*, Times-Picayune, May 12, 2013 (reporting that one shareholder meeting was so contentious that the police were called to restore order). Eventually, one side of the family acceded to a buyout proposal. *See* Pete Wells, *Brennan's in New Orleans Walks the Tightrope of Tradition*, N.Y. Times, Jan. 20, 2015, at D1.

135 *See* Jaskiewicz et al., *supra* note 8, at 121 (noting that "since nepotism discriminates against non-family members, it has been characterized as detrimental to society").

136 Elizabeth S. Anderson, *Integration, Affirmative Action, and Strict Scrutiny*, 77 N.Y.U. L. Rev. 1195, 1203 (2002); *see also* Melvin L. Oliver & Thomas S. Shapiro, Black Wealth/White Wealth: A New Perspective on Racial Inequality 4 (2006) (noting "relatively low level of entrepreneurship").

137 *See* Ezra Rosser, *The Ambition and Transformative Potential of Progressive Property*, 101 Cal. L. Rev. 107, 137–38 (2013) ("Residential segregation dampens wealth growth among African American homeowners by 'suppressing their home equity' but has the opposite effect on white homeowners.") (citing Dorothy A. Brown, *Shades of the American Dream*, 87 Wash. U. L. Rev. 329, 336–62 (2009)).

138 Anderson, *supra* note 136, at 1203–04 ("Residential segregation, by depressing housing appreciation and reducing access to credit, therefore depresses black business startups, upon which

If background conditions of inequality limit entrepreneurial opportunities, then, in the aggregate, the insular practices of family businesses might exacerbate racial division and inequality.

Moreover, the influence of "nonmarket" values in the workplace is not necessarily something to celebrate. As noted earlier, businesses like Hobby Lobby may seek exemptions from generally applicable laws based on the religious convictions of their controlling shareholders. Yet, the religious values espoused by business owners can conflict with the interests of their employees in access to reproductive healthcare, or, conceivably, of customers in access to goods and services regardless of their gender, race, or sexual orientation.[139]

Even if business owners do not seek or obtain exemptions from otherwise applicable laws, the owners nevertheless have wide discretion to run their businesses in a manner consistent with their values. In doing so, they may intend to benefit their employees and other stakeholders by including them within the compass of the family's own values. For example, Hobby Lobby's mission statement of core values includes, among other things, "[s]erving our employees and their families by establishing a work environment and company policies that build character, strengthen individuals, and nurture families."[140] However, when wealth empowers business owners to inscribe their values into the structure of the marketplace, requiring others to abide by values they may not share, the confluence of economic and social power exacerbates the problem of wealth inequality.[141]

On the other hand, so long as there are multiple businesses in the marketplace, and employees and customers are not forced to deal with a single player, there ought to be room for businesses to represent a variety of social views. In order to achieve a wider economic equality, it is important to ensure that the marketplace is open to everyone. Excluding religious individuals whose personal values conflict with society's values would coerce a choice between deeply held principles and access to economic opportunities. Recognizing this tradeoff does not require us to condone invidious

black communities disproportionately rely.") (citing THOMAS D. BOSTON, AFFIRMATIVE ACTION AND BLACK ENTREPRENEURSHIP 76–79 (1999)).

139 Two state courts recently rejected claims by small-business owners that they were entitled to refuse to provide services for same-sex weddings based on religious objections. *See* Craig v. Masterpiece Cakeshop, Inc., 2015 WL 4760453 (Colo. Ct. App., Div. I., Aug. 13, 2015); Elane Photography, LLC v. Willock, 309 P.3d 53, 60–64 (N.M. 2015).

140 *Our Story*, HOBBY LOBBY, www.hobbylobby.com/about-us/our-story (last visited Mar. 13, 2025).

141 *See* Purdy, *supra* note 95, at 1 (observing that wealth inequality relates to "the conception of citizenship implied in any picture of democracy: what it means to have standing in the political community and among other private individuals, and how wealth structures these relations").

discrimination, or to agree with the Supreme Court that Hobby Lobby need not follow federal law regarding worker healthcare coverage.[142] Nevertheless, if the goal is to widen economic opportunities, the laws regulating access to the marketplace should find ways to accommodate even those whose values depart dramatically from accepted mainstream principles.[143]

In sum, family businesses should be evaluated in the context of a society that is already, and for other reasons, characterized by tremendous inequality. Wealth inequality is a problem that implicates the state, the family, and the market. A comprehensive response to wealth inequality must involve all three institutions. By compensating for state inaction and by tempering the harshest edges of the market, family businesses have the potential to play an important role in ameliorating inequality.

10.3 CASE STUDY: BOCA GRANDE

Boca Grande illustrates the potentially transformative impact of business ownership – creating opportunities that would not otherwise exist – and how family values can be combined with a hard-nosed approach to business.[144] The founder and majority owner of Boca Grande, David Grillo, did not go to college. Instead, he had worked since he was a teenager, first in his father's construction business and then in the restaurant industry. Eventually, David grew tired of helping other people become wealthy and decided to take the risk of starting his own business with his wife and a few trusted partners.

In the pages that follow, I describe Boca Grande's business model at some length, largely allowing David to tell his own story, because I think that he captures a crucial insight: That it is possible to care deeply about the quality

[142] *See* Burwell v. Hobby Lobby Stores, Inc., 134 S. Ct. 2751, 2774–79 (2014) (concluding that the contraceptive coverage mandated by the Patient Protection and Affordable Care Act infringed upon the religious interests of Hobby Lobby under the Religious Freedom Restoration Act). For a defense of the Court's holding, see Lyman P. Q. Johnson & David Millon, *Corporate Law After* Hobby *Law*, 70 BUS. LAWYER 1 (2015).

[143] The tension between accommodating and regulating the distinctive values advanced by particular family businesses seems to implicate Robert Cover's identification of "nomic" communities. *See* Robert Cover, *The Supreme Court 1982 Term, Foreword: Nomos and Narrative*, 97 HARV. L. REV. 4, 31 (1983) (arguing that "private lawmaking takes place through religious authority, contract, property, and corporate law … [and] from time to time various groups use these … devices to create an entire nomos – an integrated world of obligation and reality from which the rest of the world is perceived"). The "norm-generating autonomy" of nomic communities can provide "the germ of meanings alternative to those of the power wielders." *Id.* at 32, 62. Professor Cover concludes: "We ought to stop circumscribing the *nomos*; we ought to invite new worlds." *Id.* at 68.

[144] This case study is based on a February 13, 2023, interview with David Grillo. I asked a few questions, but the bulk of the interview was conducted by my student, Zach Palmer.

of the products and services you offer, to take care of your employees, and to hold true to your own values while still insisting upon running an efficient operation that can compete in the marketplace. In other words, there is no need to indulge in a romanticized vision of family capitalism to see that family values can balance a focus on profitability with a sense of social responsibility, contributing to the effort to build a better society.

Ownership and Management Structure. David is the executive chef and majority owner of Boca Grande. He wrote the menu, developed the concept, and holds a 51 percent stake in the equity. As David put it, "From the front door to the back door, this is my mental property." Boca Grande is organized as an LLC with flow-through taxation. The management team of working partners includes David's wife, Cheryl, and Adam Cabot, whose father is a significant investor in the business. David stated, "I didn't expect Adam's dad to invest and Adam not to come along." They all work together to do whatever is needed. In terms of titles, Adam is the general manager, and Cheryl is the marketing director and catering sales director. She handles outside sales and guest services. Adam focuses on the front of the restaurant. David's responsibilities concern food logistics, training staff, and overseeing the schedule for the kitchen.

In addition to Adam's father, there are a few investors who are family friends. Two went to college with Cheryl at Furman. Another is a close friend of David's and a chef. David explained that there are three groups of outside investors; collectively, the outside investors have a 49 percent stake in the business. Apart from Adam's connection to his father, the outside investors are not actively involved in the management of Boca Grande. David said that he told the investors he wanted "a little bit of money, not a lot" because he didn't want to be in debt to them. Two of the investors made clear that, in their view, David needed to have the controlling stake and to have sole managerial authority to make business decisions. A lawyer David consulted confirmed that it was important for him to have a majority stake. The investors' contributions are not loans, so they are repaid only if the business earns profits. Already, in year two, Boca Grande is on track to pay back nearly all the capital that was invested.

Heritage. David is the youngest of five boys. His parents were Sicilian, and his father's cooking reflected the regional influence. Some of David's earliest memories involve helping his father in the kitchen. "Dad cooked all day Saturday and all day Sunday, and I'd get up with him and cook with him." David recalls that his father would put a little bit of seasoning on a napkin, "and I'd taste the seasoning, and I'd have to guess what it was. And he would do that to me all the time, and that was how I got to learn very intricately different flavors. Sometimes he'd have me taste vinegar poured in a spoon. 'Here taste that.' But I learned how pungent things were, and I learned how spicy things were, and I learned how aromatic things were, because he wanted me to understand that."

David's mother suffered from schizophrenia and was not able to function in society or hold a job. She was heavily medicated. David's father supported the whole family, so there wasn't much money. When David was seven or eight, he took over cooking for weekday family meals from his mother. "I made a deal with her, that if my brothers took on all the chores, I'd cook and do the dishes. And so I did." It was a great learning experience. "Well, if you've got four older Italian brothers, and you screw up dinner, they don't tell you. You know real fast. They were my biggest critics." David said, "That's a lot to do with how I learned cooking."

Another formative cooking experience involved David's father's friend, R. J. Moore, who owned the Exxon on Rosewood Drive in Columbia. Mr. Moore was part of the "Gamecock community" and had forty years of autographed black-and-white photographs of players all over the garage. "This was when Sparky Woods and Coach Morrison were [at the University]." David's father would cook for after-parties that Mr. Moore hosted at the gas station for Gamecock fans, "and a lot of times the coach would come, and the players would show up, and Todd Ellis used to come there just for my Dad's meatball subs. And we would take the hydraulics in the shop and lift them to table height and put plywood and tablecloths on them." The after-parties might have 200 or 300 people. David explained, "I learned about bulk cooking from my Dad doing that. Most of my cooking I learned from him." (David added that he also learned about sauces watching Julia Child and Jacque Pepin on PBS.)

Career Path. David's first job in the food industry came after he heard Van Halen "shredding" on the radio. When he asked his father for a guitar, his father told him that it was "Devil's music." As David recalls, his father said that "he'd have nothing to do with it, but if I found a job and saved up my money I could buy my own guitar." When David was fifteen, he worked all summer for minimum wage at the snack bar of the state farmer's market. He bought his first guitar and taught himself to play.

David also worked at his father's construction company from the time he was twelve until he was seventeen. He learned to trough concrete, to put up siding, and to do roof and shingle work. Right before he was eighteen, David got a job washing dishes at the Appleby's on Devine Street. He spent about two years, working eighty hours a week washing dishes. David would stay late, off the clock, to learn how the line worked. He asked the kitchen manager how to write a schedule. When the kitchen manager asked why, David said he just wanted to know. One thing led to another: "I figured it out, and I started writing the schedule for free. And then I started doing his produce orders. And then I started doing the truck orders. And then I started writing the prep sheets. And then I started working on the line." When the kitchen manager was moved to another store, he told the general manager that David had been doing all the schedules and truck orders, and that he should get a shot at running the kitchen. At the time, David believes he was the youngest kitchen manager at any of Appleby's approximately 600 locations.

David did well in the new role: "I ran the living tar out of that kitchen. And I ran it so well they put me on the road opening stores and also fixing kitchens that were not making money." David provided expert assistance at several locations throughout the Southeast.

Meanwhile, David was still playing guitar and wanted to find a job that would allow him to play in bands. The Appleby's job involved late nights. David went to work for the Original Pancake House. "At the time, they were closed at nights, so I could close up shop, take a nap, go to band practice, and start gigging on the weekends." For about five-and-a-half years, David pursued restaurant work and music at the same time. Sometimes, he would work a full day, drive to Atlanta for a show, play until two or three in the morning, sleep in the back of the van on the way home, unload the van, shower, and head straight to work.

In 2000, David moved with a friend to Austin, Texas, and lived there for about a year. He learned a lot about Latino food and Mexican American food like burritos and tacos. "That's all you make there, you know." Apart from the culinary education, Austin was a disappointment. "There was no metal to be had there." David discovered that the metalhead subculture was shunned and that the music scene was all about the purity of country and western. After 9/11, David decided he wanted to come home. His parents were getting older. Also, David added, partly tongue in cheek, "Texans don't like people from South Carolina, and I don't like people from Texas much."

When David returned to South Carolina, he worked at a TGI Fridays as kitchen manager for about five or six years. "I took that store from $28,000 to $30,000 a week to $80,000 to $85,000 a week." David met Cheryl and Adam there. Cheryl was working as a bartender at the time. They dated for several years while they both worked at TGI Fridays. Later, after David left, she worked for Hilton doing banquet sales for Ruth's Chris Steak House, and then for a restaurant in Greenville. When David needed someone to handle catering sales at a restaurant that he was managing, he asked Cheryl, and they have been together personally and professionally ever since.

David recalls that Cheryl bought him a copy of the book, *What Color Is Your Parachute*, and he found the personality assessments very helpful. According to David, the book "does not tell you what you should do when you grow up, but it helps you calculate what you think you are best at based on these traits." After reading the book and reflecting on his own personality, David realized that he should be a chef owner, not a kitchen manager or a general manager of a business for somebody else.

Becoming a Chef. David always had a talent for cooking, and he had years of experience working on a kitchen line, so he joined the American Culinary Federation (ACF) to get certified as a chef. Once he was certified, David got hired as a chef at a fine-dining restaurant in Chapin. After two years, the restaurant closed, "Mostly because it was fine dining in Chapin, which was … the wrong food for the wrong market, you know."

The next job came along quickly: "The day we locked the doors, I got a call from a friend of mine who was the food director for BlueCross BlueShield about some guys looking to open up a taco joint." David interviewed with the owners of Cantina 76, and it was four weeks later that the original location on Devine Street opened. David's contributions were instrumental: "I wrote that menu, costed it out, put the recipes together, recruited, went into kitchens with people that knew me." The restaurant was profitable within a year's time. In David's estimation, they went from a 400,000-dollar investment to 10 to 11 million dollars a year. "We opened five stores total in twelve years." David facilitated the expansion, drawing upon his experience at Appleby's.

Overall, David benefited from his time at Cantina 76 in terms of "experience, exposure, and connections." He was able to "show the local food and beverage scene what [he] had to offer." Although people may not respect restaurants like Appleby's or TGI Fridays, "those systems are second to none." The food is mostly microwaved but it's good for what it is when prepared properly. The restaurants "run tight margins, and they run good training, and they get you in a regimen of understanding workflow that is almost military, and that's how I run all my restaurants."

In about 2006, David started teaching in the culinary program at the University of South Carolina. He still teaches classes on sauces and knife skills. David also worked eight seasons (2007–2013, approximately) at the Augusta National, in the clubhouse, the Caddyshack, and doing private dining. He stopped around the time his first child was born. The Augusta National job involved nearly eighteen-hour days, and if rain delayed play, could involve more unscheduled time away from his regular job at Cantina 76.

Ultimately, though, he realized that he was working hard to make other people money and that he was not going to be treated like an owner. David said that "when Covid hit, I had some time to think and clear my head." As he put it, "There was enough money to go around at Cantina for everyone but me." He felt it was time to try his own restaurant. Even if the restaurant did not succeed, he would be able to say that he had tried it.

Boca Grande. The restaurant opened in April 2021 and beat projected sales for those first nine months by 300,000 dollars. In 2022, sales doubled. It was a full twelve months, and it helped that Cheryl came on board selling catering. In assessing the reasons for their success, David also mentioned that they broadened the menu and responded to customer comments and suggestions. As a chef, David likes to talk to customers, especially new customers, about their experience. "Is there anything you didn't like? Is there anything we can do better? You've just got to be okay with feedback."

The business has twenty or twenty-one employees, mostly part time. The eight members of the kitchen staff are full time and average over thirty hours a week. For the size of the restaurant, the kitchen is leanly staffed but very experienced, and David said that the kitchen staff live by two mottoes: "crush, kill, destroy" (the catchphrase of a robot on the television show *Lost in Space*) and "positive mental attitude" (from the hardcore DC band, the Bad Brains). Industry standard is about 900 dollars an hour in revenue with three cooks, and Boca Grande maxes out around 1,300 dollars with a nine-dollar burrito.

David has experienced situations where the owners of a business take what they can get without "paying you to the level they claim to believe in you." Now, as an owner himself, David acknowledges that there is a disparity between his own profits and what staff are paid, which is part of how capitalism works, but he said that "it is a lot closer to fair." He does not drive a fancy car, but his bills are paid, and he has been able to put money aside to send his children to college. Boca Grande's employees get benefits, they are off on Sundays, and they get major holidays.

David insists on cleaning as you go and efficiency – minimizing steps. At other restaurants, David said, "I would have guys who would run to the cooler and get one thing. Then they'd read the recipe and go back for something else. Make a list. Grab it all at once." Also, "You can only have one thing in front of you at a time when you're prepping. So that was a discipline that I practiced for seven years while I was at Cantina, and at the Masters. No matter how bad the situation I was in, I would only keep one thing in front of me, I would do that one thing, wipe down, clean up, sanitize, start over, start the next thing." That approach sets the right example for employees who follow David's lead. David also tries to create a happy work environment. "It's probably the Mary Poppins in me. It's okay to whistle while you work." No matter how busy it gets, no one yells. David is at the restaurant sixty hours a week and doesn't want to be miserable.

For seventeen years before Boca Grande opened, the same location was occupied by the Happy Café, owned and operated by Susan Hodges. They knew each other by reputation, and David believes that it made the transition easier for her to hand over the location to someone she respected. For his part, David was glad to step into a spot that was already known for having a quality restaurant and with good foot traffic. Although David strives to provide a great working atmosphere and exceptional-quality food at reasonable prices, his prior experience in the world of "corporate" restaurants like Appleby's and TGI Fridays gives him an appreciation for the need to create efficient systems and to manage costs carefully. A restaurant owner must understand the market and hold everyone accountable.

Business Risks and Resilience. David acknowledged that wars and other major external events can disrupt supply chains and shake up the business environment in unpredictable ways. He noted that COVID-19 was the first major pandemic in 100 years since the Spanish flu and that it is unclear whether that will continue to be an issue. He is hopeful that we are past the worst of it. In general, David said, "You try to create a business that is somewhat bulletproof. The only way to do that is to know the market you are in. I've lived here my entire life except for a little over a year in Austin, so I know this market. I try to hold onto the core values that I know make businesses successful." In that regard, David looks at businesses like Lizard's Thicket, Groucho's, and Rush's "that have survived everything." David identified his approach as a "quality casual, fast vibe" that people in Columbia want. "I want to leave my baseball hat on when I go into a restaurant in Columbia."

At Boca Grande, the food is sourced regionally and mostly made in the restaurant, except the tortillas and cheese. David explained that it is sometimes slightly more expensive to buy from local vendors, but the food is fresh and costs tend to be steadier when there are spikes elsewhere in the market, so it is more reliable. David tries to spend money on the things that matter – the quality of the food and the people making the food, and then set prices at a realistic margin. Boca Grande caters to children and aims for flexibility in the menu so that it can accommodate people with food allergies. For example, the brisket is made with just salt and pepper, so David can guarantee it won't cause a problem for someone with a gluten intolerance. And there is a big vegan and vegetarian menu: Boca Grande sells almost as much tofu as pork.

Although it can sometimes be difficult to separate family and business values, David said it has not been an issue to have his wife Cheryl working with him. They worked together previously at TGI Fridays and at Cantina 76, and they have learned to leave work at work. When they are home, they try not to discuss business-related issues and to be fully present for their children. "If you're not all in with your wife and kids when you are at home, it's not going to work." Also, having his wife involved in the business can be helpful because she is levelheaded and helps him to avoid overreacting to situations, which he jokingly ascribes to his Sicilian background.

David noted that no one drinks on the job and taking alcohol out of the equation helps. David mentioned a truism in the industry that there are "three things that break up family-run restaurants: alcohol, cocaine, and the hostess." In a corporate structure like Appleby's, those risks were reduced, partly because everything was in writing. "So, it was beneficial to open up the manual, 'It says right here you can't show up to work intoxicated, okay, so I have to let you go because the book says so, okay?'" David contrasted the "cut and dried" Appleby's approach with the "Wild West" that you sometimes find with mom and pops and said that the key is to stay away from the "shenanigans." The "systems and legalese" of corporate restaurants are effective; the only problem is that the restaurants tend not to make good food. David's goal has been to put together the stability and the resilience of a corporate restaurant structure with real, local food.

David keeps his lawyer Thomas Kilpatrick on call in case something bad happens at the restaurant, like a slip and fall or someone chokes or has a heart attack in the building. More generally, David said that access to legal advice is "crucial to the business." Before starting Boca Grande, he spoke to a couple of local business owners, and they told him "to find a good lawyer and a CPA." Mr. Kilpatrick has guided David through a few situations and has a copy of the LLC agreement and the lease agreement on file. Another issue David mentioned is the cost of the lease. Boca Grande's lease is much more affordable than comparable space in locations like Cardinal Crossing, and he said that it is often a mistake to look for the fanciest spot – unless you have deep pockets.

Finally, David said that chefs generally help each other out, and that the goal is for no one to fail. David has helped to build that culture. At the ACF, David was certified as an executive chef. Later, he served in leadership for ACF as Treasurer, Vice President, President, and, for years, Chairman of the Board. (Today, he is just an active paid member.) David has also been on boards for the Department of Agriculture, Farm to Table, and the Fishmongers' Association. As the owner of a small restaurant, he feels that he is part of a community, and that he is not in it alone.

Plans for the Next Generation. Boca Grande currently operates at a single location on Forest Drive in Columbia, South Carolina. Even though the restaurant has been popular, David rejected the idea of franchising the concept. “If Ace Frehley left Kiss and tried to start another version of Kiss and called it ‘Smooch,’ it would have bombed. It’s too hard to duplicate something as special as those four people.” As further support, David cited the difference between David-Lee-Roth-era Van Halen and the various later iterations of the band. “That’s what happens with these places. This place is what it is because it’s me, J. D., Sammy, Adam, Cheryl, Will; it’s the chemistry between the people who are here. If I were to grow this business, it would either be a food production mentality, like make my tortillas, bottling hot sauces for the local grocery stores, things like that, or it would be opening up a different concept – in this community.”

David and Cheryl’s daughters are nine and six. David joked that they have already started working in the business. His oldest “will run a tray, and she’ll ask, ‘Do you need any silverware or hot sauce?’” They come to the business when they have days off school and like to “buzz around” and help with customers in the front. When asked about them being on payroll someday, David said that would happen only if joining the restaurant is what interests them. “I don’t have dreams of them doing that one day, because that’s what my Dad had for me. Taking over the construction business.” David does not want to put that pressure on his own children and wants them to find their own path.

Boca Grande is a family business, even though it was not inherited and is not meant to be passed down. David refused to join his father’s construction management business, because he understood that he should not live his life trying to do what his father wanted. Yet, David learned to cook from his father, and his passion for food seems to be an inherited trait. Maybe a further lesson, then, is that what we leave for our children is more who we are than what we do.

Afterword

My grandfather Jack Perlmutter was a printmaker and painter whose work brought Coney Island and New York City to life for me long before I had a chance to visit. His woodcuts, etchings, lithographs, and paintings, though not photorealistic and often incorporating abstract design elements, were rooted in his personal experiences growing up in New York and the photographs he took as source material. From the 1940s through the 1980s, Jack was rarely without his camera, capturing whatever caught his eye. He developed the photos himself in a basement darkroom, a place I remember vividly: the mineral smell of turpentine; the dim red light as Jack carefully moved photos from vat to vat; and the clothespins he used to clip each picture to a taut string to dry.

Now, as I scan batches of his negatives onto my computer, I can accomplish in minutes – and without a darkroom – what once took him hours. The photos themselves are treasures, not just for Jack's artist's eye, but because the photos preserve a lost world: elongated cars with fins; men strolling the Coney Island boardwalk in button-down shirts and top hats; the bell bottoms and antiwar protest placards of the 1960s; and, in the background, an array of local businesses long since shuttered or sold. To name a few: Barato's Distributors; S. Beckenstein Fabrics; C. A. & Son Fish Market; Double Hey Rice Shoppe; European Woolens; Fleischers Clothes; Katzin's ("Big or Small We Fit 'Em All"); Lonnie's Coffee Shoppe; Leo's Fancy Fruits & Cigarettes; Paragon Oil; Sol's Fruit & Vegetables; Weitzman's Delicatessen; and Wo Kee Chop Suey.

Sometimes, an internet search helps fill in the story. Take Paragon Oil, for example. According to a detailed Wikipedia entry, the company was founded in 1925 by five brothers – Henry, Irving, Robert, Benjamin, and Arnold Schwartz.[1] The two eldest brothers began by hauling sacks of coal

[1] Paragon Oil, Wikipedia, https://en.wikipedia.org/wiki/Paragon_Oil (last visited Jan. 2, 2025). Note that there is a different Paragon Oil still in business today, apparently unrelated to the Paragon Oil company captured in my grandfather's photograph.

on their backs, selling it to heat local homes and businesses. Later, they designed oil heaters for residential buildings, a venture that proved successful and eventually led them into the fuel oil distribution business. After World War II, Paragon Oil secured a significant government contract to supply fuel for Europe's reconstruction. By the late 1950s, the Schwartz brothers sold Paragon Oil to Texaco for an estimated 75 million dollars. For the Schwartz brothers, whose parents had immigrated from Ukraine, business ownership took them in a single generation from backbreaking manual labor to considerable wealth.

Despite their cultural and economic importance, family businesses like Paragon Oil are "either absent or treated as an exception ... [i]n prominent theories of the firm."[2] In the legal academy, family businesses have received scant attention. Yet, family businesses are different from other businesses, because they require the participants to balance family and business relationships, values, and expectations. This book has argued that family business law rests on three principles: (1) intimacy; (2) integration; and (3) inheritance. Ultimately, the goal is to support the voluntary participation of family members in a shared venture by protecting and shaping their expectations. Accordingly, family business law should offer a resource that interprets the parties' negotiated bargain in full context and that also compensates for what family members cannot anticipate or adequately address regarding their business venture.

From the standpoint of the legal academy, the development of family business law as a field offers three principal payoffs: descriptive, methodological, and normative.

Descriptive: State corporate codes create a centralized management structure that facilitates economic investment. The corporate structure, as supplemented by contracts among participants and legally imposed fiduciary obligations, is said to have supplanted the kinship ties that were once a necessary ingredient for most business ventures. US legal scholars have, therefore, proceeded on the assumption that family ownership is a peripheral phenomenon. But this assumption is wrong. The continued prevalence of family businesses in every sector of the economy demands an explanation.

Methodological: The erasure of family businesses from descriptive accounts of the legal landscape reflects a deeper methodological problem.

[2] Susan Clark Muntean, *Analyzing the Dearth in Family Enterprise Research*, *in* THEORETICAL DEVELOPMENTS AND FUTURE RESEARCH IN FAMILY BUSINESS 3, 4 (Phillip H. Phan & John E. Butler eds., 2008).

As a discipline, business law rests on the false (and gendered) view that the marketplace and family life exist in separate spheres.[3] Law-and-economics reasoning reinforces the divide between families and markets because it asserts that businesses are comprised of individuals rationally pursuing their own economic advantage. In family businesses, however, the values of the marketplace and the values of the family coexist. When applied to family businesses, therefore, economic rationality is too limiting a concept. Employers may be parents or children; co-owners may be spouses, siblings, or cousins. Family business law offers an explanatory model capable of accounting for both family and business systems.

Normative: What is the role and purpose of business associations in society? When evaluating business associations, that is said to be the "fundamental question."[4] A complete answer should include consideration of family business characteristics that can promote the public good or undermine it. For example, family businesses are justly celebrated for providing a ladder of opportunity that can expand the middle class, and family owners often act as stewards of long-term value. In these respects, family businesses offer a model for other businesses to follow. Yet, it is common knowledge that family businesses are vulnerable to destabilizing family conflicts. Also, if family businesses reward family members at the expense of other stakeholders and entrench privileges across generations, they can create dynastic wealth that is in tension with our commitment to equality. Finally, as exemplified by the Supreme Court's decision in *Hobby Lobby*, a controlling family's religious convictions can affect employees and customers. These issues deserve closer scrutiny by business law scholars.

[3] A critique along these lines was made powerfully by Frances Olsen in *The Family and the Market: A Study of Ideology and Legal Reform*, 96 Harv. L. Rev. 1497 (1983). More than forty years later, however, the separation persists. Business law and family law are distinct fields with little crossover. Although women are present in the workplace in far greater numbers, issues concerning marriage, parenting, elder care, and the like are not considered relevant to business law.

[4] John R. Danley, The Role of the Modern Corporation in a Free Society (1994); Elizabeth Pollman, *The Making and Meaning of ESG*, 14 Harv. Bus. L. Rev. 403, 408 (2024) ("Corporations and their role in society and purpose have been the subject of perpetual debate, going back to early corporations."); Elizabeth Pollman, *The History and Revival of the Corporate Purpose Clause*, 99 Tex. L. Rev. 1423 (2021). At one extreme, Milton Friedman argues that "the Social Responsibility of Business is to Increase Profits." N.Y. Times Mag., Sept. 13, 1970. Other commentators advocate for a "stakeholder capitalism" concerned with the wellbeing of employees, customers, and society. *See* The Moral Responsibility of Firms (Eric W. Orts & N. Craig Smith eds., 2017).

Although family businesses seek financial returns, they can also provide intrinsic value for family members who find meaning in shared effort, mutual support, and the preservation of family traditions across generations. What younger generations inherit is more than just an economic investment. Those inherited, intangible family values are what connect the case studies in this book: Chase Oil, Burns Dance Studio, Sharp & Sharp Certified Seed, Market Basket, Inman Mills, and Boca Grande differ in many respects, but the owners would all affirm that they are not just in it for the money. The norms of family life as well as economic considerations shape the choice of investment and the structure of internal governance.[5] When individual investment choices reflect a range of market and nonmarket values and motivations, they cannot be summed in a simple, utility-maximizing formula. To make profits the sole objective of the corporate form is to endorse an impoverished view of what corporations can accomplish. The principles of family business law identified in this book offer a foundation for further analysis and development.

[5] *See* Jonathan R. Macey, Corporate Governance: Promises Kept, Promises Broken 8 (2008) ("The term 'corporate governance' includes law, policy, and social norms, as well as contracts that regulate and motivate behavior within the corporation."). Jon Elster explains that, "[a] sociological alternative to the economic approach is the theory of social norms." Jon Elster, *When Rationality Fails*, *in* Reasoning: Studies of Human Inference and Its Foundations 94, 107 (Jonathan E. Adler & Lance J. Rips eds., 2008).

Index

For EU product safety concerns, contact us at Calle de José Abascal, 56–1°, 28003 Madrid, Spain or eugpsr@cambridge.org.

www.ingramcontent.com/pod-product-compliance
Ingram Content Group UK Ltd.
Pitfield, Milton Keynes, MK11 3LW, UK
UKHW020840290926
15470UKWH00004B/1460
* 9 7 8 1 0 0 9 3 5 4 5 3 0 *